HANSI

HANSI

THE GIRL WHO LEFT THE SWASTIKA

MARIA ANNE HIRSCHMANN

HANSI MINISTRIES INC. KAILUA-KONA,HAWAII

Library of Congress Catalog Card Number: 73-81015
ISBN 0-932878-09-1

Copyright © by Hansi Ministries, INC., Kailua-Kona, Hawaii
25th Printing, April 1999, over 400,000 in print
Printed in the United States of America

To the
American People
With Love

Contents

1 An Orphan for Hitler

Mother bent over my straw bed. I looked up at the questioning, gray-blue eyes in her kind, wrinkled face.

"Mother," I whispered, "can I have a bowl of sauerkraut, please?"

Mother nodded and turned away. She ducked her gray head to avoid the low doorframe of the cottage's only bedroom. Because I was sick with an upset stomach, Mother had bedded me there on the wooden floor beside her own bed.

I listened to her quick steps moving away and followed her in my mind through the kitchen out to the stone-built storeroom by the goat stable. I could picture her every movement, for I had followed her there many times. She would enter the windowless room, light a candle, and set the burning light carefully on a rock. She always feared that our straw-thatched wooden cottage might burn some day. She would lift out the big sandstone from the top of the barrel, remove a piece of board, and move the moldy top layer of the sauerkraut aside. Then she would fill a bowl full of the crisp, cool sauerkraut which I had helped to prepare in the fall.

The kitchen door banged again, and I heard her open a drawer for a fork. My mouth began to water. I had not eaten for two days, and all at once I felt hungry. Then I heard Father's voice.

"Don't spoil her so much, Anna; she mustn't have every whim fulfilled. She is trouble enough as it is."

"She is only a little child yet, Father." Mother's voice was quiet. "She only began school last year. She has been very patient through the whole day while I was busy working. She needs something to settle her stomach. God knows there isn't much fancy food in this house to spoil her, even when she is sick."

She pushed the bedroom door open and put the bowl and fork beside my makeshift bed on the floor.

"Mother," I asked, "can I go back to the hayloft tonight, please?"

She pondered for a moment. "But what if you need me? Do you feel well enough to be alone above? What if I don't hear you when you call?"

"I am fine, Mother." I lowered my voice to a scared whisper. "You know Father doesn't like it when I am around him. And I'd rather sleep in my own bed in the hay, really, Mother."

I tried to eat the sauerkraut, one of my favorite foods in healthy days, but Father's remark had spoiled the taste. I gave it back to Mother. Without another word she moved me up to my usual sleeping quarters. She tucked another blanket over my featherbed to keep out the winter's chill. The roof was brittle and drafty.

"Mother," I asked her as I often had before, "why doesn't Father like me? He doesn't scold when Sepp asks for hot chocolate sometimes, and there is always just enough for him and I can't have any."

Mother sat down beside me for a moment. This was a rare thing for one who always seemed to fly everywhere because there was so much to do in the fields or the stable. If not that, then she had to cook another meal at the big stone hearth heated by wood she gathered herself. But here she sat and seemed in no hurry.

"*Marichen* (little Mary), I have explained it before, but I will tell you again. When you were a little baby your mama brought you to us because she was very sick. She asked me if I would keep you until she was well again. Your mama and I were good friends, so I agreed to keep you for a while though it wasn't easy for us to do so. You know how scarce food and clothing are.

Father had his hands full as a bricklayer to feed our own four children."

I nodded and watched the lantern draw ghostly shadows on the dark hay bales. I knew already what she would say next.

"When your mama died I decided to keep you, and Father wanted to adopt you, but your own papa would not give his permission. That made Father bitter. Now he thinks you don't belong here because Herr Appelt, your papa, could take you away from us anytime he wishes to do so."

Fear gripped my stomach. As I had so often before, I begged again, "Mother, don't let him take me away from here, please! I will hide in the woods if he comes! Please, Mother!"

"Don't worry, child, he will never come for you. He has forgotten you. He has never visited you even once since your mama laid you down on the wooden bench beside the stove and left you here. He is a proud man who gives himself fancy airs though he is poorer than a church mouse. Your dear mama died so young because she wouldn't listen, but married that mean fellow anyway. He put her into that early grave!"

She rose abruptly and picked up the flickering lantern. "Do not kneel beside your bed tonight, girl. It is too cold and you are well tucked in. Fold your hands and pray."

I closed my hands and drawled, *"Müde bin ich, geh zur Ruh* (tired I am and go to rest)." This was a common German prayer and I used it whenever I didn't want to pray in my own words as I knew Mother preferred for me to do.

Saying a simple "Good night," Mother climbed down the steep ladder to the ground and left me alone, staring into the darkness.

I loved the loft, though I was always a little scared at being there alone in the dark. I breathed deeply to inhale the sweet fragrance of our mountain hay which I had missed for a night. I looked out the small gable window waiting for the moon.

The moon was my friend. He chased away my fear and the murky gloom of night. Then I didn't feel alone. Besides, since the beginning of my second school year, the moon had become my ally against my foster father.

Father had forbidden me to read more than one hour any evening. He took the oil lamp away, often in the middle of an interesting sentence, and sent me off to bed. There was no way of protesting. We children were brought up to be seen, not heard.

My rebellious spirit had found a way to defy him. I always hid a school book under my pillow and I knew exactly when the moon turned into a round face every month. But tonight I didn't feel like reading, though the full moon reflected the white shimmer of the snow with an unearthly brightness. I felt too upset. My stomach might have been full of butterflies. Tears washed across my cheeks, getting my ears wet and cold. I had touched the sorest spot of my young life — one that Mother avoided unless I asked.

I would never forget the moment when I heard her explain it to me for the first time. Still very young then, I had been quarreling with Sepp, the youngest son of the house, three years older than I. He had been teasing me as he so often did, till I lost my temper and began to hammer his back with my small fists, yelling and screaming at him.

Suddenly he had turned around and said, "Look, sis! Save your breath and get lost! Don't you know that you aren't even my sister? I'm the real son here and you are just a nobody, an orphan. My mother is not your mother, either!"

I stared into his grinning face and shouted, "I am going right now and tell Mother what you said. And you are going to get in trouble!"

"Go and tell! She is *my* mother, not yours, you *Dummkopf.* Go ahead, tell her!" Sepp triumphed.

Storming into the kitchen I threw my arms around Mother's waist and wailed, "Sepp is lying, isn't he, Mother? He said thou art not my mother!"

That's when she had to tell me for the first time that I didn't belong to that family. But as she finished she said, "Now you are my girl, *Marichen,* and I will keep you as long as they let me."

Since that day the shadow of a great worry had hung in my heart. Would they ever take me away from Mother?

I folded my hands and closed my eyes.

"Dear Jesus, don't let my papa come and take me away, please! Bless Mother and Sepp and the others and —" I hesitated for a long moment, "— bless Father, too. Help me to be good so he will like me. Send my guardian angel by my bed. Amen."

When I opened my eyes I tried again my favorite but always unsuccessful trick. Mother, who had taught me how to pray, had also told me that God and the angels could not be seen. But I was certain they must become visible whenever I closed my eyes. So I always tried to open my eyes very slowly or so fast after prayer that I might catch a glimpse of the heavenly visitors before

they disappeared again. I was never fast enough to catch even
the last shimmer of an angel wing. Now even the moon had passed
the little window and my loft was scary and dark.

Papa never came, but spring did. Then summer and fall and
winter again in quiet steadiness from year to year. As time passed
my love for Mother grew deeper, but my resentment grew stronger
toward my foster father and my papa whom I had never seen. I
had learned to blame him for all my troubles, which were plenty.

Father, a short, thin-faced man with a black mustache, had strict
ideas about his household. He, the patriarch, reigned with an iron
hand. His wife and children submitted silently — except for me.
My proud, unbroken stubbornness clashed countless times with
his hard demands. He tried various ways to subdue me — by
leather belt, by locking me for a whole day in the dark storeroom
with scurrying mice, by making me go hungry.

I never dared to answer back when he scolded. I knew better
than that. But my set jaw, clenched fists, and blazing eyes signaled
temper and rebellion clearly enough. Often I provoked him into
fits of rage, and the whole family suffered because of it.

Poor little Mother! She was the go-between from year to year
and the tongue-lashings she endured so often for my stubborn
sake were my greatest and most painful punishments. Only her
pleading, tearful eyes had been able to melt my uncompromising
rebellion — but less so as I approached my early teen years.

Only for Mother I would sometimes apologize; I could do anything for her — but only for her. I knew my presence was like
acid to Father's ulcered stomach. But he was poison for my
stomach also, and together we were a taxing drain on Mother's
tired heart.

One reason I loved spring and summer so much was that it was
then possible to stay out of Father's way more often. The hard,
long winters in the Sudeten mountains of Czechoslovakia forced
people close to the little pipe stove and elbows rubbed easily.
But when the little brook began to murmur under the melting
snow and the brave, fragile snowdrops pierced the night-crusted
wet snow with their little pointed stems, heralding the rebirth of
another spring, my joy grew boundless.

Nobody could find snowbells — as Mother called her favorite
flowers — earlier than I, and Mother's eyes misted happily when

I brought her the first flowers of the year. As soon as she let us go out without shoes, my easy time began.

I spent countless happy hours gathering wild berries and mushrooms in the shady coolness of the dark green forest that came up to our back windows. I romped with the little spring-born goats and picked dandelions for their gentle mothers. I feared the bees, but loved their hum in the blossoming fruit trees. I whistled with the starlings and picked forget-me-nots for Mother. And I avoided the house when Father was home.

Harvest time brought hard work for all of us. I was so thin and small; Mother's eye would sometimes be on me when I tried to straighten my tired back, and ever so often she found an excuse to send me in to easier work. But she toiled on and on, weeding, cultivating, digging winter potatoes, baling hay, pulling cabbage, and all the while silently accepting Father's criticism for over-protecting me.

Fall brought brown, plowed empty spots around the house. I hated the color brown, which became to me a symbol of new confinement to the house with Father around. My two favorite colors, blue and green, vanished. The blue sky turned gray with clouds, and the green pastures were bare and ready for deep blankets of snow. As nature went to sleep, I often longed to be one of Father's bees that wintered in.

But one fall, September 1938, brought new colors, symbols, and changes of pace into my life. On a sunny autumn day when the leaves burned red splashes into the deep blue skies, strange soldiers marched down the country road bearing a flag redder than the most flaming leaf. In the middle of the flag was a white circle with a black cross. But what a cross! It had hooks on all four ends. The soldiers sang as they waved that flag. Horses and riders, tanks and cannons poured over the mountain ridge, and our little German village held its breath and skipped a heartbeat while the inhabitants watched from behind the windows and waited.

They didn't have to wait long. Almost at once the army loudspeakers announced the peaceful intentions of Hitler who had sent the army to "free" the German brothers "oppressed" by the Czech government since the disgraceful Verdict of Versailles of 1918. The army train was bringing not only a *Gulasch-kanone* (field kitchen), but a whole new future for everybody. So people dared to step outdoors and the children were first to make friends with the smiling soldiers.

Mother watched for a long time and listened carefully to all the announcements and messages over the loudspeaker. Soon we all knew the whole story. Adolf Hitler, Germany's Fuhrer, had sent his troops to make Sudetenland part of the Third Reich. Hitler pledged his word that hunger, unemployment, and hardship were over for everybody.

Mother nodded thoughtfully, then murmured softly, "Maybe Jesus sent that man Hitler into our land to bring an end to the depression. Things couldn't get any worse than they are now!"

And things did not get any worse; there was much improvement right from the start.

Father had longer hours of work at better pay. He seemed more pleasant — at least for a while. School got more exciting, too. The Nazi party brought many gifts from Germany into our poor community, and the gift I enjoyed most was several boxes of new school library books for the unlimited use of anybody in our tiny country school. I read and read and read — and Father raged again!

My teacher, a secret follower of Hitler for years, became overnight the acknowledged hero of the village, and everybody sought his friendship and advice.

It didn't take Hitler's troops marching into Czechoslovakia to make my teacher an object of hero-worship in my eyes. He and I had been on best of terms for a long time. I was his right-hand helper in the one-room school, tutoring primary students while he taught the upper grades. After school I baby-sat his children without pay. He encouraged my passion for reading just as Mother did.

Mother had nothing new for me to read anymore. I had already read every printed page in the cottage several times, even Mother's Bible and the hymnbook.

Teacher gave much of his own time to advance me scholastically, and one day it became clear to me why he pushed me so hard. Not too long after Czechoslovakia became a protectorate of the Third Reich, Nazi educators began testing every student. Along with thousands of other teen-agers, I accepted the challenge. Yes, I would pass those tests. I would show everybody that students of simple country schools were as smart as city kids. *Herr Lehrer* (Mister Teacher) laid his hands on my shoulders and said, "I know you can do it, Maria! You can make it to the top!"

What top? I soon found out. Hitler was picking young people all over the country for special training in Nazi schools. They were selected by special qualifications, not by force. It was a privilege and an honor to qualify. After the first two tests it stopped being a game for me. It became hard work and stiffest competition. By the time I had been selected to represent my county in the next testing-round for the entire Sudetenland, I felt scared. The county supervisor tried to prepare me gently.

"Maria, your teacher is very proud of you and so are we. But now you are matching yourself against the top students of many counties. I hope you will not be too disappointed if you are not selected. From this testing camp only a very few will be sent to Prague to be specially trained for Nazi youth leadership. It is next to impossible for an untrained mountain girl like you to make the top."

That did it! Yes, I knew I was only a skinny peasant girl who looked like a boy except for the long blonde pigtails. I knew how clumsy I was, too, and that I had never been in a county office before. But to call me "untrained" — well, that was a polite way of calling me dumb. That was a challenge! I *would* make the top! And so I did.

When I returned to my own school after ten days in testing camp, my classmates stood up and cheered. So did *Herr Lehrer,* and I thought I saw his eyes become moist. Even Father smiled, and my head whirled!

To think that a poor orphan girl such as I would have such luck! I had been chosen from among many thousands of students to be further educated in one of Hitler's special schools. It was a great honor. On top of that, I would go to Prague, the capital of my homeland — a place I had longed to see ever since I had been able to read. I had never dared to dream that big, and had never seen anything beyond our small county town. I bubbled over with joy, and the envy of the village people made me lift my head high.

The only one who did not rejoice with me was Mother. She packed my meager belongings, and during my remaining days at home her tired shoulders hung lower than usual as in her quiet, quick way she tended to the many tasks of a hardworking, frugal cottage woman.

She looked burdened and helpless in an unspoken grief. It puzzled me, but it was not my place to ask questions.

The struggle for survival has furrowed deep wrinkles into the faces and hearts of the people of the Sudeten Mountains. They are sparing of words and diffident in display of affection. For me to ask the cause of Mother's sorrow would be unthinkable.

She called me before sunrise on the day of my departure. She had the customary bread, soup, and potatoes ready before I had my long hair brushed and braided. Then we loaded my large, rope-tied, wooden box on the small rack wagon, and knelt down for prayer before we left the house. Then Mother kissed me. Kisses were shy, awkward, and only for those who left home for good. She had so kissed each of the four older children when they left. Now I too was leaving, the last fledgling to fly from the nest.

Without speaking, we pulled the wagon up the little hill past our brown, plowed-under rye field, past the partially harvested potatoes. Then Mother stopped.

"Turn around, child," she said. "Look once more before you leave home. Childhood is waving farewell and you are stepping out today into a big, wide world. But there will never be anything more precious than this spot, be it ever so simple, for it was your home."

Tears filled my eyes. Mother could sound so poetic and wise on special occasions. I stopped to turn and look. How I loved the little white cottage beneath the big cherry trees! Would I ever see it again? Would I ever hear the tall fir trees sing again in the morning wind? Would I ever lie among the wildflowers in the soft grass, watching the summer clouds sail past, and dreaming young dreams?

"Mother," I asked softly, "will Father ever permit me to come back to visit? He didn't even shake my hand to bid me farewell this morning. I know he is glad I am leaving. He doesn't think this is my home. Thou art the only one who made it home for me. Now that I'm leaving, Father is closing the door on me, isn't he?"

Mother didn't answer, and her short, labored breathing told me that her heart was giving her trouble again. She didn't need upsetting thoughts. We both reached for the rope and moved on. I did not let myself look back even one last time after that. The only way to live with this most sensitive spot in my soul was to ignore it. And after all, did I not walk toward a great new future?

I was the only passenger who climbed onto the old cannonball, and as the conductor helped me with my box the train whistle shrilled impatiently while the sooty locomotive started to hiss and smoke. I stood at the open train window, smiling down into Mother's sad eyes.

Sparks and cinders flew around her small figure. The morning wind loosened stray wisps of her thin white hair which was combed straight back into a tightly-braided bun. Her expression puzzled me. Her eyes held the kind of agony I had seen only twice as long as I lived with her. Into my excitement and anticipation crept a strange, foreboding fear as I wondered why she looked so troubled.

The first time I had seen that helpless look was when she had told me I had been born of another mother — that bitter moment when my world had broken apart and we suffered together.

The second time I had seen the same agony in her eyes was only a few months before I left home. Just a year after Hitler's troops occupied Czechoslovakia, war began. All the young men were called to bear arms. Sepp, Mother's youngest son, was drafted. It was not the parting that concerned Mother the most. She knew that men must go to war. Every generation in Europe followed this pattern. Grandfather had fought in the Franco-Prussian War — Father served several years during World War I, just after he and Mother had married — now Sepp's turn had come. But after the first World War Mother had become convinced that her sons should not carry rifles and kill human beings. This was her great burden. She knew Hitler would make no exceptions for Sepp, for Nazi rules were iron rules. She was aware, too, that the village party leader considered her thinking dangerous and cowardly. "Heil Hitler" for everybody — that was it!

Sepp himself had not been disturbed about the matter as he made ready to leave. There were the daily radio announcements of victory from every fighting front, and he was young and strong and eager to win the war. He looked sharp in his new German uniform; and before he left, a girl in the village had whispered a sweet promise into his ear. The future belonged to him. After all, war would soon be over. But Mother seemed to know different as in choked grief she bade her boy good-bye.

Now why should Mother look at me in my hour of parting with the same heartrending anguish? I did not leave to go to war. Didn't she realize how lucky I was, how happy and eager I felt? This should not be a time for sorrow, but for rejoicing because I had been chosen! They had selected me, a nobody, an ugly duckling, to go to the new Nazi school in Prague after all those grinding tests. Someday I would be a youth leader for the Fuhrer. My honor in being selected would bring honor to her; I would make her proud of me. Why couldn't she rejoice with me?

The train jerked hard and began to move. Mother lifted her drawn face, stretched out her worn hands toward me and over the clatter called in a heart-strangled voice, *"Marichen, Marichen, don't ever forget Jesus!"*

I smiled and shouted back, "Don't worry, *Muetterlein* (Mother dear)! How could I ever forget you and God?"

I felt so relieved! Was *that* why she had looked so perturbed? Why should Mother worry about such a simple matter? Hadn't she taught me to love God? Had I not prayed beside her from baby-hood? Didn't I know my Bible? And what about the many hymns I knew by heart? We had sung them together in our garden veranda some evenings. Could I ever forget those precious moments of worship when the whole family would sit in the glow of sunset, and after Father had read from the Bible Mother's soft voice would start all of us singing, singing — until the neighbors would open their windows to catch a few strains of our little family choir. I tried to harmonize with Mother's melody, lower or higher, never taking my eyes from her face and kind eyes. I would never forget God, and to me God was like Mother and Mother like God. Whenever I prayed to my Friend, Jesus, I could picture him only with kind, blue-gray eyes like Mother's.

The train gathered speed and noise. In the receding distance stood a lonely, black-clad figure waving a white handkerchief. I waved and called, *"Auf Wiedersehen!"* until the train rounded a curve and I saw her no more. The bright morning sun mounted a spruce-wooded hill hiding the view of the village and our cottage. A last time I strained out the window to see the hills, the village, and the white cottage, but it was all gone, and at that moment it struck me that I would never see the place again. I swallowed the lump in my throat and fought tears for just a moment; then my eager anticipation took over and my heart began to sing again. I listened to the train wheels and they sang with me; "Let's go to Prague; let's go to Prague; let's go; let's go!"

2 "SIEG HEIL! SIEG HEIL!"

Surely I was dreaming! I would wake up and find myself in my warm hayloft, rubbing my sleepy eyes and feeling disappointed that it was only a dream! How could it be true that I, a fourteen-year-old peasant girl, was permitted to be in Prague?

I stumbled from the train and dragged my box out, holding tightly to it and my coat. I felt dazed, helpless, scared, elated, and unbelievably fortunate. No, I did *not* dream. I had arrived in Prague!

"Die Goldene Stadt" (The Golden City), we German young people called Prague admiringly after a Nazi-produced movie featuring beautiful pictures of the city. But oh! She was so much fairer than her pictures. I fell in love with her that very first moment.

I stood for a while watching thousands of strangers surge to and fro in the busy, crowded depot. I had never seen so many people in a crowd before — how many people were there in the world? The masses moved me toward the gate and I wondered in which language I should ask for the way to the streetcar. I spoke German, my mother's tongue, and Czech also. Knowing how deeply the freedom-loving Czech people hated the German regime and the German language, I felt uncertain what to do.

Timidly I approached a uniformed official and began to inquire of him in German. I switched quickly to Czech as I noticed resentment in his polite face. He gave directions and soon I sat on a streetcar bench with my eyes searching out the window. That was an unforgettable ride through a golden autumn afternoon.

I knew at once that afternoon which parts of Prague would be my favorites: The "Old Town," an idyllic part of the original settlement dating back to the ninth century; Charles Bridge, over 1600 feet long, dating from 1357, guarded by two massive towers adorned with statuary; the majestic Moldau River, the largest river of my country, spanned by twelve famous bridges.

"Mother Moldau," they call her because her waters mean fruitfulness and transportation for Bohemia. Unhurried, deep, and queenly she flows, carrying ships and boats under the old bridges, past flowery gardens and lovely parks.

I also saw sights of a different kind. As the antique streetcar rattled its long way through the streets and across bridges, Hitler's bright red flags with the white circle and the black swastika waved in the autumn breeze from every great building and market place. Czech inscriptions had been painted over with German words. German soldiers, officers, and SS men thronged the sidewalks, for the pride of the Czech nation, called "Praha," had become the German city "Prag," and century-long traditions had been changed to please the German conquerors.

When at last I arrived at my school I wondered if I had lost my way and come to the wrong place. It didn't look like a school. The gate opened into a small park, beautifully landscaped with fountains and statuary. Large trees bordered the walks and the entrance to the main building. The school itself was a white stone mansion. Wide, hand-carved wooden doors and slender, high windows gave it the appearance of a fairy-tale castle and I wondered if I would be allowed to enter. I waited for a few scary moments before I pulled the chimes and the friendly door opened wide.

After I had been registered and welcomed, I found my bed and *Spind,* as we called our wardrobes. Then I met some of my classmates. In the evening, feeling subdued and bashful, I sat busy with my own thoughts in the luxurious dining room where we would receive three simple meals a day. I learned that the mansion was the confiscated estate of an immensely wealthy Jew. The idea disturbed me. It still bothered me when I slipped quickly under the blankets of my bunk bed. The mattress felt strange — I was used to a strawbed. I also had the habit of saying my prayers beside my bed, but it would embarrass me to do that here! I wondered what Mother would think about all of it. The thought of the little Bible which I had found tucked among my stuff as I unpacked made me feel uneasy and confused. Weariness enveloped me and I wanted to dismiss all bothersome thoughts. Well, someday I hoped to understand it all.

Before long I found myself well adjusted to my new way of life and with youthful enthusiasm I faced my new opportunities. My shyness left me, and I bounced around as my usual confident self, ready to lead and to compete with the best of my class. I studied hard, learned to obey and salute in wordless submission, and soon received special recognition from the student body and faculty. I could forget that I had been an orphan girl dependent upon the mercy of a poor foster home; I felt accepted and needed.

Someone began to call me "Hansi" — I'll never know who started it. In just a matter of weeks even the teachers picked up my new nickname. It fit so well! I was slim and bony, built like a boy. I acted like one, too, but everybody seemed to like me as I was, so I stopped worrying about my missing feminine curves and enjoyed life and my new name.

Each day the memories of my childhood faded a little more. It seemed as if I had never lived any other life than my new Nazi school life. Mother seemed very far away and almost unreal.

How I loved school! My teachers could bring everything to life. History fascinated me. People long dead stepped out of the pages of my Nazi history book and lived again for me. They became my friends, or enemies. They acted proud, heroic, or cowardly; they loved, fought, suffered, died. My vivid imagination lived and acted with them as my heart learned a new theme — "Adolf Hitler and the Third Reich."

Hitler was with us every hour, though he lived in Berlin and we in his school in Prague. His sayings were quoted in every class. His doctrines were our most important study. His book, *Mein Kampf,* lay under the nightlamp on every bedside table. Our teachers practically worshiped him. They would undoubtedly lay down their lives for him and the nation. All our instructors were young, picked for their enthusiasm, ability, and devotion to the party. Though they demanded obedience and strict self-discipline, they were kind, warm, understanding, and fair.

One teacher I loved above all others — our music teacher. Slim, petite, always smiling, tastefully dressed, she wore her hair in blond waves framing a pleasant oval face. Her main attraction was her eyes — big blue ones, true, firm, but understanding and kind.

Late one afternoon, several weeks after I had arrived at that school, I first decided Miss Walde was someone special. It had been an especially hard day, with many examinations. Our endurance had been tested, as it was so often, to our limit. Our last test had been scheduled in the music room, and we marched into that place feeling played out and nervous. The girls urged me to be first to try the oral test. I complied, grinning as I stepped up to the grand piano. The late afternoon sun streamed through the high windows and threw golden ornaments over my teacher, the instrument, and the soft oriental rug beneath it. The dark-paneled room seemed dusty and hot. My teacher asked me to sing a German folk song for her, one we had studied a few days before. I had been braced for some difficult requirement, and her gentle request threw me completely off. I threw my hands before my face and burst into tears. Before I could compose myself, the whole group of girl students sobbed with me, not knowing what to expect next.

The teacher turned on her piano stool in surprise. She waited, smiling, while I searched for my forgotten handkerchief, then she pulled a snow-white handkerchief out of her dress pocket and handed it to me. Deeply embarrassed over my emotional conduct, I dried my tears.

When each girl had found her composure again, Miss Walde stood up and laughed sweetly. Then she said, "You are dismissed! Go for a walk in the sunshine, do anything you please, and report on time for supper."

"But — what about our music test?" I stammered. "Did we all fail?"

"Oh, no," she said reassuringly, "you all passed. Go out now and relax. We will have some more tests on another day."

Shouting our *"Dankeschön,"* we hurried out of the music hall and stepped into the afternoon sun. Separating myself from the group, I went to my favorite spot of the estate, a white bench nestled among large lilac bushes. Even though the lilac was not in bloom, I loved that place because it was a hidden cozy nook. Whenever I needed solitude for my dreams or problems I would go to "my" bench. Trying to bring order to my stormy, puzzled thoughts, I stared at the dainty white handkerchief still in my tense hand, and relived the last hour in the music hall. What a teacher! How good and noble she had been! How understanding and generous! What could I do for her to show my gratitude? I knew what she would say.

"Little Hansi," she would say, "grow up pure and clean and give your life for the service of others, for our glorious Reich, and for our Fuhrer, and it will be enough reward for me as your teacher."

Yes, I would do what she expected. I would grow up to be like her, firm and dedicated. Her blue eyes puzzled me. I could not escape the feeling that I had seen those eyes before I came to Prague. But where? They were eyes I loved and respected. Where had I seen them before?

As time passed, Miss Walde and I developed a silent friendship. She could not show any preference to any student — that would have been unfair. But we both sensed that we were made to be friends. I studied hard for every subject, but music with her was a privilege, not work. She opened a new world to me. She slipped free tickets into my hand for concerts and opera. She lent me her books. She helped me over my stage fright when singing solos. She taught me the first steps in choir directing. Her blue eyes approved, disagreed, encouraged, and pushed. Only one doubt clouded my mind, perplexing me more and more urgently.

Among other subjects, we had one period daily of "Study of Semitism," taught by a young SS officer who had been disabled in battle. Every day he hammered into our minds the story of the Jews as the Nazi Party saw it. Using *Der Stürmer,* an anti-Semitic newspaper, Hitler's *Mein Kampf,* even the Bible, he built a damning case against the Jews, maintaining that it was their destiny to become extinct.

I listened attentively, and in my heart a battle raged. I had been brought up with the Bible and prayer and faith in Jesus Christ. Nobody had challenged them. Now, listening to this teacher's convincing arguments, I felt puzzled. Something was wrong either with him or with me. I grew restless and uncomfortable as I tried to think the matter through. Miss Walde noticed that I seemed perplexed, and raised her eyebrows in silent question. I uncertainly shook my head; I could not talk about it. It pained so much that I would not open my heart to show the storm inside.

I still prayed once in a while as Mother had taught me. Of course, not on my knees as Mother's custom had been, but lying in my bed I would give God some of my sleepy thoughts. According to Mother's religion, prayer was talking to Jesus. But Jesus of Nazareth had been a Jew, and the Jewish people were condemned. Now, why would the Son of the eternal God have to be a Jew if those people were so bad? Didn't it show poor judgment on God's part? Wouldn't an all-knowing God have seen that it was a mistake? And could a modern Nazi student still pray to that Jew, Jesus, without violating our code of living?

I lost weight. Food was not plentiful, and we lived on rations. But even those small meals did not taste good to me and I frequently gave part of my food to my hungry roommate. I could often feel the blue, searching eyes of my favorite teacher rest on me, but I dared not meet them.

One afternoon, having a few minutes free time, I walked quickly to my favorite spot. As I approached the bench, I saw my teacher friend sitting there. Her face had become more serious lately, and her smile carried a hidden sadness. We all knew why!

She was engaged to an SS officer. I had seen his picture several times in her room. He was a tall, handsome young man with sparkling eyes, blond, curly hair, and a proud, sophisticated smile. He had been stationed in Prague several months, but now he had left for the front in Russia. Miss Walde was waiting for a letter, and we all waited eagerly with her. She remained as warm and efficient as usual, but behind her self-control and her smiles we knew she carried unshed tears.

I sat down quietly beside her and watched the windswept clouds. She didn't talk. I knew she waited for me to begin.

I turned to her and said haltingly, "Miss Walde, I'd like to ask you an unusual question. I hope you don't mind!"

She nodded, so I continued. "Do you think that a German youth can be a good Nazi and still pray as folks did in the olden days?"

"Maria Anne," she answered, "I appreciate your question. It shows me that you have a deep longing to do right. But there are two ways for us. The old way is the way of our parents, who live by their old-fashioned knowledge and will live by it until they die. But Hitler has been called by providence to show us young people a better and more scientific way. German youth have a calling, a task to do, for the Supreme Being and Hitler."

Miss Walde spoke persuasively. She shared her deep convictions. I knew she believed what she said.

Well, if she believed in the new religion, it was good enough for me. Yes, she believed in God, too, only a different God, without the stain of Judaism.

"But what about prayer?" I asked.

She smiled again, and promised to give me a little book to read. It would explain everything, she said.

The book, *Wanderer Between Two Worlds,* contained the life story of a well-known Nazi writer. That evening I began to read it. From the beginning his style fascinated me, and I could hardly stop reading to take part in the evening activities.

His chapter on prayer impressed me most. As a growing boy, the writer had decided to put God to a test. Taught by his mother to pray for protection, he boldly decided one morning not to pray, to see what would happen. As expected, the day went by without tragedy, and the next day. After a few days he dispensed with prayer for good. Then the author challenged the reader to try the same experiment and see what would become of old-fashioned childish prayer.

I tried it the next day, and it worked! I tried it the second day. Nothing happened. The book must be right. I was big and strong enough to take care of myself. That suited my independent spirit just fine. Dejection left me.

The only thing that bothered me was the thought of Mother. I could still see her at the train station with pleading eyes and hear her say, *"Marichen,* don't forget Jesus."

Mother would never understand my new way of life; she was set in her old beliefs. I didn't worry about Father. I had never cared for his concept of religion anyway. He served a different God than Mother did, and his zealous fanaticism had never left any room for love or communication with his own family and had just made me rebellious. I didn't want to let Mother down, but we had a new world in the making, a new ideology for young people, and the older people with their old-fashioned ways had to be left behind.

I read that book over and over again. I kept it beside my bed and memorized whole paragraphs. I lent the book to other young people and quoted its statements in letters to my friends. The book had shown me a new way of life. It meant victory, honor, fame, national pride. My last reserve had fallen. I had changed gods. I laid my burning heart and life upon the altar of my country — for Hitler.

At that time I heard one of Hitler's many speeches over the radio. We listened to all of them, but that address was something special, given at one of the annual sport festivals for the Hitler youth. How that deep voice could send chills down my back!

"Hitler Youth, you are my youth," he said affectionately at the end. "I believe in you and I claim you, for you are the Germany of tomorrow, *my* Germany of tomorrow."

Thousands of voices drowned out the rest of his words. Young voices responded the way we all felt. *"Heil! Heil! Sieg Heil! Sieg Heil! Heil Hitler!"* We could imagine the sea of outstretched arms, the eager faces, the exultant shouts. Tears ran down my cheeks and as we heard the national anthem over the radio we all stood with outstretched arms to join in, but I was too choked up to sing.

Yes, we all belonged to Hitler, even little me. For the first time in my life I felt someone claimed me as his own — and I *wanted* to belong to him.

Later that evening I went to Miss Walde again.

"Teacher, why did the Fuhrer never get married?"

She gave me a strange look, hesitated for a moment and then said with a gay smile, "The Fuhrer belongs to all of us, Maria Anne; he could never choose one of us above everybody else, or would that seem right to you?"

I shook my head. It made perfect sense to me that the great and wise Fuhrer would feel like that. Yes, we all loved Hitler. He belonged to us and we to him. And if I had to make the supreme sacrifice someday and lay my life down for him, I would be willing to do so. Hitler's war raged and his youth stood ready to die! Fuhrer, command; we obey. Heil Hitler!

₃ Could It Be Love?

As war raged on for three years, the difficulties and perplexities of life intensified. We had all expected final victory much sooner than this, and sometimes I wondered why it took our soldiers so long to finish up. I knew that it was only a question of time until Germany and my Fuhrer would win the war; then we could go on with our Nazi program, teaching the nations our new and better way of life and building a world where peace and brotherhood would reign forever — or at least for the thousand-year Reich that Hitler was planning.

I trusted Hitler and my teachers with the simple credulity of a young girl who had stepped out of her small, innocent world and her hayloft into a new, strange life. But sometimes it seemed so hard to put all the pieces together. Even Hitler's book, *Mein Kampf,* had puzzles for me — so many great words and strange ideas I had never heard before. I couldn't understand many things in the Nazi books I read, but I felt content to trust. Someday I would be grown up and wise like the Fuhrer, I thought, and everything would fall into place. Until then, all I had to do was obey and do my best, though it seemed more and more difficult to do so.

We had never dreamed that the war would bring such hardships. Food became so scarce that I almost forgot how it felt to be "full" after a meal. Sometimes after dinner my classmates and I would go down to the kitchen to beg for an additional piece of black bread, but the Czech cook would always throw her hands up in despair and wail in her broken German, "If I give you bread now, I shall not have enough for supper. Then you will have growling stomachs during the night. Oh, you poor girls! You need more food. You are growing teen-agers and your stomachs have no bottom anyway. Oh, what shall I do with you?"

We would turn around and smile. Disappointed, hungry smiles, sure, but what did it really matter to feel a bit hungry if it was for Germany's great future? We would walk back to class singing — singing one of our beloved marching songs that told of victory and of flags waving in the wind.

Duties pressed after classes. I spent many evening hours at the railroad station — the same huge station where I had arrived short years before as a scared, skinny, self-conscious girl. Now I wore a uniform. Colored strings in my tie marked me as a Hitler Youth leader of rank, and with self-confidence I didn't hesitate to give orders to Czech people when necessary. As refugees flooded in from the East in ever increasing numbers we handed out bits of food to the women, children, and elderly people, hour after weary hour. We comforted the frightened, gave first aid to the sick, and helped in any way we could, though forever handicapped by the meager food and medication supplies and interrupted by screaming air raid sirens and other war routine.

I loved to do military hospital duty. We visited wounded soldiers, took wheelchair patients for walks, or dated blind soldiers and went with them to the park or to the movies. One of my favorites was a dark-haired, tall fellow named Erwin. A grenade had exploded in his face and robbed him forever of his eyesight and handsomeness. His delight when I took him to a movie made me forget my own weariness. I watched his upturned young face in the darkness as he listened eagerly to all the sounds of the movie while I whispered to him the descriptions of the pictures he could not see. After the movie I took his hand to lead him back to the military hospital. "Little Hansi," he said quietly, "do you know how much I want to see you?"

A big lump formed in my throat. "Yes, Erwin," I said; "I wish so much that you could see — not only me, but everything . . . the city, the stars, the river . . . everything!"

"I wonder why I had to lose my eyes," Erwin continued. "I wouldn't mind so much to be without arms or legs, but my eyes — it's so dark and lonely where I am!"

I fought tears and couldn't let him know; I had to be brave and give courage.

"Erwin," I said, and I knew I was only adding to the problem, "I don't know why your eyes are gone; I don't know why other soldiers are in wheelchairs; it is all so hard to understand. Most of all, I cannot understand why the other countries hate us Germans so much that they have to start war with us. Why is everybody trying to destroy our new Reich? All we want is space to live. Hitler says it is because we are the master race and they are all jealous. But why, Erwin, why?"

Erwin grimaced. "I lost my chance to be one of the master race, Hansi; I am a wreck, and would be better off if the grenade had killed me."

I squeezed his hand and my tears began to roll. "Erwin," I said warmly, "remember that the individual is nothing and the Reich must be first. We might not understand everything, but there has to be a deep meaning to it. Someday we will understand."

"I was once as idealistic as you are, little girl," Erwin said hoarsely, "but your ideals get lost when you grope like an idiot from bed to bed, and try to get the food from the plate to your mouth. All I know is that my life is messed up and I can't find any reasons good enough to help me accept my tough luck."

I had no answer. I held his hand, and before I left him I kissed him gently. My mind refused to let his words influence my devotion and loyalty to our great German cause. Though my thinking sometimes became blurred after accumulated hours of uneasy sleep, days of struggle to fit studies with volunteer service, and cold hours in the air shelter, I had confidence that the Fuhrer knew what he was doing. His frequent speeches never ceased to inspire me. The war would soon end in certain victory.

Erwin and I never saw each other after that. I had to leave Prague for several weeks to do some student teaching at the city where my sister lived. We knew each other very casually, but there at her urging I went to meet my real father for the first time. It was almost boring to me: we shook hands like polite strangers, and we both acted defensive.

"So, you are a Hitler Youth," Papa said with a thin smile. "I never dreamed that one of my daughters would bring me such honor!" He sounded sarcastic, and we both knew it.

"I am not your daughter, sir," I said icily. "And what I do with my life is none of your concern since you never worried about me when I was a child and needed you."

He opened his mouth and his face reddened, but then he closed his lips tightly and turned away.

I shrugged my shoulders. What was it to me? I belonged to a movement and to my Fuhrer — he didn't. I wouldn't even shake hands with his second wife, a Czech peasant woman. I was ashamed to claim either of them.

I couldn't wait to get back to Prague. My school was my home where I was accepted and secure. How much I loved it!

The highlight of each school day was the arrival of the mailman. Mail was the only thing that was plentiful besides duties. I liked letters and I enjoyed writing. I would write in the bomb shelter at night, during class recess, and whenever I could find an unoccupied minute. Almost daily I received a handful of mail from friends, including soldiers and officers. We knew how our boys waited for messages from home, and we all tried our best not to make them wait.

Mail did not always bring sunshine. Often it brought heartache. Sometimes a letter addressed to a soldier would be returned to the sender stamped, *"Gefallen für Führer und Vaterland"* (Died for the Fuhrer and fatherland). How those few words under the name of the soldier would blow out the light in our hearts and eyes! Many of these boys had worked together with me in the Hitler Youth organization, and when they had left for military training and the fighting front, I had promised to write faithfully. I had kept my promises to all of them.

The first of my letters to be returned was to Fluntl, a friend of my early teens. A tall blond, he had joined the SS troops. I had liked and admired him for his striking smile, frank blue eyes, bubbling enthusiasm, and sincerity.

For weeks I couldn't believe he was dead. I didn't cry; a Nazi youth was not supposed to cry, for it was the highest realization and greatest honor to die for our cause. I knew that Fluntl had believed in his calling and most likely had died with a heil for the Fuhrer on his lips. Self-sacrifice was the greatest goal for any human being! Would tears not degrade his noble death? I controlled my tears, but I could not control the numbness in my soul. Why did he have to die?

The same question haunted me more deeply a few months later when I took part in a training session at the Nazi welfare headquarters in Reichenberg. My sister Margret and I had corresponded after we visited with each other during my student teaching, and I had accepted her invitation to stay with her during that summer. We wanted to know each other better though we didn't seem to have much in common.

One sunny summer afternoon Papa stepped into the house. I rose to leave since he and I avoided each other by wordless agreement. He waved me back. His face looked ashen and very old.

"Margret." He almost whispered it. "Margret, my girl, you must be brave for your children's sake!"

My sister's form swayed and her big blue eyes revealed that she knew the message.

"Is he dead?" she said.

Papa nodded. "Sit down, girl; sit down. He has died for our leader!"

He gave me a quick look and bit his lips. I got up and left the room. I knew that Papa didn't belong to the Nazi Party, and I had the impression that he wanted to say something nasty. But why? It wasn't Hitler's fault that Margret's husband had to die at the Russian front. But whose fault was it? All that dying made no sense, not even for those who were left behind. Margret had two stepchildren and a little baby of her own to care for. The father *couldn't* be dead, but he was!

Margret, however, was better off than many others. Sometimes letters would come back to loved ones with those fateful words: *"Vermisst an der Russischen Kampffront"* (Missing at the Russian front). We dreaded this more than the death note, for it spelled uncertainty, imprisonment, perhaps Siberia. It kept the people in the homeland in mental agony for years, hoping that in some way the missing boy might survive and return home.

Mail helped to keep the war going. As everybody knew, headquarters had ordered that in case of emergency, mail must be delivered even if food must be left behind. The boys could stand hunger as long as they had mail. And it worked both ways. How much easier it was for us to forget the meager lunch, the aching stomach, the dizziness from missing sleep, when we had interesting letters to read.

One sunny spring day in 1942 I slipped out of class to receive my mail. Among other letters I noticed a long, dignified, white envelope with strange handwriting on it. And what handwriting! Handwriting had been of special interest to me ever since I had read an old book on graphology in the school library. That bold, large script fascinated me, but there was one small problem. The writing was partially so illegible that I couldn't make out the name of the sender. I checked the address again. Yes, the letter was addressed to me — so I tore the envelope open and began to read. Then I sat down with an amused smile and called for my friend Liese to come and see.

Well, who would have thought of that! Several months earlier Liese and I had written letters addressed to an Unnamed Soldier. Someone at Hitler's headquarters had started a campaign for more letter writing from the *Heimatfront* (home line) to the *Kampffront* (fighting front), and had suggested the writing to unknown soldiers. Since mail to the fighting forces had to be marked *"Feldpost"* and did not require postage, the idea had caught fire. Almost everybody was writing to at least one unknown soldier.

Since I liked the looks of our dark-blue-and-gold Navy uniforms best, and none of my friends had ever joined the Navy (the normal choice for most of them was the SS), I had marked my dainty little letter: "To an unknown sailor of the German navy." As we wrote on that rainy fall day we imagined our unknown servicemen to be handsome, dashing heroes. We dropped our letters into the mailbox, laughing gaily with the excitement of the idea.

Nothing came of the letters, just as we had expected, and soon we dismissed the incident from our minds. From the beginning we had felt uneasy over it, anyway. It seemed strange to write a letter to a man without being asked by him. This didn't fit into our concept of etiquette or our strict code of proud womanhood.

Six months later I held the answer to my forgotten letter in my hand, and my curious classmates kindly offered to help me decipher anything I couldn't read.

I liked the style and vocabulary of the letter; the writer, whose name was Rudy, sounded friendly, polished, and very intelligent, and I was impressed. The letter came from a Navy officer's training school, and the young man sounded busy and ambitious. I answered the same day and he replied promptly.

From letter to letter Rudy began to occupy a more special place in my heart, although I was not willing to admit it even to myself. His big handwriting demanded a lot of stationery and his letters soon became known to our mailman and to our matron for their bulkiness. As the letters came in more and more frequently, my friends teased me about it, and that made me furious. How ridiculous! Why couldn't I have a perfectly innocent, platonic correspondence with a nice young Navy officer who seemed to have common interests and ideals similar to mine, without being accused of starting a love affair? Love affair with what? A box of letters, a picture, and a few books he sent to me?

His picture told me that he had dark, soft eyes, and a very warm smile. But I had no idea how his voice sounded, how tall he was, or how he walked or laughed. I didn't know enough about him to like or dislike him. Or did I? After all, wasn't I writing to many dear friends whom I cared about deeply?

In the fall of that year I received a telegram from Walter, a Marine who had been my close friend for quite a while. My letters to Walter had helped him through happy and lonely hours as a soldier and countless love affairs in past years. His telegram asked me to come at once to see him off before he went back to the Russian front. I knew that as a Marine officer he would be sent to the forefront of the most critical battles. Heavy-hearted, I handed the telegram to the *führerin* (lady director) of the school.

"You may go, Maria," she said kindly. "I wouldn't let everybody go, but I trust you."

My eyes burned and I felt the blood rush to my face. "You *can* trust me," I said. "Walter and I are friends, but I am not his girlfriend — and I am puzzled about this telegram!"

Walter looked serious and withdrawn when he shook my hand to welcome me at the military station in Poland. We made small talk and I checked into a guest house put aside by the army for family members of officers.

The school had given me food-ration stamps for three days. We went into a restaurant to eat. We talked about his reassignment to the Russian front, and I let him know how deeply concerned I felt. He had just recuperated from bullet wounds in his shoulder, and did not look strong enough to face the oncoming Russian winter.

"I would like to be engaged before I leave for Russia," Walter said right out of the blue.

It took me by surprise. "You, Walter, becoming serious with a girl? Well, I never thought I would see the day when you would settle down! Who is the lucky girl?"

"Maybe it's you, Maria Anne. Will you marry me?"

I stared into his open, handsome face and those big, kind eyes which had turned dark blue with deep emotion. Slowly I shook my head and watched his face turn red and dejected.

"Why not, Maria Anne? Would it be so hard for you to love me?"

My eyes studied the handsome figure across the table, from the blond, wavy hair to the broad shoulders decked with the stars and gold of his gala uniform to the big, strong hands which reached over to take my hands.

No, it wouldn't be hard to love that good-looking boy with that deep, masculine voice. As a matter of fact, he was the personified dream of my teen years. He looked so German and strong and prince-charming. He was everything I ever wanted.

"Walter," I said warmly, "it would be easy for me to fall in love with you, but I don't think it would work. You come from a long-established, officers' family with the best German pedigree and tradition. Your family expects you to marry within your own social circles. You keep forgetting that I am an orphan girl with peasant background, and your parents would reject me."

"Nonsense, *Liebling,*" Walter retorted. "You know that Hitler has resolved the problem of social caste in our country. As long as you are *Arisch* (not a Jew) and qualified to have healthy children, you are my equal."

I felt my face reddening and I shook my head again. "Walter, I belong to the Hitler movement. They have given me education, status, and home. I can't just drop everything and suddenly become a little housewife, even for someone like you. That wouldn't be fair to the Fuhrer!"

Walter looked straight into my eyes. "Maria Anne, be honest with me. Your reasons don't sound convincing. Do you love someone else?"

I shook my head vigorously.

"What about that Navy man you correspond with? You mentioned him in your letters several times.

I felt the blood rush to my face again. Walter had a vexed smile.

"Listen, little girl," he said. "There has been a change in your letters to me since you started to write to him. Please, be honest with me!"

I shrugged my shoulders in helpless embarrassment. "Walter, there is nothing to tell, honestly. I don't know him. We have never met. I like his letters very much, but you should know me well enough by now — I don't let myself fall in love easily. I only know that I have to meet that boy some day before I can give my heart to anybody or I will go through the rest of my life wondering if I missed out on something. Will you give me time?"

I left that same night on the train. Before I climbed into the crowded railway carriage, Walter took me into his arms and kissed me for the first time.

"*Auf Wiedersehen,* my dear, precious friend," he said in a low voice. "I wish you all the luck in the world; you deserve it. And tell that Navy man to make you happy."

Tears blinded my eyes. I wanted to protest, but I couldn't. Somehow I knew his words were final, though I considered his jealousy about "that Navy man" unfounded. I felt confused and sad. Walter was hurt, and was leaving to face Russian snow-storms, loneliness, and maybe death — and I had added to his hardships.

"I'll write you every day, Walter," I called as the train pulled away. "You are my best friend!"

Walter turned away without answering.

How much mail from my unknown Navy man really meant to me, I admitted to myself only after we had corresponded for more than a year. All at once the bulky letters stopped. One week, two weeks, three weeks, five weeks passed.

I waited and worried. Would my last letter to him come back someday with that dreaded stamp on it — *"Vermisst?"* I feared to ask for my mail. Eagerly I listened to the Navy news during "radio hour" in the evening, especially the U-boat news. Rudy had become a third officer on a submarine that year, and I knew something about the odds against those men.

The girls began to tease me again, in a sympathetic sort of way. They seemed slightly puzzled that I would worry so much about a stranger. I denied my concern too loudly and convinced nobody. I began to reason with myself; was I not being absurd to have that man so much on my mind? Maybe he cared nothing about me. Or did he care as much as I did? Why did he write such long letters so often?

Maybe his boat was lost. Maybe he had just decided to stop writing. No, deep inside I knew that my young officer was not dead. He couldn't be. I had to meet him someday, somewhere. He had become part of my life. I had to believe in him and his future.

When after long weeks his next letter arrived, the matron waited until after dinner to give it to me. She said she knew I wouldn't have bothered to eat if I had been given my twenty-page letter to read, and I was already too skinny.

I tore the parcel-letter open, struggling to hold back the happy tears and caring nothing for the teasing remarks of my friends. I had a letter to read, and I read it hurriedly the first time, carefully and slowly a second and third time.

Rudy had been out for many weeks. *Feindfahrt* (patrol), they called it when the boats cruised the ocean and hunted convoys. His letter was a diary, and there had been no opportunity to mail it for many weeks. Certain things they were forbidden to mention, but whatever was permissible he told. I didn't care how many ships they had torpedoed or where his boat had operated; all I wanted to know was about him personally. In one part of his letter he wrote, "When I stand on the bridge during the long hours of my night watch, I look up and see the stars, and I wonder, Maria Anne, if you are asleep or if you are looking at the same stars. Someday, my dear pen pal, we are going to meet each other, and I cannot wait to see you."

That night I looked at his picture for a long, long time. I knew every line of his face by heart, but I had to study it anew.

After I had put the picture down and turned out the lights, I slipped quietly to the window behind my bed and lifted the tight shades a few centimeters. I knew it was against the rules, for every house in the country had to be darkened at night; any beam of light could betray human dwellings to the bombers, which found their targets anyway with deadly precision night after night. Nobody in his right mind ever lifted a shade before morning dawn — but I had to! I had to see the stars just once in a while, for they had been my friends since earliest childhood.

I had watched those wandering lights from my bed in the hay-loft many a night and had talked with them in my heart.

Now the time had come to talk to the stars again. I had greetings to send! Somewhere a small U-boat sailed on a wide ocean. On it stood a young navy officer with brown eyes and a high, intelligent forehead. He might look up at the stars tonight. Would the stars take my greeting to him? Would the stars tell him of the shy love in my heart and the dreams I couldn't help dreaming? Never would I dare to put my feelings into words. Our friendship seemed so precious and frail that words could have destroyed the beauty of it.

When I let the shades down and slipped under my coarse blanket, Micherle, the girl in the bed next to me, begged, "Sing us to sleep again, Hansi, please."

As so often before, I sang for the girls gladly. They relaxed and so did I. All the melancholy hits I had learned from the radio I sang softly into the darkness — the sad words of love and loneliness and war that tore hearts apart, and while I sensed some of the longing tears that were shed in some beds I finished with my favorite song: "I know that someday something wondrous will happen and I *know* that we shall meet again —" When, Rudy? When will we meet?

4 Prince Charming at the Door

As total war raged in the summer of 1944, we girls were shipped out of the city into the Sudeten mountains. Germany had forgotten what vacation meant; so had we. At nineteen, I became leader of a group of girls engaged in hard farm labor. Our male farm hands had gone to the fighting fronts. Desperately the women planted and hoed and harvested, learning to do men's work and do it very fast.

Our arms ached as we raked and pulled and lifted from early morning to late afternoon. But we all understood. The farm wife where I worked was sweet and motherly, but she looked haggard and overworked. Each day she slipped some extra food into my apron pocket. I tried to return my appreciation in diligent labor. We became the best of friends.

The extra food, the summer sun, and the large amount of exercise in the fresh air did me many favors. No longer so bony, I also acquired a healthy tan. My hair, worn in a pageboy style, had grown long over my shoulders, and the sun had bleached it almost blond. War seemed far away in our out-of-the-way camp. No air raids disturbed us as we slept in the quietness of the whispering evergreen woods. Every morning the singing birds awakened us. The morning dew glistened like a thousand diamonds over the pastures when we marched out to the villages for work. When we stood around the flagpole to salute, our voices shouted the pledge with vigor. This was the best summer for me since my childhood — and Rudy still wrote long letters regularly.

Late one afternoon we checked in from the village, took ice-cold showers, and prepared for supper and evening training. Most of the girls gathered at the athletic field around a girl with an accordion for square dancing and happy chatter. My duties as a subleader made me late, but I hummed a tune while brushing my hair and creaming my sunburned arms. Then I fell to musing again. I hadn't heard from Rudy for a while and I tried hard not to worry. It was disgusting that I couldn't get that boy out of my head!

It was almost time to leave for the city again. Soon we would have to pack and return to Prague. How I hated to leave! The summer had been so peaceful. Sure, there had been some friction with that *Führerin*. She was the assistant camp director, and she and I had not been able to get along; but outside of that it had been a dream of a summer. The only thing missing to make everything perfect would have been a visit from — well, no sense wishing again. Rudy would never be able to come to this remote place. Why should he, anyway?

Starting down the stairway opposite the entrance, I whistled a tune and threw back my long hair, resolutely tossing my head to indicate my determination to stop my silly dreaming.

All at once I stopped short. Through the high, sunflooded open door stepped a Navy officer. His face looked very familiar. Yes, I knew every line of that face by heart — and I wondered if I were dreaming! Then I panicked and fled back up to my quarters. With shaking knees I sat on the edge of my cot and tried to control my beating heart and racing thoughts. I didn't know a girl could feel so terribly scared and so happy all at once. Oh dear, what if he didn't like my looks? What if — I began to brush my long hair again, reset my service pin on my blue house uniform, check myself for invisible spots and blemishes, and wish with all my heart that fairy tales could be true and I would turn into a beautiful princess — but I didn't!

Presently I heard my name being called. Summoning all the courage I could find, I walked slowly down the stairs and reported respectfully to the leader in charge. With an amused twinkle in her eyes, she pointed at the Navy man and said, "You have a visitor, Maria Anne. Come and welcome him!"

I looked full into his smiling face and extended my hand to him. Rudy smiled broadly and said, just a shade too lightly, "Well, here I am, little Hansi!"

I nodded and managed to stammer, "Yes, I can see it —" I could feel myself blushing.

Since my superior had never seen me speechless or self-conscious before she first looked puzzled and then she laughed a hearty laugh. That broke the tension in the room. Rudy and I also began to laugh, and I finally managed enough self-composure to welcome him and invite him to join the group outside under the big tree, where everybody square danced.

Suddenly aware of the sensation Rudy's appearance created, I got my self-confidence back quickly. Proudly I introduced him to my friends; behind his back they gave me little signs of approval or envy. I beamed with delight.

When the supper bell called, Rudy was invited to dine with us. He was seated beside the camp director, a woman of high leadership rank and strict manners. I fulfilled my supervising duties, but I couldn't stop my heart from beating loudly, especially when I stole glances across at Rudy's place. A born charmer, he carried on a gallant conversation with the lady of the camp and at the same time he watched me closely with, it seemed to me, a look of slight amusement. By the end of the meal the *Führerin* of the camp was so favorably impressed by his gentlemanly behavior that she had me signed off from further duty for the evening and the next day, even before I dared ask. Since she had never done such a thing before, this created an even bigger sensation among the girls.

After I had changed into my uniform and returned, we walked slowly out, aware that many eyes watched us. Once outside the campus we turned toward the sunset. We walked in an enchanted world, glowing with golden-red and purple. A strange silence hung between us as Rudy took my hand to help me up the hill. We stood there for a long time watching the fading colors of the evening sky.

We had both felt so close to each other in our letters. Though we had never mentioned this in words, our deep feeling showed between the lines of every page. Now we recognized that the hour of testing of our friendship had come. Both of us feared that one wrong word, one untrue gesture, could break the tender thread. Our friendship now had to face reality. I did not look up as I felt Rudy's eyes searching my profile. Slowly the golden twilight turned into velvety darkness.

"Are you disappointed, little Hansi?" Rudy asked gently.

I shook my head too vigorously and quickly replied: "No — are you, Rudy?"

He denied it too, but we both knew we lied. Yes, we both felt disappointed. Not that either of us didn't like the other; we were just different from what the other had expected. Dreams are perfect; humans never are. Two and a half years of unreal friendship had suddenly come to an end, and our dreams were irretrievably gone. Would our ties prove strong enough to face reality and go on?

We were determined to give it a try. Sitting on a log, we began to talk. I had so many questions to ask, and I sat and listened as he told me about his life.

He was the only son of a well-to-do, long-established family in a German village in the province of Silesia. His only sister was two years younger than Rudy. His father owned the best *Gasthaus* (inn) and a meat business. Rudy had never experienced poverty or want.

He had been the idol of his grandmother, who lived in the same house. The maid of the house, faithful old Selma, called him "Prince" and treated him as such.

"I must have been a typical 'spoiled' boy," Rudy mused, "and I sometimes wished I had not gotten away with as much as I did — but Grandma never denied me a wish and even now my parents may grumble but I get whatever I desire."

As Rudy reminisced about his childhood, I could picture that cute, small fellow so easily — a boy living in his lone dream world amidst all the attention and fuss three women showered upon him, trying hard to be tough and excelling in all the boys' activities of the village, especially in sports. He coasted through school, succeeding without trying. During his teen years he attended the *Gymnasium* (secondary school) in the province's capital of Breslau. There he had too much freedom and money on his hands. Then the war!

"I volunteered to the Navy after the *Abitur* (final secondary school examination), and my grandfather said I wouldn't be able to stand the hardships. I told him that on my first leave home after basic training I would return either with the rank of an officer, or with the Iron Cross!"

"Did you return with one of the two?" I asked eagerly.

"I had both, my rank and the medal." Rudy sounded pleased and proud in a nonchalant way, though his voice stayed soft.

"Rudy, how did you get your medal?"

Silence deepened a while before he answered.

"I don't like to think about it," he said at last. "It was after I had begun my duty as a machine gunner on a patrol boat. We were guarding convoys. One particular day we escorted a big convoy through the Straits of Calais. About twenty Spitfires and as many bombers attacked us."

"What are Spitfires?"

Rudy laughed. "I am sorry that I expect so much war knowledge from you, little Hansi. Spitfires are English fighter planes. And it is those Spitfires which the patrol boats have to reckon with. The bombers always concentrate on the convoy, but the fighter planes try to wipe out the antiaircrafts on the patrol boats. Those planes have a rather unique way of diving down at the boats." Rudy kept his voice casual. "They first shoot into the water, and the bullets splash a little path toward the boat. Then, when they have a good aim, they really let you have it."

I shivered, and Rudy moved protectively closer to me. Silence hung again.

"Rudy, how did you get the medal?"

"Well, I shot down two Spitfires that day, and did a few other small things."

"Like —?"

"Oh, the two men who had handed me the ammunition were knocked out and after the attack I noticed that our boat still was running in big circles. We did that so we wouldn't be a steady aim for the fighter planes. So I got out of the straps of my antiaircraft gun and looked around and the deck was a mess. It finally dawned on me that something must be wrong up at the bridge. I raced up and everybody was either dead or disabled. The rudder man was dead and had slumped into the helm. I took his body out and turned the rudder wheel to midships. Then I gave orders to stop the engines. At that time I wasn't able to run a whole ship."

"I am glad that you are now with the U-boats," I said, relieved. "That isn't so dangerous for you because you are under water."

Rudy laughed again. "That's how little girls picture U-boat war, don't they! U-boats are very seldom under water, little Hansi. We submerge only when we attack by day or when we are attacked. By night we try to get away on the surface even when we are chased. We can move faster."

"Are you often chased?" I tried to sound casual.

"Well, things were not too bad until 1943. We definitely had the upper hand in the Atlantic Ocean."

"Did it turn bad after America entered the war? I always wondered why they had to in the first place. We never did anything to them."

"No, it wasn't that. We could sink their boats faster than the United States and England could build them. Our problem began with something we couldn't put our fingers on for a while. The English call it radar. It was the most spooky thing when it all began. We were so used to relaxing during the night, nearly always operating on the surface, even when we wolf-packed enemy convoys. It is next to impossible to see a little U-boat in the darkness of the night, so we never paid much attention to enemy planes except during the daytime. Then one night the floodlight of an enemy fighter plane caught us, and we couldn't shake the light by zig-zagging."

"Why didn't you submerge?"

"We finally did, but we knew that we were a dead duck. Very often a U-boat cannot submerge to a safe depth as fast as a fighter plane can come around on a second run and dump all its depth charges on us. Luckily they missed us!"

"Why did they find you in the first place?"

"We had no idea for months, and those weeks were living hell for all German U-boats and Admiral Doenitz. We lost so many boats —" Rudy's voice turned very low and he reached for my hand. ". . . So many of my best friends died — I sometimes wonder why I got through all of it without a scratch. Some of those who died right beside me were so much better and nobler than I am. I do so many foolish things whenever we come back to the ports."

"What *is* radar?" I interrupted.

"Radar has made our patrols suicide missions," Rudy said tensely. Then he stopped as my hands tightened. I had sent a message — I felt scared! Scared for this beloved stranger who wasn't a stranger and who talked about death so matter-of-factly.

He laughed suddenly. "Little girl, have I come such a long way after such a long time to talk about war to you? Don't worry; *we* know now what radar is and we will soon have means to counteract it. We will soon have different boats, too. They can stay for months under water and I expect to be called on one as a second commander. And the war will soon be over!"

It was good to listen to him. He sounded so young and yet mature. I knew why he had never gotten hurt during all those years, but I couldn't tell him that. Destiny had brought him safely to me, because I *had* to meet him or my heart would have been empty and wondering forever.

I watched the stars appear above us, one by one, until the night sky became a diamond-sprinkled dome that surrounded us with new assurance. The disappointment had gone; he really was as I had pictured him all along.

And all at once I felt, too, that Rudy had received my greetings all through the past years; for the stars began to talk to us again, and we sat and listened. The stars stepped out of the sky and began to shine within my heart, and I felt that two lights shone in my eyes as we walked hand in hand back to the camp. We both had lost something; our pen pals had left us, but we had found something more precious.

The next day found us happy and at ease with each other. We felt as if we had seen each other many times in the past. I showed him the beautiful countryside, and in high spirits we climbed some hills. Proudly I showed him off to "my" farmers. My motherly friend acted a little shy, but seemed impressed by all the "brass" and medals. She got busy, and in short time she had fixed sack lunches for us. She wouldn't listen to my suggestion to let us both help her with her work before we left. We strolled to my little hideouts around the country where I had sat and written to him and dreamed of the time we would meet.

When I least expected it, Rudy took me into his strong arms to kiss me. I quickly freed myself from his arms and shook my head.

Rudy looked utterly baffled and distressed. Why couldn't he understand? I knew that he had kissed many girls, but he and I — couldn't he understand that it had to be different? For years we had treasured our friendship as something very special. Would it have to go as most war affairs did — passion, kisses, jokes, fights, leaving a bitter taste in the mouth when it was over? Never! I couldn't fall in love, fall out, and fall in again as some girls do.

Maybe I was a dreamer, but I believed someday there would be a great love in my life. I couldn't possibly end this unusual friendship with Rudy in any cheap way, or as an everyday love affair.

Rudy listened seriously to my attempt to explain how I felt. Then, lifting my chin gently till I looked right into his eyes, he said, "Maria Anne, have I given you any reason to believe that I would like to use you in any cheap way, or for a fleeting love affair? You have become a part of my life, my great inspiration! I cannot picture my life without you and your letters anymore. You are the type of girl I want to marry someday. Would you?"

Had I heard right? He hadn't by any chance proposed to me? How could he? We had met each other just the day before. I buried my face on his shoulder and as his arms gently enfolded me I looked up. His eyes assured me that my heart had found the great love of my life. Yes, my heart had found its home and his lips found mine.

Later as we sat in the sun, he talked to me about our future together. Suddenly he said, "My little Hansi, here I am talking to you about our future home, and I am just realizing that I know hardly anything about you. All we do is talk about me and my life; tell me about yourself, your childhood, your family —"

I shrugged my shoulders. What could I tell him? About the little house by the woods, and about my hayloft? Would he understand? He had grown up so differently; he had financial security and the luxuries of life even during the war. Could I tell him of the time when Mother stood at the train station worrying because I might forget God? How could he ever understand? He had a nominal Protestant background, but religion meant nothing to him. He was a Nazi, like me; and he trusted in Hitler and the future of the Reich. What was there to tell?

"Rudy, there isn't much to tell about me. I am just an orphan girl brought up in a very religious foster home. My foster-father was a bricklayer, my real papa a gardener. I am poorer than a mouse and just lucky enough that I was selected by the Germans after our occupation to be educated in Prague. You know that I am a youth leader and I plan to advance." I took a deep breath because memories hit me.

"I never thought much about marriage because it would interfere with my future plans. I have wondered before —" my memory saw myself sitting across a table from a distressed blond officer saying the same words, and I felt a sharp pain. "Wouldn't I let everybody down if I got married? I must serve the Fuhrer and Germany someday in a special way to repay all the free education I am getting."

"I have a better idea." Rudy grinned. "Why couldn't we do those things together? As soon as the war is over I plan to go into the Merchant Marine, and I will often be gone. You can fulfill your calling and teach. I will not demand all your time."

I smiled, relieved. How simple everything was; how great and how simple! The time had come to stop worrying and let go. The great moment of my young life had arrived. I had found my love, and I could trust myself in his hands. Rudy was intelligent, mature, and wise. He had the answers to all my problems, and I was an ignorant little girl who wouldn't stop worrying.

But now I knew that somebody loved me, and for the first time I dared to love back. War, torpedoes, bombs, death — all seemed impossible as we sat close to each other in the flowering pasture with grazing cows on one side and stately evergreens on the other. Above us fluffy white clouds drifted in the bright summer sky over the hazy mountains. Maybe I was dreaming and would wake up to find everything gone and gray, but I would enjoy the dream while it lasted. With new confidence I looked into Rudy's face. Then I looked at the golden band he had put on my finger. At the wedding our rings would be moved from the left hand to the right.

The next day we traveled together to Rudy's home. We didn't feel quite as carefree as we had the day before. Rudy was obviously nervous and I dreaded facing his family. We made small talk and laughed about our funny remarks, but we both knew that we were two scared young people who might be heading into opposition.

Rudy's parents, his sister, and the maid stood in the doorway to welcome us, and in spite of my awkward shyness I couldn't help feeling amused when I noticed how Rudy hid his left hand behind his back. So did I, for neither of us had taken our golden bands off before our arrival.

Rudy's mother was a short woman, but stately, with silver-streaked dark hair and restless brown eyes. "We welcome you to our home," she said with a polite smile. Her eyes did not smile with her, but examined me coolly while we shook hands.

Rudy's father, a very short but heavy man with watery blue

eyes, pulled me down to kiss me on my cheek. His red nose spoke of a liking for liquor and he wheezed with each breath. Rudy had told me of his father's weak heart, and now I worried more than ever; how would Rudy announce our quick engagement without hurting anyone?

"Maria Anne and I are engaged," Rudy said casually and we both brought our left hands forward — I with the intention of grabbing his right hand because all at once my knees felt like soft butter and I couldn't breathe.

The smiles froze on their faces, but Annemarie, Rudy's sister, saved the moment and broke the shocked silence.

"I am so happy for both of you," she said warmly, embracing both of us at the same time. "Come in and feel at home. Dinner it waiting!"

We stepped in and Selma, the maid, took our coats. I soon found that Selma was not a hired worker but a long-time friend of the family. She had begun her service as a young girl when she began working for Rudy's grandparents during the early years of their marriage. When Rudy's parents inherited the restaurant and the butcher shop, Selma also came to them. Rudy and his sister were the third generation of that family she had loved and cared for.

"Our prince has brought home a princess," Selma announced proudly to the guests in the homey, dark-paneled guest dining room as we walked through the restaurant to the family dining room. The whole house breathed secure wealth and old-fashioned taste. I saw a carved, dark mahogany table set with china and heavy linen. We sat down to delicious, rich food, well-prepared by Rudy's mother, who never left the cooking to anyone else. Rudy had talked about her gourmet cooking and seemed very proud of it. Her eyes softened a little when I told her that I hadn't eaten so well in years.

Annemarie, who sat to my right, chattered gaily and urged me to eat more than I could. My stomach churned into knots.

I liked Annemarie from the first moment I saw her. Only two years older than I, she acted as if we were already sisters. Her eyes had the same hazel color as Rudy's. She was about my height, but slimmer, and she reminded me of an expensive china doll I had once admired. She looked so delicate and very special to me.

Annemarie tried her best to make my stay comfortable. She

shared her bedroom with me, and I wondered how it would feel to be the only daughter of a wealthy home who had a whole room with heavy oak furniture, ruffly curtains, and a bed canopy to herself. But it was too hard for my imagination.

I felt awkward and uneasy around Rudy's parents. Maybe they felt uneasy too! Our engagement had taken not only his family but the whole village by surprise. However, the "prince" and I spent every moment with each other trying to get fully acquainted; we did not worry or care unduly about anything or anybody else.

How our time flew! We tried to ignore the fact that parting time approached, hoping that by ignoring it we could stop the hour from coming. We had a small engagement party with red roses and fancy wines, which almost scared me in its richness and strangeness. Then Rudy and I rode in a horse-drawn buggy to the train station. The little country train brought us rapidly to Breslau, capital of the province of Silesia. There our two trains were to leave in opposite directions in the afternoon.

We arrived before noon, and Rudy took the opportunity to show me his beloved city during our few remaining hours together. For seven years he had gone to school in Breslau, and he knew every corner of that picturesque old place. We ate a few bites in a small cafe, paying not only with money but also with ration stamps provided by his mother. At last the moment came when we had to return to the railroad terminal. For each other's sake we had put on smiles and made lighthearted conversation, trying to disguise how we felt about parting.

Rudy had to leave first. After checking out our suitcases we walked down to the platform and found the train. Rudy's compartment was in the first class, reserved for the "better" element of society even during the days of total war. He reserved his place, stored his suitcase away, and stepped down once more from the train. I had determined to be a brave sweetheart up to the minute of his leaving, and I forced a smile. Trying to cheer me up, Rudy took me into his arms. "Don't be sad, my dear Hansi, we shall see each other soon again. Be my brave little girl meanwhile and wait for me. We shall write each other every day."

That did it! Hiding my face on his shoulder, I burst into uncontrolled sobbing. He pulled out a spotless white handkerchief and began to wipe my face tenderly. I looked up into his kind face and again I felt premonition, that dreadful feeling of danger ahead that I had known when I left my mother to go into Nazi training. Why was I so afraid? I tried to control myself, but it was no use. I cried bitterly, while my heart felt like a stone.

The conductor raised the signal plate and blew the whistle. Rudy kissed me once more and then had to let me go and swing himself onto the already moving train. His face showed the strain of the hour and a deep concern for me. Struggling to calm myself, I finally managed to smile through my tears, but I could not speak. The train gathered speed, and Rudy's waving, navy-blue arm with golden stripes and stars grew smaller and dimmer in the distance.

Even after the train had disappeared, I still waved. Then I stopped waving to wipe my tears and began to search for my own train. How I found it and got on it I couldn't remember later.

Would I ever see him again? Would he come back from war? What lay ahead of us? For a few short days I had experienced the warmth of love, the joy of togetherness, the security of having found a home for my heart. All I could think of was Rudy. All I wanted was to be with him. But the trains rolled on into the evening — mine toward the east, his toward the west. Each minute tore us farther apart, while the sun died and the day turned into a long night.

War waited for him; the big city called for me. I cherished the memory of some wonderful days, and the slim golden ring on my finger. As I lifted my hand to feel his ring on my hot face, the golden metal felt cold and strange, just like my lonely heart.

Train wheels sang again, and this is what they sang: *"Ich liebe Dich; auf Wiedersehen. Ich liebe Dich —"* (I love you; good-bye. I love you —).

Beloved sailor, good-bye.

5 Specter of Death

I held Rudy's letter in my hand. "My beloved little bride," he wrote. "It is just like a dream that you and I finally met. Remember that I love you and that we have a long life before us to get better and better acquainted. Wait for me and don't be lonely, for my heart is always with you until I come back and take you in my arms never to let you go again . . . with many kisses . . ."

Tears streamed again. It wasn't only that I missed him terribly; I felt utterly confused and scared. Everything seemed so easy and simple while we were together. It had also been easy to write to him as an unknown serviceman for so long. But I didn't feel prepared to answer love letters; I didn't know how!

Of course Rudy could write those with ease, and so affectionately. He wrote nearly every day. Still I could not shake a nagging fear that this was all an unreal dream. Sometimes I even found myself wishing we were still on undefined terms, when I could hide my deep feelings for him safely behind poetry and profound thoughts.

Rudy came from a home where he had been cuddled, pampered, and loved all his life; I spent my childhood where show of affection was considered weakness. The only time I had ever fondled anything was when as a young child I had· been given a pet goat one spring. He and I had been inseparable. He often jumped on my back and nibbled my ear. In return I pressed my face into his coarse white baby-fur and squeezed him tight, but only when nobody was looking. Once I even kissed him good-night, for I had read in a story about families kissing each other in the evening. But Sepp saw me kissing my goat and teased me for weeks. I was mortified.

How does a young peasant girl act when she finds herself engaged to a sophisticated prince charming who is wise in the ways of the world?

My letters changed very little. They were long, sharing my innermost thoughts, but oh, so shy when it came to the expressions of love.

Shortly after our engagement, Rudy celebrated his twenty-second birthday. With small means and much thought, I wrapped my gifts for him. Two books, a little scrapbook filled with my own poems and drawings, candies saved from the dinner table for weeks, and then my letter. It took all my courage but I finally managed to do it. For the first time I ended my letter: "I send you all my love and a kiss, your little Hansi."

Rudy's answer was charming. He thanked me for my gifts and at the very end he tucked in a small P.S. "Little Hansi, do you give kisses only on birthdays? Too bad that birthdays come only once a year!"

I could picture Rudy's amused smile behind the words, and I put my head on his long letter and cried.

I was afraid. Afraid of his demanding love and of myself! Would I make him a good wife? Did I have it in me to make him happy? I was so exhausted; the demands of war and studies seemed to go beyond my strength. And as time went on, I felt a strange note in Rudy's epistles. I asked him what was bothering him, but at first he ignored my questioning.

After three months he told me the truth. His parents, practical and business minded, had disapproved of our unusual romance from the beginning. They tried to discourage Rudy from continuing our relationship, and their arguments had the force of parental authority. Rudy's home was very dear to him, and family disharmony proved highly disturbing to his easygoing nature. At last he could hide his problem no longer and told me about it.

I had no choice. I pulled my golden band from my finger, wrapped it in cotton, and sent it without any written message to his parents. Then came the harder part, to write my last letter to him. This is what I wrote: "Rudy, today I sent my ring back to your mother. There is no question in my mind that I must never stand between you and your parents. I should say, your mother and you. I know how much your home means to you, and I know also that you must never give up your home for my sake.

"I do not know why your mother is against me. I realize that you are wealthy and yours is a very respectable family, while I am only an orphan girl. But Rudy, this part of life I couldn't help; it is not my fault. You know I am trying to find my calling. I might be poor, but I can be proud. I have dedicated my life to the Fuhrer and our fatherland, and I shall do my best.

"Rudy, I never did anything wrong to your mother or you. The only thing she may hold against me is that I have trusted you and that I loved you. May you both forgive me for that!

"I do want to thank you for those wonderful days which we spent together. Somehow I knew from the beginning that it was only a dream and someday there would be a rude awakening.

"Rudy, you know me well enough; you will understand that there can never be a coming back for us. I have nothing but my pride to protect me, for I am all alone in this world. We must forget each other, and I will do all I can to forget my love for you because my heart has no more right to love. You have been the first and only one I ever trusted enough to love, and it might sound bitter when I say that I wish I had not dared to trust you. It is well said that one doesn't know love until he feels love's anguish. But it seems a lot of ache for a few moments of happiness. Maybe I was never meant to love a man. Maybe I must live only for my work. I don't know if I shall ever dare to love somebody again.

"For your future I wish you only the best and much luck! May you come back unharmed from the war to your family, and may your honorable mother find a girl for you that will make her and you happy!

"For the last time I send you my greeting and my love. Farewell! Maria Anne."

My heart swelled with bitter resentment. I felt humiliated and, oh, so lonely! I had not only lost my love — I had lost a sister, too. For Annemarie, Rudy's sister, and I had become best of friends and were corresponding regularly. But as I had feared all along, it all had been a mistake — a pipe dream, a fairy tale with a cruel ending.

I did not cry a single tear. The hurt was too deep, the storm in my proud heart too great, to find relief. I busied myself with my duties and studies, lying awake for long hours waiting for the air-raid sirens to sound. I had no more desire to see the stars, so the shades stayed shut tight. Autumn mornings were chilly, and we felt the coal shortage as we shivered in our classrooms. Frosts browned the last purple flower beds as mother earth prepared for a cold winter sleep. My numb heart followed her example.

It took iron self-control to march out every morning into biting rain to salute the dripping flag. I hadn't felt warm for days; there was no place to get warm. The rooms were damp and clammy. Our food rations were meager, but it didn't matter to me — I wasn't hungry. One morning I stood before the flagpole saluting when a wave of dizziness overcame me. I forced myself to march back into the house. Then I collapsed.

They put me in a youth hospital in Brünn, a smaller city. We had excellent treatment, but I was too sick to notice or care. "Contagious jaundice infection" was the diagnosis. The epidemic had raged for weeks, and the hospital was overcrowded. Before long I had lost the robustness I had gained in the summer. I grew pale and emaciated. I tried not to think too much, for life seemed a strange puzzle with no answers.

Days turned into weeks. My lady doctor ordered new X-rays for me, which revealed a stomach ulcer. Sitting down at my bed-side, the doctor gave me a motherly smile as she asked, "Little Hansi, is there anything that bothers you — any kind of heart-ache or worry or problem? You are so listless and withdrawn."

"No." I shook my head defiantly and proudly. I wasn't willing to admit even to myself that anyone could throw me off balance. And Rudy was a closed issue.

A few days later, after my eighteenth birthday in November, the nurse brought me a forwarded letter. The envelope revealed Rudy's familiar handwriting, and the return address showed that he had again been promoted. *"Oberleutnant zur See,"* it read. I wondered if he had been called to his new position as second commander on one of the newest U-boats, as he had expected. How proud his parents would be! I wondered if my pride would permit me to open his letter. Yes, I tore the envelope eagerly and read. It was an affectionate birthday message. I read it over and over again, especially the sentence, "Little Hansi, I couldn't let your birthday go by without sending you my warmest wishes —"

No, it was no use. I had to be firm. Quickly I folded his letter up, put it into a new envelope, and mailed it back to him. Rudy didn't know I was so sick, and I didn't want him to know.

Slowly I regained strength and finally one afternoon the doctor promised that I could leave the hospital the next day. I rejoiced. That night, which I thought would be my last one in that house of sickness, the air-raid sirens forced us all out of our beds and into the shelter. Huddled in blankets, we listened indifferently to the droning of the enemy bombers. We always asked the same question: Would the bombers pass over us, or would our own place be their target for the night? We found out all too soon. The bombs exploded nearer and nearer. We knew that the bomb that would hit us would come without singing, so we just sat and waited. By far the hardest attack I had ever experienced, it left us tense and terrified.

At last the siren sounded the departure of the airplanes, and we were allowed to climb back up to our rooms and into our beds. But sleep would not come. We had opened our shades to watch the burning city. Gas and electricity were out, and nurses used flickering candles to take care of some very sick youngsters. The night sky was red from fires and dense with smoke. As I looked out at the dreadful scenes of destruction, I thought of the many lives that had been snuffed out. Nagging questions again tortured me.

All at once I noticed some nurses excitedly run to and fro whispering. I slipped out of bed, still numb and cold from hours in the shelter, and joined the nurses.

What was the problem? Somebody, they said, had detected a dark object on the back ramp of the building, which proved to be *Ein Blindgänger,* a bomb that for some reason had not exploded when it hit the ground. Either it was a time bomb that would explode in a matter of minutes or hours, or it was an ordinary bomb with a short circuit in the releasing device. In any case, the bomb was close enough to demolish the small hospital if it exploded, and shatter the windows and sliding doors in our faces.

Since any strong vibration, even a loud scream, could explode the bomb, the patients could not be taken down to the shelter nor could the building be evacuated. There was no place to go, for everything around us was fire and ruins.

Noiselessly I stepped up to the back window. In the glow of burning houses across the river I saw the pear-shaped object in its dark outline. Some others stepped up beside me as the news spread quickly through the ward. The nurses had tried to hide the news, fearing panic, but without success. Some patients pulled their blankets over their heads, others cried softly — but everybody tried to avoid commotion and fast movements.

I pressed my hot forehead against the cold window glass. Death and I faced each other again, and my heart started to argue with the grim visitor. I had so many questions to ask, and nobody would answer.

Who was I? Why was I born? Where had I come from and where was I going? If I had to die that night, what could have been the purpose and reason for my existence? Why must "self-sacrifice" be the highest fulfillment for a human being? Everything seemed shallow and intangible in the face of death. My high ideals and goals seemed powerless to comfort. I imagined that the Grim Reaper sat out there on top of that metal object and grinned into my bewildered eyes.

My heart cried out for more understanding and more insight; but smoke covered the fading stars, and the dawn had to fight its way through charred ruins and clouds of dust. Everything within and around me seemed vague and empty. We just stood motionless and waited.

As soon as it was light enough, a noiseless crew appeared. Obviously the men were prisoners, as an armed guard marched behind them. Since we young people had never heard about concentration camps and political prisoners, we had no idea who those sad, gray figures were. They moved in cautiously, like cats, toward the bomb and examined it long and carefully. Then one man bent over while others handed him some tools. Ever so precisely he began to take the detonator apart. At last he stopped, nodded, got up from his knees, and wiped his forehead. The bomb was *entschärft* (disarmed), and the prisoners carried the different parts away.

Normal life resumed in the ward, and a nurse ordered me back to bed. With a last look out the window, I turned away. I had seen the Grim Reaper walk out of the yard. Once again he had turned his back on me as he returned to the smoldering city to find more prey among the ruins. But I had a strange foreboding that we would meet again!

After a few days, as soon as a certain amount of order had been established and trains were running again, I was dismissed. I reported back to school at once in spite of my doctor's recommendation to take a vacation and recover my full health. Where should I go to find rest? The little house in the woods was so far away, and I hadn't heard from Mother for a long time. Mail was delayed. Too many trains and tracks were being destroyed. Rudy was not mine anymore, and I had no right to go to his comfortable home in eastern Germany. Possibly his parents and sister were not even there anymore. I had heard rumors that the Russians had already broken through into Silesia and the refugees had fled through winter storms to get away.

No, I had nowhere to go, and I was eager to work again. My staff leader received me gladly, for every willing hand was needed to meet the emergencies of total war. Week after week we struggled and toiled, often sharing our small food rations with refugees and wounded soldiers who seemed more hungry than we. My stomach gave me terrible pains. Ulcers demanded certain kinds of food, but who cared about such trivialities?

Miss Walde's big blue eyes watched me with increasing concern. She insisted that I would take off every so often and go for a *bummel* (stroll) through the city. It was unheard of in school to be that favored, but I was so pale and painracked most of the time the other students didn't object.

One sunny spring afternoon I strolled listlessly through the old town square, stopping at a small stand which offered some pale postcards and homemade curiosities for sale. It always astonished me how the Czech people managed to "sell" things out of nothing; for the total war had scraped away everything usable. There was no safety pin, toothbrush, stationery, or any other luxury to be found anywhere. Our shoes were soled with wood and the tops were cloth. My only shoes had holes, my uniform was faded.

In deep thought I rummaged through the postcards, a rarity, trying to find some suitable pictures to send to friends, when a very pleasant low voice made me jump.

"Mein Fräulein, brauchen sie einen Begleiter?" (Miss, do you need an escort?)

Annoyed, I looked over my shoulder. I detested street introductions of any kind, but what I saw softened my indignation.

There stood a tall young officer in the uniform of the signal corps, his right arm in a heavy cast carried in a sling. The handsome face was marked with a deep scar across the left cheek. His smile was so pleading and boyish that I had to smile in spite of myself.

"All right," I said, holding my head high. "Just come along."

He introduced himself and chattered gaily, ignoring my cold replies, asking about the history of the castle and other famous spots. That did it. Anyone so interested in my beloved Golden City was my friend. I thawed out fast and soon we gossiped like old friends. I learned that Kurt was stationed in a military hospital near my school, had spent three terms of service at the Russian front, and expected to be sent out again.

"This time I don't have to travel far." His smile turned grim. "The Russian front is only a day's travel from here!"

He took me back to school that evening and asked gallantly to see me again. I had no desire to be around any men, but did not have the heart to turn him down. There was something about him that fascinated me though I couldn't figure it out. It took me several dates to realize what was so unusual –– the expression of his gray eyes.

He had the most contagious smile a person could have, but his eyes never smiled with his mouth. They were serious, intent, full of introverted emotions. As we learned to know each other better, I understood some of the reasons.

The memories of two Russian winters, being captured in Stalingrad, the wipe-out of his battalion where all of his comrades died and only he escaped, paying for that escape with two frozen feet and frozen parts of his face — it was obvious he had volunteered for war as a young, innocent boy; he had returned a sober, mature man.

One afternoon as we walked along Mala Strana, a famous street leading to the river where the towers of the Charles Bridge reached into the golden sky, he stopped and looked into my eyes.

"Hansi, I have never talked about this to anyone, but I want to share it with you. You remember when Stalingrad fell?"

I nodded. I could see it before me — we had hovered over the radio when the Fuhrer himself had announced the great tragedy and assured us that the death of our soldiers was the sure seed for our future victory.

"Well, my best friend was caught there." Kurt had a far-away stare. "We do not know yet if he died or was captured. But we have whispered tales among us that when the Russians closed the ring and we couldn't get through with food or mail anymore except by air, that the last wireless messages we got from within was the call, 'Send us Bibles! Send us Bibles!' Hansi, why on earth did our boys call for Bibles to help them die? I don't know much what a Bible is like; isn't it a Jewish book of some sort?"

I was too shocked to say much. "Kurt, did they give them Bibles?"

"Yes, they dropped all the Bibles that could be found. There were not many around, you know. One fellow who escaped after capture told me that our soldiers would beg for just one page to hold in their hands, and they would cry and read it and kiss it. Those poor fellows must have gone nuts to act like old women. I can't picture my friend like that at all. He was tall, proud, and strong and very idealistic. Just to think about it insults my memory of him."

We were crossing the Charles Bridge as we talked, and we stopped to look down into the deep green waters. I saw myself again standing behind the window the night the bomb had threatened that youth hospital. I remembered again the deep helplessness that had enveloped me in the face of death.

"Self-sacrifice is the highest fulfillment for a human being," I repeated slowly to Kurt. "That's what the Fuhrer taught us, didn't he?"

We stopped walking and I formed my thoughts into words with hesitance.

"I know the Bible, Kurt. I was brought up in a very religious foster home. It's a good book, but it is outdated and not relevant anymore in our days. It is a book for cowards and weaklings."

My mind pictured Mother bent over the Bible by the flickering, dim light of an oil lamp, and a sharp pain of guilt pierced through me. I felt that my words betrayed Mother, for she was no coward nor a weakling. I knew her inner strength, her noble thinking. But she and I had parted ways; I had left her and her beliefs and had given my undivided allegiance to the Fuhrer.

"Kurt, you faced death so often, what did *you* think when you thought of the end?"

Kurt's face resembled the carved stone faces above us. "I never faced it, little girl. I always knew that I would make it somehow, and I did! I don't care if it is highest fulfillment to die for the

Vaterland; I don't want to. I want to live and enjoy life to the fullest, every moment of it. Life is shorter than a breeze and I want to squeeze out every pleasure possible. Life is cheating us, anyway!"

Suddenly I knew what Kurt carried in the depths of his eyes, something he had tried hard to hide: life-greediness. They all had it in their eyes, all those soldiers returning from Russia — Walter did, too — and Rudy! I began walking again.

"Kurt, do you know why I love this bridge so much?"

Kurt looked surprised. "What does this old bridge have to do with what we were talking about?"

My eyes followed the grey, carved stones of that most famous bridge, over 1600 feet long, dating back nearly six hundred years, and my hand caressed its aged smoothness. Gothic saint figures with flowing stone robes and golden haloes looked down on us in unhurried stoicism. Above us fortress Hradčany with its buttressed walls a thousand years old, and the cathedral in the glory of Gothic and baroque wealth soared into the sky. For me they were triumphant melodies in stone, timeless inspirations to mankind, a never-ending source of peace and security to my troubled heart as long as I had been in Prague.

"Kurt, we are standing in the midst of the past and the future. Look around. History comes alive. I love history, and history is the key to understanding life and death that we talked about. Man takes himself much too seriously. We are each just a small link in a chain, a string in the human web of long generations, and we live on forever in future generations. That *is* the answer to death, isn't it? Listen, Kurt, can't you hear how those old stones talk? They tell us that countless generations have walked this bridge before us. Mozart stood here and was inspired by this beauty to give us his great music. He is dead, but his music lives. The builders of the cathedral died long, long ago, but their work lives forever. It's what we do that can live on after we die which gives meaning to life and death. And Stalingrad is a monument too — for future generations of our great Reich."

Kurt searched my face and I felt his eyes groping, but I avoided his hungry look and turned away from him. "Let's go back to school." I shivered. "It's getting cool!"

Silence stood between us on the way back. I knew what Kurt thought. He didn't care about the future or history. All he wanted was to live the present at its fullest. But I didn't feel that

I could help him with that, and I deliberately closed all the doors to my heart.

There was no sense in giving anyone encouragement. I was not interested in anybody, not even my dear pen pals of many years — not even Walter. I had resumed correspondence with Walter and my Hitler Youth comrades who were not either missing or dead after four years of war, but I had nothing to give any of them but friendship, and I never made a secret of it. But I could not understand why I was not left alone by them. Kurt came back for more strolls and dates, and I enjoyed exploring the city with him. But why? My mail was voluminous and I could never write often enough to satisfy my correspondents. I finally discussed it with Walter in a letter. I found out that Walter had been engaged, too, and had broken the engagement after a short time as I had.

"Little Hansi," he wrote in reply to my question of why men asked for my friendship when I had so little to give, "you don't know what makes us males click, do you? You see, there are two types of girls in this world, the first type we seek out when we come back from war, eager to find pleasure and relief. The other type is the woman of our dreams, the girl we someday hope to marry. You are the girl men want to marry. For marriage is more than sex and flirtation; marriage is a friendship. I consider you my very best, maybe my *only* friend I have in this world. My engagement broke because I chose against better judgment. She had nothing to offer but bedroom furniture and herself in it. Out here in the misery of war we men don't want bedroom letters; we need more. We need what you offer. You care, and I know it. If I ever were in deepest trouble, I would come to you first, and you would never let me down. Friendship is the highest form of love, and your greatest gift to me is that you are true to your ideals. Don't ever change! No man will let you go because of this, Hansi. And I am the last one to give you up. Some day I shall come back."

I laid down my head and cried — cried for the first time since I had written my last letter to Rudy. Walter was wrong! Some men did let girls go who stay true to high ideals and believe in a great love! Some men use girls like trophies to build their masculine egos. Some men write beautiful letters, put a golden band on a girl's finger, but are not willing to accept the responsibility that comes with love. I sobbed out my bitterness and my loneliness and my frustration that I couldn't forget Rudy — because I still loved him and it was all so senseless and hard. But after that I felt better and my stomach didn't hurt quite so much all the time. I gained back some weight and was able to shoulder greater tasks. And just in time, for an unusual task needed my full strength.

₆ Twilight of the Gods

One day I had to report to a refugee children's home in the city. Berlin headquarters had given orders to evacuate all the children under government care from the city of Prague. I wondered why — but I had learned to follow orders without asking questions. I knew that the leaders of our Reich could be trusted.

I found about thirty children ready for the trip, with little knapsacks on their backs. In good spirits and eager to go for a train ride, they ranged in age from five to twelve years.

My written orders gave me the destination, time of train departures, and authority to use any train for transporting the entire group and myself.

Not until the youngsters formed marching ranks to leave did it dawn on me that I was solely responsible! No other adult could be freed to help me. I had thirty fidgety children and an order — that was it!

How I managed to get all those wiggly youngsters on the train I will never know, but somehow they got crammed in. When the conductor checked my papers he told me that we had to change trains in the next city. Oh dear, I didn't know that our final goal was way out in the country! A small cannonball train would take us there.

The bigger youngsters helped the little tots when it came time to change trains. I got them all safely out, across some tracks and to the place where the country train puffed and hissed in full steam ready to leave. Then my heart sank. The train was stuffed full of people — Czech people mostly — who eyed my large group and me with open hostility. I explained the situation to the conductor, but he pretended not to hear. I went to the station manager and showed my papers. He didn't even look, but slowly raised his disk to give the signal for the train to leave. Some of the children began to cry and I got very scared and very angry.

"Sir," I said in the Czech language, "if you let this train go without putting these children on, I shall call for SS help!"

The change in that man flabbergasted me. The train had started to move, but he blew a shrill whistle and the train halted. The official screamed some orders into one railway car and the passengers grabbed their luggage and stepped out, wordlessly, making room for the children to board the train. I said a friendly thank you in Czech but there was no reply — just faces of stone. The station manager raised the disk again and the train pulled out.

After roll call to account for all the children, I opened the window to look back, and saw some displaced passengers shake their fists at me.

I squeezed myself in beside the smallest child in my group and the little curly-haired tot put her head trustingly in my lap. She was tired. So was I — tired and bewildered. I felt terribly guilty and didn't know why. Or did I? For the first time in my life I had used my authority as a Nazi leader to threaten someone and the reaction to my threat was harder to take than the fear of being stranded with thirty children — the fear which had motivated me to yell at that man in the first place.

My thoughts tumbled. Why had the Czech people obeyed without protest? Were they *that* afraid of the SS troops? Of course, the SS was the arm of Hitler's authority in all the land, but they were only obeying orders, just as I did. I was responsible for those helpless children, wasn't I? But my feeling of guilt grew and I felt as if I had betrayed someone, but I didn't know who it was.

When we finally arrived at the small city where a new, makeshift children's home waited for those refugees from the east, the air raid sirens were screaming alarm. The children crowded around me at the depot while the train pulled away in haste. The railroad station was completely deserted so I led the group to the air-raid shelter nearby, but the door was locked from the inside. The children wailed. I got their attention and ordered total silence, then I explained our next moves. The children would line up in single file, hold hands, and follow me. No noise, just walking fast in the shadow of the apartment houses, close to the walls so we couldn't be so easily seen. If the planes attacked we had to lie flat behind any shelter available or just lie flat on the sidewalk.

The many little feet moved in rhythm behind me as I led. There was no other noise or sign of life on the street except all those small wooden soles tapping sharply in the dead silence — *eins-zwei, eins-zwei* — and in the distance the mean rumble of planes — bombers. They sounded like Father's bees. As they came nearer, nearer, nearer, my childhood panic grabbed me. I wanted to run, run, run! But I remembered Mother's words; *"Marichen,* don't run, bees sting only when you fight or run. Stand still, stand still, and the bees will go away!"

I stopped, and thirty pairs of feet stopped dead with me. I motioned for the children to step back deeper into the shadow of the buildings. As the airplanes droned nearer I thought I could not only smell the chemical stench of exploding bombs, but also smoke and torn human flesh. Then the planes' hum got softer, friendlier, and was gone without attack. The sirens screamed a high-pitched signal that the danger had passed for the moment.

One hour later the children sat around tables and eagerly sipped hot soup. It was meager fare for dinner, but they knew nothing better and they were happy and relieved. So was I. I could return and report: *"Befehl ausgeführt"* (order fulfilled). I had done what was expected of me — but why did I feel so horribly guilty about threatening that Czech railroad official? After all, what choice did I have? Was there any choice in the world?

One day at the end of March 1945 we got orders from headquarters to leave Prague immediately and go home. Perplexed, I reported to my leader in charge and asked for permission to stay. First of all, I had no place to go, and besides, there was still so much work to do. How could we all leave?

My *Fuhrerin* shook her head firmly. "No, Maria Anne; orders are orders. The city is no longer safe for you girls. The Russians are standing east of Prague."

I shook my head naively. "Why worry about that? Hitler will never let Prague be conquered by the enemy. He loves this city!" Had not he spoken over the radio the day before and promised that victory would come soon? With the new miracle weapons our German scientists were getting ready, Germany would be able to rout our enemies within days. The end of the war was in sight. Couldn't I stay?

"My girl, you must leave today," she replied. "Don't you have any relatives?"

"Yes, my sister in Reichenberg. I don't know her very well because we did not meet each other until a couple years ago. Her husband fell on the battlefield in Russia. Maybe I could stay with her for a few weeks until I come back to school."

The railroad station had no answering service, so I had to go on the streetcar to find out about the possibility of trains leaving. I also stopped by the military hospital and told Kurt good-bye.

The trains no longer ran on schedule; everything was chaos. But I was told there might be a train leaving that night, so I went back to the school to get my things.

My superior wrote an emergency ticket for the train and I left, wondering about the strange expression on her face as I bade her *"Auf Wiedersehen."*

My suitcase in one hand and the last day's mail in the other, I made my way to the railroad station. The air seemed tense with hostility and foreboding. Perched in the overcrowded streetcar, I ignored the hostile glances I got from the Czechs. I was too occupied with my own worries.

I had a card from Walter, scribbled partially by him but finished by a nurse. He had been badly wounded again and was in an emergency hospital at a harbor city of Lithuania. There the wounded waited for troop transport ships to take them to northern Germany. His words contrasted starkly with his weak handwriting — a message of joy that he was coming home.

Then all at once it hit me — the news I hadn't paid attention to the day before. The Russians had torpedoed several hospital ships a few days ago. The ships had been clearly marked as hospital ships and were loaded with hundreds of wounded soldiers and officers shipped from Lithuania to northern Germany. There were no survivors.

No, it couldn't be! Walter hadn't gone through all that hell of war for five long years to be murdered when he was helpless, wounded, and jubilantly on his way home? He was the only son, the idol of his proud, well-to-do parents. I couldn't picture that handsome face of his fighting with the icy waters of the Baltic Sea, going down, down into a watery grave. No, no, no! It was too cruel to be true. Tears overwhelmed me; I couldn't hold them back. Times had passed when I was too proud and strong to cry. Five years of war had left my soul bruised and raw; I was numb and confused from all the heartaches, and tears were welcome relief.

The trip was long and often interrupted. Fighter planes attacked our moving train and left the railcars stranded on the tracks for most of the night. Passengers cried, cursed, moaned, and prayed while I sat motionless at the window staring into the dark.

Reality was slipping away and I felt like an actress on a stage, pushed into a play by an unseen power. But I didn't know my lines; I was like a puppet manipulated by an outside force. I knew nothing of what the next act would bring. I felt helpless.

In my mind I could even hear the music to the play — Richard Wagner's. His was my favorite music, though I often wondered if I had favored him first because he was Adolf Hitler's most loved composer. Wagner's music had become part of my life and my emotions. Yes, I could hear it, the motif of the "Trauermarsch" from *Gotterdämmerung* (Twilight of the Gods). My spirit longed to be brave, but premonition and loneliness nearly suffocated me.

Why couldn't I be without fear of death like my favorite heroine in the Nibelungen epic? Brunnhilde, Wagner's Valkyrie. I could never hear Wagner's dramatic opera music about her without shivering in awe. Why did Hitler love *Der Nibelungenring* the most? The end of it was dissolution, nothingness, death by choice. Why would he teach us by his example to love music of annihilation when he was building a Reich for a thousand years? Why was life filled with conflict and contradiction? How long would I have to wait before I could go back to Prague?

O Prague, you great prima donna! I am eager to go back and live in the shadow of your beauty, listen to your heartbeat and discover more of your ancient, wise soul. Why, oh, why did I have to leave the place that seemed more like home to me than any spot in the world?

Margret looked weary and the children skinny and listless when I walked into their little house. Food was terribly scarce and I was suddenly one more mouth to feed — no wonder I didn't get a joyful reception. I determined to leave as soon as possible, but where could I go? Gloom and foreboding filled the air, while a clock ticked the time slowly away and the flower-painted cupboards in Margret's tiny kitchen showed more and more empty spaces. We all seemed to be waiting, numbly waiting — for what?

7 CRUSHED

Weeks later I learned the Russians had entered the eastern edge of Prague a few hours after I left. My train must have been one of the last to pull out of the terminal unhindered before the terrible blood bath took place that reports described as inhuman.

Czech nationalists killed hundreds of Nazis and fought the German troops savagely while the Russians held back at the east side of Prague to let their Czech friends do the dirty work. Death had missed me again. Why? Most likely the woman who had forced me to leave and had saved my life lost hers, for she stayed.

Only one day after my arrival at my sister's, Kurt stood before me again. I thought I was seeing a ghost!

"What are *you* doing here, young man?" I demanded.

"I came with the same train you did." Kurt had his impish grin again. "I just couldn't get to you because the train was so overcrowded. They shipped me to a safer place to get well so I can fight again." He grimaced and I laughed.

I had a feeling that Kurt had pulled some strings or just walked out of that hospital in Prague after I had told him good-bye.

Whatever the case, he was alive because of it, and I was grateful for that.

Kurt and I saw much of each other for several weeks. He was so pleased when time came for his cast to be removed. He exercised his fingers by the hour and he could use both hands again.

One balmy evening we walked through the park and sat down under a blooming jasmine bush. The air was heavy with its intoxicating fragrance. Kurt looked at me and said bluntly, "Let's get married, Hansi — tomorrow!"

I laughed in his face.

"I am not joking, girl," he said, irritated. "I mean it. We can get our license within twenty-four hours. You know how fast the military works by now. We can be married by tomorrow night!"

"That might be so, Kurt," I smiled, "but why should we get married?"

"Because I want to sleep with you!"

"But, Kurt, that is no ground for marriage." I felt myself blushing. "You should know me by now. I marry only because of love, and we are not in love!"

"Maybe not. I know you are not; maybe I love you. All I know is that I want you and I can't have you unless I marry you!"

I laughed again. "Kurt, you couldn't get me whether married or unmarried unless I was ready for you. Why would you go through all the trouble of marrying me just to have me? There are enough girls in this city who will be yours for the asking!"

"That may be so, Maria Anne, but I don't want any of them. I want you. And I want you more than anything I ever wanted in my life; I can't eat or sleep any more, you are so much on my mind!"

I could understand how Kurt felt, for there had once been a man in my life who possessed my heart that much. But such love was not real. It ended in disillusionment and pain.

I shook my head. "No, Kurt, I would never do that to you; I doubt that I ever marry."

"Is it because you still love that Navy man?"

"No, I don't think so, Kurt." I felt very defensive. "Actually, he wasn't even my type. I don't go for brown hair and dark eyes; I go for the German type!"

"Well, at least I qualify by eye and hair color," Kurt said sarcastically, but I interrupted him.

"Kurt, have I ever quoted you my favorite saying?"

"Oh, you quoted so many sayings to me, little dreamer, but I don't know which one of your favorites you mean."

"Rein bleiben und reif werden, das ist höchste und edelste Lebenskunst." (To stay pure and become mature, that is highest and most noble art of life.)

"You are a hopeless dreamer, girl," Kurt said, very agitated. "Look, dear, the Russians are already close to this city. I have to leave the day after tomorrow. If you listen closely you can already hear the rumble of the artillery. Wake up, girl, life is just about over for you and me!"

"What do you mean?" I cried. "Life is over? Sure, it will take some more hard weeks to finish this war, but we'll be fine after that. As soon as our new miracle weapons are brought in, the Russians will leave and I can go back to school!"

Kurt gave me an incredulous look. "Hansi," he said very kindly, "the Russians will be in this city, right here, within days or short weeks. Nothing will stop them. Stop waiting for Hitler. Why don't you live it up with me — we have so little time left — all you've known in your young life is hardship and duties. Hansi, today we live, who knows when we die!"

"No, Kurt," I said and big tears burned my cheeks. "You are wrong! I shall not doubt my country and Hitler nor our victory. You don't know what you are saying. Those many friends of mine who died for our cause — how can it all end in death and defeat? Never, Kurt, never! As for you and me, I am your friend for life. That's all I have to give!"

Kurt jumped to his feet and for the first time I watched him lose control of a temper I didn't know he had.

"Fine, you dumb girl," he shouted. "Go ahead and save your ideals for the Russians! Your pure body, your dreams, all of it! They will rape you and teach you! Just wait for them. Save yourself for the Russian hordes. Just save it all for them!"

He stomped away and left me behind with his words ringing in my ears but not making sense. Kurt had gone mad to even think such horrid things and I sat and tried to understand why he would threaten me so. But it was hard to reason it out.

He came back the next day and apologized and I saw him off the following morning as he left for war again. There was no smile on his face, only resentment. His eyes shouted the same words in silence that he had screamed at me under the tree, but he said nothing, and I knew that he was wrong.

On another beautiful day shortly after Kurt left, Admiral Doenitz, Rudy's commander, spoke over the air. We sat before my
sister's radio and listened intently. Doenitz had, by Hitler's last
will, taken the reins of our leaderless nation to carry on. In a
matter of hours, even though it was not officially announced, the
whole country knew and whispered from door to door that Hitler
and his mistress Eva Braun had committed suicide!

We were stunned. Why would Hitler do such a ghastly thing?
Hadn't he promised to lead us to victory? Still, I didn't question
Hitler's decision. I couldn't understand, but I trusted that our
hero knew what was best for the nation and in that mysterious
act of "self-sacrifice" had shown a way for us. I could not enter-
tain the thought that Hitler, my god and idol, could have used a
coward's way out of a predicament of his own making.

Two days later the Russians marched into Reichenberg. I
stared into those strange faces as the soldiers tramped and rode
in past my sister's house toward the city center. I stood behind the
window curtains and watched, numb with fright and unbelief, and
waited! Yes, I knew that Hitler was dead — but I still trusted him.
I knew that Hitler's promises would be fulfilled; it was only a
matter of time!

When Admiral Doenitz announced the total surrender of Germany to the Allies, my stupefied mind refused to believe it. I
picked up the screaming baby and held her while the radio
blared its mad message. Mechanically I did what was expected
of me, but I could neither speak nor bring order into my thinking.
I felt myself falling into a bottomless pit and I knew I was dreaming a horrible nightmare. Soon I would wake up, wouldn't I?

The nightmare seemed to get worse. The children begged for
food, but we had only enough to feed them once a day. In the
nights we could hear women scream in neighboring houses, and
we knew that Russians were on raping forays. My sister and I
didn't dare to sleep at the same time; we would take turns staying
awake to listen. As soon as we heard steps approach our house
we would hide. And as I hovered in dark corners of my sister's
attic, shaking with fear, hiding myself every night, I would hear
Kurt's shout: "Go ahead, save yourself for the Russian hordes.
Save yourself for them!"

It was only a question of time before I would be hunted down
by the lustful, drunken soldiers. I would rather die than let myself be touched by one of those brutes. No, Kurt, I might have

been a foolish dreamer, but nobody would ever degrade me that much. I wouldn't let them. Maybe I should follow my friends and Hitler to the last and die by choice. But was it right to kill myself? For what cause would I die? Was there anything left in this world to live for? Save yourself — die — for what?

I was not the only one who felt past all hope and full of despair. Many Germans did what I contemplated; they followed Hitler to the bitter end and committed suicide.

One of my former summer chiefs in the department of NSV (Nazi welfare work) had been a friend to me up to the day of the Russian occupation. I had gone to him after Kurt had threatened me about the future, and Mr. Braun has reassured me that victory of Germany was sure. It couldn't be any other way. I knew that he meant it. He believed in the Fuhrer with as much fervor and dedication as I did — or more. When the total surrender of the German Third Reich ended its existence, he and his devoted wife prepared a last good meal for themselves and their five children. They put poison into the last dish and never got up from the table. They were found after days, slumped over their empty plates, horribly discolored from the poison. Other Nazis didn't have to take their own lives; someone else did the job for them.

One day shortly after the surrender, I was compelled with many other women to work for the local Communist administration. We were assigned the task of weeding around the city crematorium, a busy place during those days. There were so many corpses to dispose of, and the chimney billowed smoke.

All at once our monotonous work was interrupted by some terrible screams from the inside of the building. We were all used to screams by then. Women screamed at night when soldiers broke into the German homes for rape and robbing. People screamed when the Russians decided to raid streets or public places for Germans who had forgotten their white arm bands which marked all of us as *Nemci* (Germans) and made us defenseless "game" for anyone who felt like hunting. Screams we were accustomed to by then, but those moaning cries sent chills down my spine. Such agonized wails by a deep masculine voice — what could have happened?

After a while two Czech National Guards brought a man out from the crematorium. We recognized him as Dr. Helmer, a well-known German physican of the city and a prominent figure of the

Nazi regime. As he was led away, he wept and groaned loudly, wringing his handcuffed hands in hopeless agony.

Later a Czech city employee told us that during the night someone had forced himself into the Helmer home and strangled the mother and four children. Then to make sure that all were dead, the killer had cut their throats. All five bodies had been brought to the crematorium, and then the authorities had brought Dr. Helmer from imprisonment in a Communist labor camp to identify the victims.

"They didn't warn that poor man beforehand either," said the Czech employee indignantly. He seemed deeply moved by the heartbroken expression of grief we all had seen and heard. "It is not right to treat anyone like that. And what is it the four little children did that they had to die so horribly?"

We nodded, but nobody answered. We Germans knew better than to say anything, for we could have been shot if we had expressed the same thoughts. But what a storm I hid behind my impassive face!

How was it possible that life could have become such a cruel nightmare from one week to the next? How much could a person stand before cracking up? For several days and nights those screams stayed with me, tortured me, frustrated me with the great "why" about the meaning of suffering and death. There was no answer as I stared in the darkness of the tiny attic I squeezed into while hiding at nights to escape prowling soldiers.

I felt myself falling into a deep abyss of confusion, and my derangement became so intense that I felt as if I were two persons. One was numb with fear and shuddered about all I had to witness; the second watched the first in amazed unbelief, sure that I was only dreaming and would wake up soon to my orderly, idealistic life of the immediate past. But the nightmare held on, and I felt myself falling deeper into horror and bottomless darkness. I thought my cup of woe was full and I would have to end my life if more would be added, but I did not know about the tenacity and the instinct of self-preservation in a young life.

8 Slave Women

One morning I was required to report at a
Communist labor center for the usual daily assignment in the city.
But soon I found myself perched high on an open truck with many
other girls and women. We were swiftly transported across the
German-Czech line deep into the interior of old Bohemia. By late
afternoon we arrived at a huge farm, Communist style. The place
had several buildings, including large barns. Surrounding the farm
was a high stone wall with two gates. Evidently the estate had
been the manorial domain of a rich Czech proprietor, recently
confiscated.

The new manager and overseers, we soon discovered, had been
picked from the ranks of the farmhands who had served the
land owner. These new bosses had little aptitude for their posi-
tions but attempted to compensate with shouting and arbitrary
orders.

Dazed from hunger, we climbed off the vehicle and faced a
brute of a man, our new overseer. He shouted some commands,
and I understood that we were supposed to climb up a shaky
ladder that led into a kind of attic in the barn. There we found

a few old cots, and some fresh straw spread on the floor — our new sleeping quarters!

In my heart raged a storm of hate. Realizing how easily they had tricked me into a labor camp, I hated myself for having been so gullible. I looked around. There was no chance of escape; we were far from German territory. The white band on the left sleeve marked us as Germans. The walls were high, and the whole place swarmed with hostile, suspicious people. We had no choice; we might as well submit quietly.

The next morning, after a meager breakfast, we were ordered at sunrise into the fields. The new regime demanded production, and our overseer was more than eager to put on a good show. He rushed us mercilessly from the first minute.

We worked doggedly. My suppressed fury speeded my work. As the sun rose, the heat became unbearable; we had no water. Putting my rake down, I crossed the field and faced the sullen overseer. "The girls need water or they will not be able to work very well," I said in Czech. "We are dizzy, and some will faint." His eyes and mine met for some seconds.

I thought he was getting ready to strike me, but instead he forced a sly smile on his face and replied, "Very well, you girls shall have some water, just because you asked for it, Manjo (Czech for Mary). I see that you are a fast worker, Manjo. I hope you will become my helper in many ways!"

I turned silently and walked back to my work, thinking, "Who does he think I am? His 'helper,' ha!"

"Control yourself, girl; control yourself," I murmured as I dug my nails into my clenched fists. I had to learn to be quiet or it would make things worse for me and the others.

We got drinking water that first day; but there were other days when the man's ugly mood controlled him, and we had to work without water. Girls fainted, women screamed, and the frustrated overseer used his fists to urge us on. But he never bothered me. Somehow he treated me with a reluctant respect and left me alone. He knew that the girls had made me their spokesman, and my influence on them could be felt as we reached our work quota. I had the girls organized so that two or more able workers would take a weak or unskilled girl in the middle. As soon as a girl lagged behind, we faster workers stepped in and helped her so she could catch up. This way we protected each other from beatings most of the time.

In spite of our efforts, our group diminished in size. Nobody bothered to discuss it. Life had become a nightmare of hunger, thirst, hard work, and fear.

The days would have been bearable, but the nights! A few days after we arrived, the soldiers stationed in the next village found out about our German girl group. That night they broke into our sleeping quarters, led in by our grinning overseer. I was one of the few who got away unmolested.

The following night the Russians were back in larger numbers. It was impossible for any of us to hide or to get away; they had stationed a soldier with a cocked gun below the ladder.

I felt my blood drain from my face, and my knees shook. Again I had that incredible feeling that it was not really me facing those drunken, vulgar intruders, but that I watched in unbelief a horror play enacted on the stage of life. I knew not the outcome of the drama, but only one thing. I would not let them touch me; I would rather die.

By the dim moonlight filtering through a high window, and by the light of their flashlights, the soldiers mustered us girls. My best friends among the girls cried, "Manjo! Talk to them! Tell them we are Czechoslovakian girls, not Germans."

Yes, it was true we were Czechoslovakian citizens, but because our mother tongue was German, the Czechs didn't claim us anymore. The hate of those days exceeded belief.

I didn't speak Russian, but Czech is related enough to the Russian language that I could communicate on a limited scale. I faced the soldiers and shrieked, "Leave us alone! We are Czechoslovakians!"

Most of the Russians drew back. Into their brains, befuddled with drink and passion, struck the word "Czech." They knew better than to assault Czech girls. They could be court-martialed for that and they knew it — so did we!

One soldier called the overseer.

"Tell them that we are Czechoslovakians," I pleaded with that leering man. "Please, tell them. They will go away if you say it, and it is true!"

The overseer gave me a malicious sneer, then he turned to the soldiers. "They are *Nemci,*" he said. "Have them!"

Hate toward that spiteful man surged so intensely I forgot my fear. "You beast," I hissed, and bit my lips so hard I could taste blood. "You ugly beast!"

The overseer turned abruptly away and left us with the Russians. The soldiers grabbed again. As one pulled my friend Helga from my side, she held on to me.

"Please, leave her alone," I begged. "Please don't harm her!" I spoke Czech.

The Russian had already thrown her on a cot and pinned her down with one elbow while holding on to a pistol with the other hand. She still clung to my hand, pulling me toward both of them.

"If you don't keep your mouth shut, you'll be next," the soldier told me with a contemptuous, appraising look. He talked in Russian, but I could understand all too well. His expression told me what words failed to communicate. He turned his attention back toward Helga.

His foul breath struck my face. Nausea choked me breathless but I held on to Helga's hand. "Helga, don't fight. He will kill you," I begged her over and over.

Helga didn't fight. She lay still, her face like a white stone. I watched that Russian defile my friend and my thoughts tumbled like a rockslide down the mountains.

Was *this* what my teachers had called highest fulfillment of womanhood? Had I kept myself untouched through all my teen life to end up with this? If this was part of the human life, I would never want any of it. It was revolting, animalistic, violent. Another ideal was transmuted into a dirty lie. Sex was not at the end of a rainbow dream as I had thought. Sex was raw lust acted out before my eyes by a drunken soldier who dared to use my best friend for it, and I shook with hate and disgust.

When the soldiers finally left, we girls huddled together like frightened little animals and whispered with each other. "Manjo, you're the lucky one — the Russians don't want you because you are so skinny," one girl said who had been raped by four soldiers that night. She was endowed with voluptuous curves, and I had often envied her for it.

Another girl who had not been raped followed the thought. "It's true, they picked only the curvy girls tonight. Maybe it's not so bad after all to be flat and skinny?"

It sounded incredible. That couldn't be the only reason why she and I had gotten away untouched. There had to be something more to it than that — but what? I thought of the many stories I had heard before I came to this place.

My sister's mother-in-law, a woman in her late sixties, had

been molested and hurt so badly that she bled for days. My
great-uncle, a man I had never met, had to watch drunken Russians assault his wife and his twelve-year-old granddaughter.

I looked at Helga. She didn't speak at all. I knew her life
story; she had been engaged to an officer of the German air force
and had twice missed her wedding by days. The second time was
just before the Russians broke into the city. All she ever thought
or talked about was her handsome fiancé and her future with
him.

"Helga, don't take it so hard," I whispered. But I didn't sound
convincing, only surprised that the girls who had been raped were
willing to go on living and able to talk about it.

"Manjo, what if I get pregnant?" Helga whispered, and she
sounded so desperate. "And what will my Werner say?"

"Don't think about it," I answered. "Someday life has to be
better again and you . . ." My voice trailed off — what could I
say?

As the weeks went by, I suffered with Helga as I watched her
fight the morning sickness of a dreaded pregnancy. . . .

Life after that night became more and more of a nightmare.
Our chances for undisturbed sleep were slim. Shame and death
seemed close from one moment to the next. Nothing kept me
going but pride, hatred, and stubbornness. I was more determined than ever that I would never surrender to anyone, but
would fight and scratch like a wildcat until they shot me.

So far, I had never needed to fight to protect myself. Did some
unseen power take care of me? It seemed so. The other girls noticed and asked, "Manjo, what kind of good luck charm do you
have? Nothing happens to you. The overseer is leaving you
alone, and the soldiers didn't bother you. You never faint in the
fields."

"Nonsense," I replied. "You know better than to be supersti-
tious. Good luck charms are old women's tales. There is nothing
special about me."

But deep inside, I began to wonder. It was the same feeling
Rudy had told me about once when he survived so many close
calls. Something really seemed to protect me, but what? The religious convictions of my childhood had been so thoroughly brain-
washed out of me that it did not occur to me that God might

have been my Defender. The whole situation seemed so incomprehensible, but it was real.

On the other hand, I didn't know how long my good fortune would last, and I was not eager to take any chances. After that first visit of the soldiers I began to look around with a purpose. We knew they would be back again, and we knew that nobody would bother to stop them. The overseer seemed pleased that he could be of service to his Russian friends. The other girls and women depended on me for advice and help. It was almost as if they had made me their lucky charm. So I had to find a solution.

The first thing to do was to find a hiding place. But where? We had to stay within the court because the gates were locked at night, and the Russians enforced a merciless curfew. Czechs, Slovenians, and Germans alike were subject to it.

Then I found it. At the far end of the large farmyard stood an old barn half filled with straw and hay. The building could be entered by a small side door after the large doors were closed at night. We tried it. Late every evening when we could hear the overseer snoring, we noiselessly climbed down our old chicken ladder, sneaked across the courtyard one by one, and slipped cautiously through the small door into the straw. We dug individual "caves" in the fresh straw, and it seemed more comfortable than in our former sleeping quarters. Each night the entire group migrated to this place, where we enjoyed better rest and greater security.

With the coming of summer heat, tensions mounted and tempers grew short. We thought of little else than our need for more food and rest. We stopped counting days. We had no calendar. We staggered through the days with scarcely a thought for the morrow, because all was hopeless.

One day in midsummer everything went wrong. We were not permitted to take water out, and the heat had become sultry and oppressive. Thunderclouds threatened the ripening grain and made the overseer nervous. Before our eyes he hit a young mother who had stopped raking to still her fussing child. I could hardly bear to watch it without retaliation. We listened to the cries of mother and child. Then we quarreled among ourselves, and some girls cried.

Sunburned and exhausted, we finally dragged ourselves back to our quarters where, after a few bites of poor food, we climbed the ladder to the straw. Desperately I fought off sleep after we retired, because I knew that I must awaken the girls for our excursion to the barn. It was especially important that night, for new Russian troops had been coming in that afternoon, and some soldiers had seen us as we worked in a field beside the country road. Some soldiers had even stopped to inquire of the overseer. Those soldiers would know before evening where we could be found. I couldn't afford to go to sleep; I had to get us all out in time.

As I dozed, my mind began to wander. I could hardly believe that it had been just a year since I had taken part in that summer aid program in the Sudeten mountains. Yes, and it would soon be a year from the time when Rudy had come to that remote spot and we had run across the flowery pasture under smiling sunshine and fluffy white clouds. I could hear myself saying to him, "Rudy, tell me that I am not just dreaming. Oh, Rudy!"

How hard I had tried not to think of him during the past few months. What had become of him? Was he still alive? Maybe his U-boat had been blown up as so many had shortly before the end of the war. If his boat had come back, where was he? Maybe in a prison camp? How had he taken Germany's defeat? He had been such an optimistic and enthusiastic Nazi. Neither of us had even considered the possibility of a German defeat. Maybe he had committed suicide like some other officers. As I saw it, suicide might be the most noble way out of the whole mess, and I had considered it several times, especially since I had been pressed into this labor camp. But how could a person do it? I had no gun or fast-acting poison. Besides, *was* it really a noble way out? Mother would say that it would be an escape for cowards.

What about Mother? Most likely she was dead. I hadn't seen her for five years. Frail little woman, how much chance would she have had in these last months of starvation and suffering? Father was gone, for sure. He had depended upon medicine and doctor's care from day to day. It was comforting for me to picture those I loved as being dead. Better that than to go through days like mine.

Maybe Rudy had been caught by the Russians. No, I wanted him to be dead, too; not hungry as I was and hunted like a defenseless animal. It seemed so desirable to be dead!

Quietly I got up and awakened the girls. Accustomed by then to climb noiselessly down the wobbly ladder, we made our way quickly over to the barn. As I reached out both hands to open the squeaky side door, something warned me against going in. Was it a voice? Surprised, I turned around. Behind me stood the silent group of girls huddled together in fright.

I shook my head in disgust. "Manjo," I thought, "you are getting crazy and you are beginning to hear ghosts."

Again I stepped forward to enter and a second time something seemed to say within me, "Don't go into that barn tonight."

In an instant I had decided. My deep urge was clear and strong, and while I could not understand who or what was warning me, I knew I felt the same way as when I had left Mother and when I had said good-bye to Rudy. I knew that I had to obey that voice.

I whispered to the waiting girls, "I won't go in tonight."

"Why not, Manjo? We are so tired and want to go back to sleep. Look! We have been safe in that barn for many nights!" The girls began to whisper and get noisy.

"Hush," I said firmly. "You all may go in — I will not stop you. It's only that I don't want to go in myself, that's all."

The girls were undecided, but then one girl said, "Oh, no. If Manjo doesn't go into the barn tonight, I will not go in either. She usually knows what she is doing."

Nobody wanted to enter that barn. But what to do next? The same inner urge seemed to tell me. "We must leave these premises tonight," I whispered, and began to walk quietly toward the locked east gate. The girls followed me. One of my closest friends among the group hurried close to my side and whispered in fright, "Hansi, have you forgotten curfew? I hope you know what you are doing! Do you realize what a chance we are taking? Nobody is allowed out after 9:30, not even the Czech people!"

Had I forgotten curfew? Will I ever forget to the day I die what curfew means? Shot without warning if anyone with a gun saw us outside the wall. Oh, I knew, I knew! I nodded impatiently.

"Yes, Lilo, I know. But somehow I just feel we must get out of here for tonight. I don't know how to explain it. Please don't ask me any more questions, for we must hurry."

I had learned how to open the gate some days before through a kind Czech woman who had secretly befriended me. Quickly I had the mechanism released, and through the slightly open gate the frightened girls slipped out into the fields. As soon as I had closed the gate, I followed the group. The night was still, and the moon and stars seemed cruel in their brightness, for they betrayed our moving forms. Close to the woods we found a field where we had harvested alfalfa a few days before. The hay had been stacked on high wooden racks to dry out. I suggested that the girls crawl under those haystacks for protection and a little sleep. The girls obeyed without delay. Lilo and I also squeezed under one of the stacks and tried to make ourselves comfortable. But sleep stayed away that night. Death seemed near enough to touch and we were tense and apprehensive. The frogs croaked loudly in a nearby pond. Other night noises from the woods sounded strange and forbidding. We heard the barking of dogs, now closer, now fading into the distance again, as we sat with cramped muscles and waited.

At last the stars began to pale into deep darkness, then we could see signs of day in the east. Dawn was our salvation, because we knew that every Russian soldier had to return by morning light, and their army discipline was very strict. They would have left by the time we had crept back to our sleeping quarters at the labor camp.

We managed to get back in time without being detected by the overseer. After a short while he blew the whistle and we all "got up" and formed our routine line for report and breakfast.

I was very unhappy with myself. Why hadn't I let the girls sleep in the straw barn last night? Now we were all so dead tired from the crazy goose chase I started. Nothing could have happened in the night, for the night was gone and around me was a glorious sunrise, awakening birds, and a thousand dew diamonds sparkling in the morning glow. I was stupid — and I felt sure the girls thought so too. Was I going crazy?

With more disgust than usual I noticed the breakfast menu — soup, consisting mainly of water and salt and some potatoes, and some crusts of dry bread. I couldn't help wondering if the cook let the bread mold systematically before he portioned it out to us in stingy rations. How could any kitchen produce so much spoiled bread at all times without deliberate planning?

Well, it really didn't matter; we were hungry enough to devour anything edible. As the line began to move, I eagerly awaited my turn because my stomach hurt so much when I was hungry. Suddenly I felt a gentle nudge in my ribs. Looking up, I saw the kind face of that Czech woman who had been our secret friend.

"Devcatko" (little girl), she whispered, trying to appear inconspicuous, "I got to tell you something!"

"Ano?" (yes) I mumbled.

"The Russians were here last night!"

I nodded, unimpressed. Her words were really no news at all.

"Listen, Manjo. It was really very bad!" She pointed toward the kitchen. "One of those women over there betrayed you last night. She told those drunken soldiers where you have been hiding. Oh, those sons of the devil." She crossed herself fearfully. "They were so mad because they couldn't find you and made so much commotion. Do you know what they did? Those *hloupy Rucky* (stupid Russian) beasts got into the barn where you have been sleeping and looked through the straw. When they were not able to find you, they used their bayonets to jab through the straw, swearing and shouting, 'Those German pigs will squeak when we stab them!'

"Though they hunted for you the whole night," she continued, "they couldn't find you anywhere. In the name of our holy saint, where did you hide? I shall burn a candle to our Holy Madonna next Sunday for protecting you. Oh, you poor *Nemci,* I am glad that you are not hurt."

I was so horrified I felt dizzy. As she hurried off, I stammered a soft *"Dekuji"* (thank you) after her.

So it was known that we had been hiding in the barn! But who had told me not to go in last night?

I passed the news to the girls around me and their whispering went like the morning wind down the line on both sides of me. Carefully, slowly, in order not to arouse our overseer's suspicion, the girls crowded around me and implored, "Manjo, how did you know? Manjo, who told you that we shouldn't sleep in that barn last night? Manjo, what charm do you use?"

I shrugged. "I don't know, girls; I really don't know. It was just — well, I can't explain it!"

The line moved quickly on because the overseer yelled and whistled impatiently. Receiving my soup, I drank it hurriedly. I tried to bring order into my muddled brain while I chewed my hard crust of *chleb* (bread), but it was no use. Everything seemed hazy, and I couldn't channel my thinking in the right direction. Something had gone wrong with me. My memory did not work!

I tried to reach back into my thoughts, to tie past and present together, but it was no use. I tried to remember some basic things like home or Mother or the one I loved, and couldn't. Worst of all, those figures suddenly lacked names. No, it was not possible. I couldn't have forgotten Mother's name. Oh, what was Mother's name?

Obviously I was going crazy. Maybe soon my aching head would burst, and I would do something irrational and go hysterical. I knew what that would mean. If I cracked up like others I had known — the solution was simple: one or two bullets.

No, I had to get away from my persecutors while I could still make decisions. I wouldn't surrender and give that ugly overseer the devilish satisfaction that he had broken me — that he had won! No, I would fight, escape, leave, walk out. If they killed me, all right — at least it wasn't a surrender!

As soon as we arrived at our assigned place of work, I announced my departure to the girls around me. Some wanted to go with me, and I grimly nodded my agreement.

We looked at the direction of wind and sun; then when the overseer had left our field, we deliberately walked away. Woods are plentiful in Bohemia, and we hurried toward the nearest one. As soon as we had reached the dark coolness of the dense evergreens, we moved steadily northward, listening anxiously for any threatening noises.

Our overseer must have felt very sure of himself. He knew how deep we were in Czech territory. He knew also that Russian soldiers combed the area for escaped prisoners everywhere. He knew we would be caught sooner or later and be brought back.

I do not know how long we walked and hid and struggled through woods and fields. That whole escape is one gray haze of terror and endless walk in my memory. All I know is that we did reach the Sudeten territory, and the girls left one by one to seek their separate havens. At last I arrived at my sister's.

My sister Margret asked few questions after she had cautiously opened the door to answer my knocking. She quietly led me upstairs where I could hide and sleep undisturbed. I fell upon the mattress, and she removed my shoes. Her motherly hand put a blanket over me, and while I sank into deep sleep I mumbled into the pillow, "Everything is shattered, Sis; all broken up. But things will be all right after I wake up. It's just a bad dream I am having."

9 FAREWELL

I woke up startled. Where was I? Sunbeams forced their way through the cracks of the attic and hushed voices came from far away. Oh, yes, I was at my sister's place hiding and I must have slept very late.

I tried to get up. My body ached. On blistered feet I hobbled out of the room and down the stairs.

The children raced to embrace me, and the baby girl, Uta, gurgled with delight as she toddled toward me. How I loved her! It was so good to see them again, and they all looked fine except my sister.

Margret had aged years within the last months and her face looked haggard and worn. How she kept going was beyond my understanding. Brave, ingenious woman! Three hungry little girls, fatherless — and somehow she managed to find a bit of flour, a loaf of bread, a cabbage head, some greens — something to eat every day. The children got most of it while she watched them eat. The only person who stood by her was Papa — our real father — the man I had hated all my life and whom I scarcely knew. He lived out in the country beyond the other end of the city. His Czech wife had a few goats and a garden. Though it was a long way out there, every so often my sister left her children and went to get a jug of milk for Uta from Papa.

Milk was as precious as gold, but my sister fixed milk soup for me because she knew of my ulcer pains. While I sipped the hot soup, feeling guilty for eating her children's food, we talked softly. There was no safety for me at her place; it was just a matter of time before my pursuers would find me. And the next time they would take me to a labor camp farther east — oh, so much farther east! Siberia was cold, silent, and endless; there would be no way back a second time for me. My sister suggested that I stay just long enough to regain my strength before going on from there. But where would I go?

I slept and ate and slept again. My sister's meager food supplies went fast with the extra mouth to feed, and we all knew it.

"Let me go out to Papa's place and see if I can get some milk and vegetables for you," I said one morning, feeling almost like myself again. My sister looked surprised.

"*You* want to go and see Papa?"

"Why not?" I asked defensively. "Regardless how I feel about him and that witch of a wife he is married to, it's time that we get better acquainted. Besides, I want to be of some help to you! As for being safe, I think I can manage. I doubt that anyone will take me in; they usually come at night to get people."

With two empty jugs hidden in a knapsack, I started out. I was hot and thirsty when at last I arrived at my father's place.

"Well, what gives me the honor of seeing my Nazi daughter?" he asked sarcastically. I swallowed hard. The few times our paths had crossed during the war had been just in the reverse. I had been the one who had treated him haughtily and with contempt. I knew he was against the Nazis, and in my eyes he had also stooped below his German dignity when he had married a Czech woman. Besides, I would never forgive him for having forsaken me.

I met his steel-gray eyes without blinking. "I came for Uta's sake, Herr Papa," I said. "She needs milk, and Grittli is not very strong any more."

Papa's eyes softened. I knew he loved his little granddaughter, and my oldest sister was close to his heart. I handed him the knapsack.

From the bedroom came a scolding, high-pitched voice. "Who is out there, Robert? Don't you give any food away; we have scarcely enough for ourselves! Remember that everything here is mine! You wouldn't have it any more but that you're married to me, a Czech woman. Don't you dare!"

"What is the matter with her?" I said softly but with disgust.

Papa wrinkled his nose. "Oh, she is sick. Her meanness is slowly eating her guts out. I think she has cancer, but who knows?"

He stepped into the cool storage room and poured milk into the jugs and stuffed some potatoes, carrots and other vegetables into the knapsack without looking up. I watched him. Was he really that heartless, bitter stranger I imagined him to be? Was he really as proud and hard as I saw him?

He looked tall, gray, and bony. There were two deep lines around his thin, tight lips and his brows wrinkled in obvious anger because the petty voice in the bedroom still went on. I knew enough about him and his famous temper to wonder why she would suddenly dare to be so persistent in her quarreling. I knew from hearsay that he had given her many a beating in years past. Oh, yes, suddenly she had become the master in the house, sick or not — for Papa wore a white band on his sleeve like I did — and she could throw him out of his house and keep everything. She could make him a beggar, a refugee like so many other Germans who had to leave day after day, kicked out by Czechs and pushed over the border with nothing but their stigma and the clothing on their backs.

Papa handed me the full knapsack and stood up. A deep premonition seized me that it was the last time we would see each other, and it melted some of my resentment.

"Papa," I said, "I will leave Margret's place soon and not bother you any more. But all my life I wanted to ask you one question: Why did you forsake your children when Mama died?" My bitterness came back and my mouth felt dry.

Papa looked me up and down as if he hadn't heard my question. "Girl, you look like your mother. Did you know that your mama was beautiful? The only thing, your hair isn't long like Maria's. Her braids came down to her knees. Oh, she was so good and sweet . . ."

Did I see tears in his eyes? Impossible! That rough old man wouldn't know how to cry.

"Papa," I said coldly, "I asked you a question; would you mind answering me before I leave? Our paths might never cross again and I might wonder forever. Papa, why did you leave us?" I blinked in unbelief. He did have tears in his eyes!

"*Marichen,* someday you will understand. You *are* my flesh and blood and we belong to each other regardless how you feel about me. I didn't want to confuse you, child. I couldn't get you. She . . ." — he frowned toward the bedroom — "wouldn't let me. I married her because she had hair like your mama's. But she didn't have anything else like her, and I've lived in hell ever since your mama died. She was my angel!"

I felt myself softening and resented it. "Papa, if my mama was so good, why did you treat her so mean? They say she died because of you!"

"Is that what those Christians told you about me?" Papa jerked as if a needle had pierced him. "I thought they were better than that!"

"Leave Christianity out of it, sir," I said defensively. "I believe in it as little as you do, but if it comes down to facts, they were good enough to keep me, weren't they?"

"Yes, child." Papa suddenly looked very tired. "They did, and you should always be grateful to them. Now go before she finds out that it is you. She might try to harm you!"

"*Auf Wiedersehen,*" I said and shook his hand. I wanted to ask him for a glass of water, but my pride was greater than my thirst and I walked away without turning back to wave at him. I had every reason to despise him, and I was glad he went through hell with that bad woman. He deserved it, and it made me feel good. Or did it? All at once I felt very sad and alone.

My sister was very happy about the food and she cooked enough stew that evening to fill all of us up to our ears. It was a feast! I tried to forget that old, strange man called Papa and it wasn't too hard. I was too worried about myself to think very much about anyone else.

My head had been hazy since I had left that labor camp. Something was wrong with my mind — yes, with my memory. It worried me day and night. I felt like an animal in a cage. I was frightened most of the time. Whenever I tried to recall the past the fog closed in. In that fog I recognized familiar faces, places, people, but the names were gone. Names, where were all the names of the past? It had even haunted me while I had faced my Papa. I couldn't remember the name of that wretched woman who had struck from her bedroom at us — witch without name, did I care if I knew it?

I could have asked my sister. She knew that name and many other names I had lost. But I would never do that. What if she thought I was insane? Maybe I was! But not crazy enough to admit to her or to anyone else that my enemies had managed to crack me up! Not for the life of me. I was a German, a German of a lost, shattered, but great Reich. In my ear I could still hear my dead Fuhrer's voice: "They can break us but they can never bend us!"

If I had to go under I would go proudly with my head high, the way I had walked away from Herr Appelt, the man who begot me — the way I had left that miserable labor camp. Nobody would ever know that they had been able to get me down. Nobody! I hated them all.

Soon I had to make another decision. Not far from us lived a prosperous Czech family who had been friendly toward our family for a long time. The son of the family belonged to the National Guard. When he found out that I had returned to my sister's place, he visited us regularly, assuring us of his good intentions and even bringing us small amounts of bread and potatoes. I treated him politely, but laughed at my sister's suggestion that Vladislav was courting me.

I stopped laughing when our young neighbor came to see me one day and asked gravely if he might talk to me. I nodded politely, and we went for a walk. It was safe to leave the house with him beside me because his position protected me even though I wore my white armband. Vladislav, after stuttering for a while, announced that he had just received orders to bring me to the labor office in the city. I was horrified. Would he really do it?

He hesitated, then continued. "Manjo, there is not a thing you can do about it. Even if you hide, the militia will find you by and by. But —" and his round, simple face blushed as he continued, "there is one way out for you, and that is to marry a Czech man. It would change your status and you would be considered a free citizen of the Czech Republic. Well, and — and — since I feel real love in my heart for you, and since I am well able to start my own *domecku* (little home) for both of us, will you consider it?"

I looked into his red, sweaty face. Was Vladi aware of what he was doing? Other Czech men had dared to marry German girls within the last few months, and many more German girls were trying to make such contacts as an easy way out of a desperate situation. But with my young neighbor it was different! As a *narodny* (national Czech) his marriage with a German girl could endanger his future career.

I shook my head. "No, Vladi, that is not good for you and your future. I thank you for your willingness to save me from labor camp, but I cannot accept the offer!"

The young man was not easily convinced. He urged, pleaded, and threatened. After all, he had the power to take me to the officials! My mind raced. I had to have time to think.

Meekly I asked him if he would give me time to think it over. The proposal had come as a surprise to me, and I had to think about it first and ask my sister for advice.

Vladi nodded happily and smiled, relieved, and walked me back to my sister's home. Before I slipped through the door, he assured me again that not only my problems but my sister's would be over as soon as I gave my yes. Vladi would bring food for the children, and clothing, shoes — I nodded a friendly good night and went inside.

I could never marry that Czech man. I had not a spark of love for him in my heart, and I would never do what my papa had done. I had looked down on him ever since I had known him and I was prejudiced enough toward the Czechs as a whole that I would never join them. But I had no choice but to stall him. It was tempting to say, "Yes" and give up struggling, but I just couldn't do it. If nothing else, it would not be fair to him. I could not make him happy and I didn't want to, either!

In two days he would return from a patrol trip, so I lost no time. I didn't have much civilian clothing, but I hastily packed what little I did have, my dirndl, my only white knee socks, a sweater and some other small pieces of clothing in a knapsack, and my sister helped me to sew my few valuable possessions into the lining of my coat. The only document I took with me was my Catholic birth certificate. All my other important papers I laid in an airtight metal box and buried it in the backyard during the night. My report cards, diplomas, and other records were Nazi papers, signed and sealed with different stamps bearing the Nazi eagle and swastika. I didn't dare carry them on my flight from home.

Flight? Yes, I had to flee; but where? We knew that the

"leftovers" of Germany had been divided. West Germany lay far to the west of us. Now East Germany had become a Communist republic, heavily occupied by Russian troops. West Germany was occupied by the Allies, mainly Americans. Rumor had it that the Americans were friendly. There was a ration card system, and people could buy food. Not much, of course, but enough to keep alive. The American soldiers, it was said, did not force their attentions on women; enough girls liked to be *Soldaten-Liebchen* (soldiers' sweethearts) so that the Americans left other people alone. This sounded too good to be true, and nobody knew anything for sure; but just in case those marvelous reports were true I would try to go there. If I made it and found things otherwise, I wouldn't have lost anything.

One night later I left for West Germany, but not alone. Micherle, one of my former dormitory mates from the Nazi school, wanted to join me, and I didn't have the heart to turn her down. Her parents had been taken to a labor camp, leaving her alone and helpless.

My sister's children had already gone to sleep when I bent sadly over Uta's small baby bed. I loved that child! Would I ever see her again? Would I ever see anybody again? My sister put a crust of bread into my knapsack and a few dried blueberries. I knew she had taken them from her own children.

We did not say much as I stepped out the back door. What was there to say? I looked once more over at Vladi's house. Everything was dark. I wondered how he would feel when he returned the next day and found the bird flown. Would he become a real German-hater? I knew I was betraying his trust. Would he ever understand that I was doing the best for both of us? "Good-bye, Vladi. Good luck to you, and thanks for your kindness. May you forgive me that I chose freedom rather than a life of ease!"

We soon reached the borderline between Czechoslovakia and East Germany. Both parts were occupied by Russian troops and governed by Communists. Therefore the boundary was not carefully guarded, and we got across it unmolested.

We took off our white bands, which had marked us for so long as outcasts, for East Germany did not require them. Then with new hope we began our long tramp through East Germany. Unfortunately, the weather seemed to turn against us and all the other refugees who milled around all over the country. It rained for hours, for days, for weeks. We moved on as in a nightmare with drenched clothing clinging to our bodies until a merciful sun shone for a few hours and dried us a little. Our hungry stomachs woke us up at night while we tried to sleep in the woods or hide in the ditches.

There were evenings when I was so exhausted and racked by pains from my ulcerated stomach that I felt tempted to quit. For food we had only a few herbs from the woods, wild berries, and roots. Did it make any sense to keep going? Oh, yes, there was Micherle, who had trusted her life into my hands when she had joined me in my long journey. She was younger than I and less independent. She had been rendered too soft by doting parents who were suddenly gone. If nothing else, I had to keep going for her sake.

At night, whenever we were lucky enough to find a fairly dry shelter to sleep under, we would dream of food — rich, appetizing, warm, tantalizing food. We eagerly reached for it only to wake up empty and cold. We talked about food, tried to remember how certain things tasted. We did not long for fancy stuff; just a bowl of soup, a good piece of bread, fresh boiled potatoes. But there was nobody to share with us — too many refugees on the roads. The farmers and villagers kept their homes locked, the barns barred, the orchards and fields guarded by dogs and traps.

My greatest trial was still my befuddled mind! My memory had not returned after many days, and I tormented myself for hours trying to force my brain to remember. The search for my mother's name obsessed me, but I could not find it regardless of how hard I tried.

One ray of light shone, one consolation, one hope. In the darkest hours of discouragement and despair, while cold, sleepless, and bent over with pain, I was able to close my eyes and think of Mother. I didn't know her name; I couldn't remember many incidents of my childhood, but I still could visualize her as a person. Whenever my heart called for her, she seemed to be there; and my vision of her was always, of all things, in the frame of evening worship!

There she sat at the window looking out toward the crimson evening sky or the dark clouds that towered above the hills. Her blue eyes would get a faraway look, then she would start to sing. Her voice was not fancy or full, but silvery like a child's voice. She would run out of breath before the end of the phrase was reached, because her heart was not strong and she was short of breath. She loved *"Näher mein Gott zu Dir"* (Nearer, My God, to Thee) and *"Oh bleibe Herr, der Abend bricht herein"* (Abide with Me), and we all joined in. After the singing, Father would reach for the family Bible and read a psalm.

Yes, Mother's worship hours stayed with me when everything else had left me. Her peaceful face bent toward me in the darkest hours of the night and my life, and I sensed that I had lost something great. Peace — mother's peace — I couldn't give it up, lie down, and die. I had to get up every new dawn, move my stiff limbs, grit my teeth, and go on tramping through the rain, searching for herbs or mushrooms to still that hurting stomach, and moving forward — always west — looking for what?

Mother, oh, Mother, where are you? Is there any peace and love left anywhere in this world?

After crossing the larger part of Thuringia, we arrived in a small village. Something was different in that village. What? The place was stuffed to the brim with refugees. They seemed to be everywhere, but only milling around, not moving west as they usually were.

"What's the matter?" A shrug, a sigh!

"Niemandsland!"

"What is that? No-man's-land?"

"Haven't you heard about that before?"

No, we hadn't. If we had, I would never have attempted to make my way west through all of East Germany, through long weeks of rain, starvation, fear and endless nights to a cruel strip of land several kilometers wide beyond the village, set up for one purpose only: to keep people, homeless, hungry, helpless people, from going across to West Germany. But why? What was over there the Russians wouldn't want people to see?

I didn't dare to ask those questions aloud. I mingled with the crowds and just by listening I found out some hard facts all too soon. It was hopeless to try to make it across no-man's-land. Communist border guards patrolled the area heavily, twenty-four hours every day. The soldiers had orders to shoot at any moving object. There were some gruesome stories about people who had tried to cross it and had been shot, or caught and imprisoned.

It wasn't fair. It was so senseless. Why would the Russians try to keep the refugees in the *Arbeiter paradies* (laborer's paradise) when they didn't want them? There were thousands of people on the roads without food and shelter, and the Communists couldn't care less. But what was on the other side? Were Americans different? What form of government did they have? What would wait for us if we got across? According to my teachers in Prague, Americans were bloodsuckers like the British imperialists. Most puzzling of all, the Americans were allies of Russia and had helped them to beat Germany. Why would Russians now shoot people for trying to go over to their allies and friends? It was all so confusing. I couldn't even begin to figure it out and my head felt hazier than ever.

Dusk had settled over the village, and as the dripping fog rolled in from the river we shivered in our wet clothing. Clouds promised another heavy rain. Some windows lighted up behind drawn shades, suggesting warmth and a sense of belonging. How would it feel to sit near a big stone hearth and get warmed up again — warmed through and through?

On a sudden impulse, I walked up to a house and knocked! A weather-beaten sign told us that it had been a *Gasthaus* (guest house) in its better days, but naturally it was closed, for the *Gastwirt* (innkeeper) had nothing to offer anymore. Yes, I knew it was senseless to knock, and Micherle's round eyes stared at me in surprise. Had I forgotten that doors did not open to people like us? People didn't bother anymore even to look at the homeless, foodless, shelterless refugees who filled the roads. They didn't even bother to answer their knocking. But I knocked again, loud and eager, with determination.

Unexpectedly the door opened, and I looked into the kind eyes of an elderly man. "What do you want?" he asked hesitatingly.

"Sir," I stammered, "we are so cold and soaked by the rain, we wondered if we could sit for a while beside your hearth to get dry?"

He looked at us, two strange girls with their clothes dripping, the water squeezing in the old torn shoes — he must slam the door in our faces, and we would walk sadly into the night again.

"Well, come on in," said the man. "You poor girls!"

Had I heard right? The man was inviting us in?

With a humble *"Danke"* we stepped into the house, took off our shoes so we would not dirty the floor, and sat down by the hearth to dry our clothing. Oh, how good it felt to be warm! If we didn't disturb anyone maybe we could sit by the hearth until the people retired?

After a while the man came toward us with two steaming bowls of soup in his hands. Smiling, he asked us whether we wanted to eat some soup! Our hands trembled as we reached out for the bowls. We thanked the kind man over and over again.

Gratefully we handed back the empty bowls and spoons and sat quietly, waiting for the word that would send us out again into the stormy night. I felt a strong desire to talk to that friendly man about our plans to cross the border into the West. But it might prove disastrous. Still, this man had been so kind. Would he turn around and betray us if we asked for advice?

Time ticked away at the old cuckoo clock, and I knew I had to hurry. I threw my hair back over my shoulders with a determined head shake and said, "Sir, may I ask you a question?"

The man nodded.

"I don't have to tell you that we are refugees. We left my homeland, Czechoslovakia, weeks ago. We came west to cross the border, but we did not know about this no-man's-land. Sir, we've got to get across it, but we don't know how. Do you have a map of this area so we could find a way? We would like to cross tonight."

The man began to laugh. No, not malicious — it sounded like a friendly, amused laugh. But why would a man laugh under such circumstances?

"You naive little things!" he said. "You sound like a dog barking at the moon. How can you think of crossing the countryside with only a map? No, no, girls! Soldiers are out there day and night to catch you. You couldn't possibly make it."

"But, sir," I pleaded, "isn't there any way at all? I've got to leave because I escaped from a labor camp. If I stay here they will find me and put me back into one of those horrid camps."

"Yes," he finally answered, "there is one pass yet where Germans are going across, but the way is very hard to find. Only a guide can lead you through, and" — his voice became a whisper — "there is such a guide in the village. It's the ferryman down at the river. If you can pay him enough he may take you, but he is asking a lot. He wants watches, jewelry —"

I interrupted him excitedly. "Sir, we have a few things hidden in the lining of our clothing. Maybe it will be enough to please him. At least we can try. Oh, thank you, sir, for being so kind and open toward us. I do not know how I ever can repay you, but let me assure you of our deepest appreciation!"

The man nodded, rose from his chair, and said simply, "You girls may sleep in our house tonight. Not even a dog should be out on a night like this, and you girls look as if you need some rest. Tomorrow you can see the ferryman."

He led us upstairs to a room with two beds. The cover on each bed was a bulging featherbed, and there were soft pillows. He bade us good night and left.

We looked at each other, dumbfounded. We must be dreaming! People like that man didn't really exist! The beds felt real, and though the raindrops drummed on the small window, no rain was hitting us.

Before we retired, we ripped certain parts of our clothing open and laid our treasures out in a little pile. It wasn't a fortune, but the things seemed valuable enough to make a try the next morning. The only thing I hated to lose was a silver bracelet Rudy had sent me. A piece of my heart went along with it. Another thing I had treasured was my colorful silk scarf. It made a bright little bundle after we had tied our valuables in it. Then we eagerly slipped under the soft feather covers. We felt guilty to be sleeping so comfortably, for we knew how many of our fellow refugees were out in the rain.

During the night I awakened several times with a feeling of dread. "Maybe we're in a trap," I thought. "When will somebody come in and order us out? Surely we cannot sleep a whole night in a soft, warm bed!"

Nobody came to chase us out. When morning came, I awakened Micherle because we had to go and find the ferryman. She was not happy about rising early; who knew when we might sleep in a real bed again?

Careful not to disturb our kind host's family, we tiptoed out of the house and stepped into a dull gray morning. For the first time in days our clothing was dry, and we felt warm and rested. In our hearts we felt a new hope. The happenings of the last evening seemed like a good omen.

We found the river dirty with yellow-brown mud, and swiftly flowing as a result of continuing rain. We waited at the wharf, and I felt a pang of fear when the ferry appeared. What if the man said no? What if he asked for more pay? We had nothing more to give!

With a forced cheery, "Good morning," we stepped on the raft and paid our fee. The man steered quietly across, gazing silently into the water. We were the only passengers, and as we reached the middle of the river, I took a deep breath and began my speech.

"Sir," I said, "somebody has told us that you are a guide who will take refugees across the border if the pay is equal to the chance you are taking. Now, sir" — I talked in haste so he would not interrupt until I had finished — "I do not know whether our valuable things we brought with us will be enough, but look and see." Hastily I untied my bundle and laid it at his feet.

"No. I don't do such things. You know that the Russians would shoot me if they caught me doing that!"

I nodded emphatically. "Yes, I know, but look. We *must* get across. Believe me, we are not spies. We have come from Czechoslovakia and have walked a long, long way. Please help us! I escaped from a labor camp, so I ran away and my girl-friend with me. Is it not enough that we offer you? Look at it, sir. It's all we have to give, friend. We hold nothing back. Won't you take us?"

He stared at my bundle and remained silent for what seemed a long time. At last he nodded his unkempt head and said, "Ja, girls, I will take you tonight. I shall meet you half an hour before midnight, over there," and he pointed toward the hills where the evergreen woods spread. "Where the woods begin you will find a small trail leading into the underbrush. Stand behind trees till I come."

Jubilantly I pressed his hand and thanked him profoundly. Then I asked him to take the ferry back, for we had no reason to cross to the other side. Our mission had been accomplished.

1928 -- Hansi's Mama
She died and left Hansi as a
baby behind in a foster home.

1943 -- Hansi's Papa

1929 -- Sepp and "Marichen"

1928 -- Little Hansi and her Grandpa
The only visit from her own family - he died shortly after.

The white cottage where Hansi lived as a child.
Left gable window her hay loft.

Hansi's tiny mountain village of her childhood named Hutberg.

1940 --
The foster
mother
takes Hansi
to the train
to leave her
village
forever.

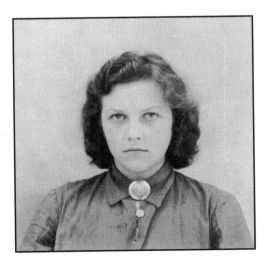

Summer of 1944 --

This is not my uniform but a
work outfit for the special
assignment during the
summer in the country when
I met Rudy. The pin has two
wheat-ears below the
swastika - but my official
emblem was the German
Eagle holding the swastika
as a sun sign in its claws.

1955 -- Hansi leaves for the U.S.A.
Her last time with her foster mother.

1957 -- Hansi's foster mother Anna
living as a displaced refugee in West Germany.

10 Escape

Time dragged by as we wandered aimlessly around. We must not draw attention to ourselves. The less a person was noticed by the soldiers, the better. As soon as it was dark enough we made our way to the woods. We knew we would have to wait, but we wanted to find the assigned meeting place. Undisturbed, we crossed fields and meadows and after some searching found the brush trail. We stepped under the trees and waited. After a while we noticed that we were not alone. Many silent figures stood under dripping trees as we did and waited. I whispered, "How will the man take such a large group across without being detected?" Micherle shrugged her shoulders.

We had another worry on our minds. Would the guide really come? What if he didn't? We had given him all we owned. What if he betrayed us after collecting our stuff?

More people arrived, among them women with children, even babies. The night was dark and foggy and it drizzled. How did those mothers keep their little ones from protesting loudly about the unearthly hour and the cold rain? Maybe the guide had advised the mothers what to do, for all the babies had diapers tied around their mouths, with their noses left open for breathing.

This muffled their little voices sufficiently for safety. Preschool children held tightly to their mothers' hands or skirts, not daring to whisper or cough.

What a relief when the guide finally appeared! He whispered orders, and the group lined up in single file. Information from the front would be given by signs, which were to be passed on from one person to the next. He briefly explained the route and some landmarks that marked the border over which we would have to run. Then the silent figures began to move forward, led by that rough-looking man who was willing to risk his life either for the pay he received or because he felt called to help. I didn't know why, and it didn't matter as long as he was doing it.

Our progress was slow because every step had to be cautious and noiseless. Flashlights could not be used (most of us did not own such a luxury, anyway), and the guide led us part of the way through dense underbrush where it was hard, especially for the mothers with children, to move without noise. Micherle and I were near the rear, while the mothers with children were in the middle of the line so we could give a hand once in a while. We had already walked for a long, long time and I wondered if these woods would ever come to an end. The darkness had become pitch black and from previous sleepless nights I had learned that the darkest hour was always before morning dawn.

Dawn was again just below the horizon and I knew it. Any other night I had longed for morning to come but now I wished for darkness to stay. Stay, night, oh, stay! Cover us, night, hide us!

I turned my head back more often. Stumbling forward I ran into trees, barely feeling the pain because I was filled with panic. If the morning light was faster than we, the Russians would see us, for the most dangerous part of our journey was still ahead.

I turned my head again, and there it was — that first nudge of morning dawn touching the black tops of the many trees behind me with a dark grey mist. Fear grabbed me and took my breath away. Then, oh, what a relief, there was finally the sign I had waited for, the sign which indicated that the Russian patrol line was only meters away. Now we were again on our own because here the ferryman had to leave us to make his way back. Now each of us would try to break through the brush to cross the border line. Micherle stood close to me waiting for my signal to run.

Suddenly we heard Russian guards shouting, *"Stoj! Stoj! Stoj* (stop)!" Next we heard shots followed by screams and then soldiers cursing and shouting. I threw myself flat on the muddy ground behind a bush, and Micherle lay close beside me, breathing heavily. The woods had opened its merciful arms and swallowed us up; we saw none of the others of our group. The shooting stopped, and all was silent again. Only our hearts beat so loudly that we felt the ground would transmit the sound to the enemy soldiers.

My thoughts raced: "Maria Anne, dumb girl, you ran into a trap. The Russians are in front of us. Shall we turn back?" Impossible! Morning was breaking, and we could never make it back through no-man's-land without being caught. This must be the end.

Suddenly we heard a child screaming. It was not far from us, calling for its mother. Dear me, why didn't those mothers watch their children better in an hour like this? This child would attract the soldiers. I worked my way toward the child, remaining flat on the ground while moving forward on my elbows and slightly bent knees.

The child was a skinny, frightened little girl, three or four years old, with blond, wet strands of hair hanging over her shoulders. I closed her mouth tightly with my hand and whispered, "Be quiet, child! The Russians will find us if you scream so loud. Where is your mother?"

I took my hand from her mouth so she could talk. She sobbed softly as she told me that her mother had held her baby brother in one arm while she, the "big sister," had held Mother's other hand. When the shooting began, *Mammi* was suddenly gone and "big sister" found herself alone in the big dark woods.

"If you stop crying, honey, we shall see if we can't find *Mammi* somewhere. Come with me over to where my girl friend is waiting." I stroked her head and wiped her tears away, and we crawled cautiously back to Micherle.

Time was running out. Morning was moving in fast, and time would work against us if we didn't hurry. I looked at the strange child who had cuddled up with childlike confidence, trusting me to find her mother. We would have to run somewhere, but how could we run if we kept the child with us? On the other hand, could we leave her alone in the woods and run away?

"Listen, we will try to make it across the border," I decided. "We cannot go back, and we will be caught for sure here in no-man's-land. We must try for the American Zone."

I turned to the child. *"Häschen* (little rabbit), we will take you along. Maybe your mother made it across, and we will find her over there. Now you must promise two things: you must run as fast as your little feet will carry you, and you must not make any noise. Do you think you can do that for me?"

The girl nodded gravely, without a word. She had already begun to keep her promise.

I showed Micherle how to get a fast grip on the child's hand without hurting her wrist in case we had to pull her, then I took the child's other hand securely, and we began to run.

First we ran down the last meters to the foot of the wooded hill. Then we had to cross a small road running through the valley, which was the actual patrol line of the Eastern guards. After crossing a deep ditch by the road we entered an open grassy area without trees or bushes to protect us. We ran in desperation, expecting bullets to hit us any moment. At the meadow's end we came to a small creek whose waters looked swift and murky from the rains. We had no chance to guess the depth of the creek. We waded into the swift water and splashed across as fast as we could. Stumbling and struggling, our main concern was to keep the child's head above the water and keep our balance. As we struggled ashore at the other side, ice-cold water ran in little streams down our hips and legs, and our coats clung heavily to us. We reached some woods again and started running uphill. We knew that the American patrol line was at the top of the hill.

Partway up, I threw myself down in exhaustion. "I have to rest awhile," I gasped. "I can't go on another step even if the Russians are after us." Micherle had lain down too, breathing in short, sharp gasps.

Why hadn't the Russians shot at us? I wondered. We had been perfect targets. Why did we get through unmolested? I could think of no answer. Did the soldiers see us and take pity on the little child between us? Soldiers may be cruel when drunk, but perhaps they have tender hearts when sober. Most of them love children. I had seen Russians share their lunches with hollow-cheeked, begging children more than once. Maybe the officer in charge was a father himself and hadn't been able to shoot when he saw those little legs running in desperation!

My eyes fell upon the child. For a moment I had forgotten her! There she stood, dripping wet from neck to water-filled shoes. Her little body shook, and her teeth chattered. Tears rolled down her cheeks, drawing straight lines on the mud-smeared face. But no loud sob escaped her blue lips; she wept noiselessly and waited without complaint. Why must little tots suffer so much? I wondered.

"Quick, Micherle, pull something out of my knapsack. There should be something dry on top. We must change the child's coat or she will catch pneumonia for sure." Hastily I pulled off the child's dripping coat and wrapped her in my dry sweater.

Overtired, she snuggled herself trustingly on my shoulders. What else could I do but pick her up and carry her? Micherle put my knapsack over one of my shoulders and then we began to climb the hill again. The child fell asleep, and with the extra load I had to use all my will power to keep going. One step, one more, one again — will the top of the hill never come? What if the soldiers should catch us just a few meters short of the goal? "Don't think, Maria, just keep going!"

I struggled on to climb some more of the steep slope, but the mountain had vanished. I walked on and lifted my foot. How come the ground was even? Where had the hill gone? Some thought seemed to try to dig into my skull, but my temples throbbed from exhaustion and fear. Keep going. Keep going. Don't, stop. You are saved. Go — stop — run! No, you made it! Thoughts at war, but my feet were too tired to walk any-more, and suddenly we had arrived! I finally believed myself and laid the child down for a moment and turned to look eastward. The dark evergreens stretched away for miles, and somewhere in those dark woods were my pursuers. Death and I had met again, and I had been spared. Why?

I bent over and looked into the child's white face. Her closed eyelids flickered, and shivers shook the undernourished little form. Gently I lifted her from the damp ground and turned to the west. I knew I had to find help fast if that child were to survive, and I was determined to find it. In the distance blinked a light.

"Let's go toward the light," I urged. "Maybe somebody will take the child in."

Steadying ourselves, we lifted the child and began to walk again, across fields and pastures, over rocks and little streams. The light came nearer while the dawn yielded to a new day.

But maybe I was just dreaming. Maybe I just thought that a new day was beginning. Maybe it was dark, would stay dark, for ever and ever — and more darkness was ahead of me. I had wished for it! I was afraid! I had escaped the Russians, yes, but would the Americans be any better? And the light in the sky, was it morning or evening? Did I really hear a lark above me? Was there anyone I could trust? Was light stronger than darkness? Would I wake up someday and know that everything had only been a horrible nightmare? Would there ever be a new morning for me?

11 From America, with Love

If I hadn't been so tired I would have noticed it: as we approached the building with the light, it did not register on our minds that the building was not a German farmhouse. I only knew I couldn't carry that child another step, and that the child was deathly pale.

I stepped up to the door and knocked. No reply. I started to beat the door with my fist, determined not to let up until somebody answered. Maybe if the farm family could see the child, they might be willing to help. All I wanted was a warm place where the child might get dry.

Unexpectedly the door opened, and there stood an American soldier. I knew he was an American. I had seen pictures of such soldiers during the war while I trained as a Nazi. I didn't remember much that I had been taught about those men; only two things: American men, living in big dirty cities, were all shooting gangsters; and they chewed gum, which was a teeth-destroying habit.

The soldier before me stood tall, armed — and chewing! "What do you want?" he drawled, moving his gum from one side to the other while his teeth gleamed at me.

I was petrified with fear, and my scared face must have spoken louder than my German words as I stuttered and mumbled my plea. I knew no English at all, and obviously the soldier did not understand my German. He gave me a puzzled look, then turned and called a name. Presently an interpreter appeared and asked me in German what we wanted.

"We just crossed over from the Russian side, and we found this child alone in the woods," I explained. "We had to cross the river and the child got soaked up to her head. She will die unless we can get her warm and dry. And please tell that soldier that he should not send us back to the Russians —" The child had buried her face on my shoulder and sobbed silently.

The next thing that happened I had never thought possible, not even in my dreams and imaginations. The door opened wide and we were invited in! Other soldiers appeared and brought a cot and blankets. They told me to wrap a blanket around the child and remove her wet clothing. Then we laid the cold little form on the cot. Meanwhile, another soldier had brought a big cup of hot chocolate. As I lifted the child's head up, she sipped the drink eagerly and greedily. Slowly I watched the color come back into her face, and her cold hands loosened their tight grip on my fingers. Gently I put her head back and told her to go to sleep. She nodded, and I stepped back into the corner where Micherle stood.

But some of the soldiers began to talk to the child. It was a strange language, to be sure, but it sounded as if they were trying to talk baby talk. They made funny faces and rolled their eyes like clowns. She sat up and watched. After a while she had lost her shyness and talked happily with those strange, big boys. They had a merry time together in spite of the fact that they could not understand each other's words.

I stood in my corner and watched, mystified. How could this all be true? Through ignorance, we had run into a situation where we were at the mercy of American soldiers, our enemies. They had taken us in and helped the child; now they were entertaining her, laughing and jumping. Why would gangsters, who hated the Germans so badly that they had come across the ocean to fight us, treat us so kindly? This had to be a big trap, but it didn't look like a trap. It seemed so real! Did I dare to think that Americans were not gangsters, just friendly human beings? Maybe I had been misinformed. Again I had the feeling that something was breaking within me. Yes, my previous concept of

American people was crumbling. Goebbel's hateful propaganda was proving to be lies again.

At last the little girl fell asleep, and the soldiers became quiet. Some had tiptoed away, and the others stood beside the cot. I stepped forward and looked down at the resting child. Well, we had accomplished what we had tried to do, and it was time for Micherle and me to leave again. The child seemed to be in good hands. I nodded a shy *Danke* and made for the door.

Before I reached it, a soldier spoke up. He motioned and tried to make me understand something. He rubbed his eyes and asked, "Are you tired, sleepy — you want to sleep too?"

So that was it! Soldiers were all alike, I thought. I shook my head in disgust and backed toward the door. *"Nein, nein, Danke,"* I whispered hoarsely.

The soldier seemed to read my thoughts. "Look," he said proudly, and pointed toward himself, "I American." His big chest seemed to widen several centimeters! He spoke slowly and deliberately, and I nodded. I understood. Yes, he was an American!

"I no Russian." He pointed toward the east and shook his head emphatically.

I nodded again. No, he was not a Russian!

"I good man." *Guter Mann* in German — it sounded similar enough to me that I got the meaning. I thought I understood and nodded hesitatingly. He grinned and showed his big white teeth.

I stared at him. Was he really good? Each of us knew what the other was thinking.

He went to a door, opened it, and motioned us to enter. We saw two cots with blankets in a small room. Most likely it was one of their first-aid rooms. He nodded, gestured, and rubbed his eyes again. "You sleepy, go rest. We — good men."

I hesitated again. It was against common sense to trust, and I knew it was better to turn and run. But somehow I couldn't! Those cots looked so good, the blankets so dry and warm, and my eyes were so heavy. I had been running away from everything for many weeks. I was so tired of running. Yes, I would take a chance and lie down and sleep while all those soldiers swarmed around. It was foolish to trust, but I would do it anyway.

With a trace of a smile I looked into the eyes of our host and nodded slowly. Politely he held the door open and ushered us in, then he closed the door carefully and was gone. Without further delay we threw ourselves onto those cots and spread the blankets over us. We went to sleep within minutes.

I do not know how long we had slept when a loud knock on the door made me jump. Frightened, I called, "Who is it? What do you want?"

In stepped a soldier in white, who proved to be an American army cook. His face was round, full, and pink. He looked healthy and pleasant. He smiled broadly, and that made his face rounder and fuller yet. A high white cap towered over his head. At the middle he seemed to be round and full also; a white apron covered a lot of waist. In his arms he carried a tray loaded with food. He put the tray down and asked with a jolly wink, "You want to eat?"

Hardly believing my ears and eyes, I nodded. We were supposed to eat something! I looked at the tray. It was loaded with food. I wondered which of all these things we would be permitted to eat. Obviously the man would eat with us. I looked into his face and waited for him to give further orders.

"Eat," he urged again, as we hesitated.

"Alles (all of it)?" I asked breathlessly.

"Yeah, all." He seemed amused.

"Danke! Danke!"

He grinned and left the room.

Our hands shook as we reached for the food. I tried to butter my bread. I had never seen snow-white bread before; the rye bread of my country had been dark and coarse. White baked goods were called *Kuchen* (cake). Why, I wondered, would American soldiers begin their day eating cake with butter and jelly, besides all the other things, some of them strange to us, just for a simple meal like breakfast! Puzzling or not, this food was tastier and fancier than anything we had eaten for many weeks, and there was so much! We also had pots of steaming coffee. It was a new taste. I had only known grain coffee before, and the new taste was tangy and bitter. But it was a drink, anyway, and it warmed us inside. When we picked up the last few crumbs, we wiped our mouths with paper napkins. What a luxury! Napkins! Unheard of in postwar Germany. Maybe we were only imagining things!

We stretched out on the cots and tried to sleep again. The cook had come in to take the empty tray away and had motioned that we should go back to sleep. But sleep would not come, and

I felt disgusted with myself. To have a chance to sleep for a few hours under real covers, in a real house, and then to lie awake! I didn't know much about coffee then.

"Let's get up," I finally suggested, so we did. We folded the blankets neatly and fished through our knapsacks for some dry clothing. Our skirts were still damp and terribly wrinkled, so we changed into our *Dirndls,* typical German garments of pleated wide skirts with white blouses and special bodices. We put white socks on and brushed our tangled hair long and carefully. We felt like new people! Stepping out into the hall, we looked around to find somebody we could say our *Danke* to once more before leaving.

The interpreter asked us to come into the office. The officer in charge greeted us with a polite nod of his gray head, and spoke rapidly. Then the interpreter said in German, "The lieutenant has contacted the Russian headquarters across the border to get some information about the child you brought in. The Russians knew about the lost child, for they caught the mother with the baby. We offered to return the child to the Russian border so it could be given back to its mother, but the Russians refused to take her back, in order to punish the mother.

"We cannot keep the little girl with us here in the barracks," the interpreter continued apologetically. "It's not the right place for her. Our office has contacted the International Red Cross in the next village. They have promised to take care of the child. Will you kindly take her to the next village and deliver her to the Red Cross lady there?"

The little girl was brought in. Somebody had been kind enough to wash and comb her hair, and her clothing was dry. She smiled radiantly and showed us her new possessions. Her pockets were filled with candies, crackers — and gum! Oh dear! After another thank you, we took the child's hand and started to leave. As we walked toward the entrance, somebody called once more. The interpreter told us, "The lieutenant said you should go right away to the office window at the Red Cross station; don't stand in line!"

"Yes, thank you," I answered. I didn't know what he meant.

As we walked away from the barracks I looked back and saw a scene I will never forget. Out of every window and door looked smiling GI faces, arms were waving and words we couldn't understand reached our ears.

I was completely mystified. Up to the last moment I had expected trouble. Now we walked away and the enemy soldiers waved after us without stopping us. They seemed to have a great time, laughing, joking — what was it that made Americans so different?

"*Danke*," I said, "*danke schön, danke.*" I knew no English, I couldn't say what I felt. I couldn't ask any questions. I walked away and wondered — wondered why those men had been so kind to us.

I understood the advice of the lieutenant, however, after we arrived in the village an hour later and found the Red Cross refugee office. People stood in line for blocks! I remembered the parting words of the German interpreter and marched boldly by the long rows of refugees, who watched us with critical eyes.

Before anybody could stop me, I said, "Please, madam, an American officer said I should come right away up to your window and bring you this little girl because —"

"Come right in," said the uniformed lady, opening the door. In we marched, while hundreds looked on and perhaps silently protested.

"Sit down," encouraged the nurse, and settled herself behind the desk.

What was happening all around us? Refugees were not treated like this. Nobody had bothered to offer us a chair or food or shelter for so long. Suddenly everybody seemed to be kind. First, the Americans giving us food and sleep, now the lady with the Swiss accent treating us like people. All these foreign people seemed to be so human.

"You girls," she said smilingly; "the American lieutenant told me over the telephone about you and the child. I want you to know that we respect you highly for saving the child while you were running for your lives. It was wonderful of you to take her with you."

"*Schwester*," (nurses in Germany are called "sister") I answered, embarrassed, "we didn't do anything special. I mean, we couldn't have left the little thing all alone in the dark woods, could we?"

"No, dear, you couldn't have left her in the woods, but many *would* have left her. We are glad that you didn't."

I smiled down at my little friend. As usual, she held tightly onto my hand or skirt and seemed to be content as long as she could stay near me. I stroked her hair while she cuddled close.

The lady continued. "We have a little problem, girls. The International Red Cross office in the next large city is trying to make arrangements for the child, but every *Heim* (emergency shelter for refugee children) is overfilled; no bed is available. It will take a few days to make room somewhere for your little foundling, and I am wondering if you two girls would be willing to take care of her until we find a place."

"But *Schwester,*" I interrupted, "we are more than willing to do so, only we have absolutely nothing for her! We gave all our valuable things to the guide who led us across no-man's-land. We have no food, no shelter, no clothing for the child, nothing. I can keep her by my side, but I can't give any care."

"Oh, I forgot to mention," the nurse interrupted gently, "that the Red Cross will provide what is needed. We will register you."

She reached for her fountain pen and some forms. "We will give all three of you ration cards for a week and some money, and I will call the hotel and tell them to give you shelter until we call you again."

Had I heard right? That woman offered us a hotel room, food, and money just because we would baby-sit a little refugee? After filling out some information blanks, she reached for the telephone and reserved a room in the only hotel in the village, which had been taken over by the occupation army. We received ration cards and money and left the office.

When we stepped out, several refugees who stood in line surrounded us and asked eager questions. "How come you girls got to go in without waiting?" asked a haggard, tired-looking woman. She was trying to keep order among her children, who fussed and kicked around her. I told the story briefly.

"How lucky can somebody be?" said one man. "Do you realize that it usually takes people eight to ten days to register, be approved, and get a ration card? And here you girls crossed the border just last night and are all taken care of already!" We smiled apologetically and left in a hurry. We had no longing to get tangled up with long lines of people who couldn't help resenting our streak of luck.

We walked to the hotel and found our room with beds ready. I put the little girl down for a nap and sat beside her until she went to sleep. So we had tried to help a lost child! All at once that child had become our talisman. How strange! We had not saved her because we expected any reward, but it seemed almost as if life was rewarding us for the deed. Kindness, I thought, must beget kindness, and hate will beget hate. Every thought, every action brings forth after its own kind.

For three days and nights we enjoyed the comfort of the hotel room. We used our ration cards and the money sparingly, but we slept a great deal and felt refreshed and rested. On the third day the Red Cross sent a message. A place had been secured, and we had to bring the child back to the Red Cross office. I did so with mixed feelings. We had become attached to each other, and the child didn't want to leave me. Furthermore, I did not want to give her up. But we had to be glad that she would be taken care of, and I tried to comfort her. Tears flowed freely as we hurried away. The last sound we heard was of the nurse trying to still the girl's screaming.

I never again heard of the child. Though I forgot her name, I often thought of her and wondered what might have become of her. Did she ever rejoin her mother? Did her soldier daddy ever come back from the war? Only eternity will give me the answers, so I must wait.

12 Rudy!

Following the country road to the southwest, we wandered along without plans. After all, we had it made; we had arrived in the West. We had refugee registration cards which assured us we could request another ration card every ten days, and even though this meant only a minimum of food, this would protect us from starvation.

What to do next? For weeks we had been urged on by one goal only — the West. Now that we had made it, we felt like boats without rudders. We began to drift. We walked slowly, passed many other refugees on every road, entered villages, and learned little tricks to make the ration cards last longer.

We saw unmistakable signs of new beginnings. In different places the people in the villages had already begun to rebuild. Children, women, and old men were busy among ruins, carrying rubbish away, scraping old bricks for reuse, mixing clay and straw for new bricks. Some stores had reopened to supply the few needs which could be supplied. Some restaurants were beginning to serve food to the milling refugees if they had ration cards and money. Every so often we treated ourselves extravagantly and bought a bowl of hot soup, though this took a big section out of our ration cards. Some drugstores had reopened, too, and tried to do business with almost nothing. They offered herbs and a limited supply of medicine to distribute for real emergencies. These supplies came from the occupation army. They also had worthless knicknacks on display for the eager refugees. It was almost an obsession with some of the homeless wanderers like us; they had to buy everything which was "free" — in other words without ration cards. It had become a habit for people to stroll through every drugstore looking eagerly for "free" merchandise. Once we were lucky enough to find a store where they sold cough drops without prescription. The stuff tasted horrible, but what did it matter? They filled the stomach for a while.

We arrived at Vohenstrauss, a fair-sized village not damaged by the war. As we wandered along the main street, we discovered a pharmacy. The urge was irresistible, as usual, to go in and try our luck. We kept our money supply up by selling part of our ration cards to people with more means, so we always had enough money. As we entered the dim old place, we noticed another young woman standing at the counter, talking to the white-haired pharmacist. Obviously they knew each other. Those villagers, we thought, had the advantage. They knew the people behind the counters and were favored over strangers. Well, that was life!

Micherle and I looked around and searched. Any offerings which would be of any use to us? Nothing we could see. Well, we could ask for cough drops. We approached the man and asked politely for them.

At the sound of my voice the young woman looked up in surprise and stared at me. I stared back into two surprised brown eyes. I had seen that person before!

"Annemarie! What in the world are you doing here?"

It was Rudy's sister! We had not heard from each other since I had returned my ring to their mother, and I had often wondered what had become of her. I only knew that the Russians and Poles had taken over her province, Silesia.

Annemarie stretched her hands out, and I took them in mine. She was not able to talk at once, as tears brimmed in her eyes. We walked out of the building, Annemarie leading the way. Little by little we began to piece our stories together. Annemarie cried while she talked. My resentment began to melt as I listened. She and her parents had lost everything; they had saved nothing but their lives. Her father had caught pneumonia and had been near death for weeks. His wife had nursed him day and night. Food had been scarce and the valuable things they had carried had to be traded for milk and medicine.

"Maria Anne," sobbed Annemarie, "you wouldn't recognize Mother anymore! She lost sixty pounds in six weeks. Father still looks like a shadow; he is so thin and pale, and he cannot climb stairs. We live out in the country because a kind woman opened her house to us and gave us an upstairs room. We are luckier than many because we have a roof over our heads and a bed for Father!"

For a moment I had to fight "it-serves-you-right" feelings. Then I felt ashamed of even thinking such thoughts. There was no need to feel good because Rudy's rich family had suddenly become poor, and we were all in the same boat. Deepest pity filled me as I looked at Annemarie. She had been a sheltered, overprotected girl, and not even the war had inconvenienced her too severely during the first four years. I tried to picture her fright and agony when they had fled from home. She looked so skinny and forlorn as she walked beside me pushing her landlady's bicycle.

"Annemarie," I said, "please take my heartiest greetings to your parents. Tell them that I have nothing against them anymore and that I wish you all the best of luck." Swallowing my pride with great effort, I added, "and, Annemarie, may I ask you how your brother is?"

"Oh, Maria Anne, don't you know?" Her eyes overflowed again. "Rudy is — dead for all we know." She proceeded to tell me why they thought so — lost boat, no mail for months.

Rudy dead? Yes, I had hoped he would be, because it was too hard to think he might be suffering in a prisoner-of-war camp. But now that I heard his sister say so, I knew that I had lied to my heart. No, I didn't want him to be dead! Life had become almost hopeful again since I had crossed over to West Germany, and I had to admit to myself that I had looked for him constantly ever since I had escaped my persecutors. I had studied lists of registered names in every Red Cross station. I had looked in every man's face in the hope of finding Rudy among the refugees. I had really begun to hope again because my heart refused to give up. My buried love had pushed and inspired me to wander on, to search, to find — to find *him*.

I had to be alone for a few moments because I was too proud to show how much I cared. Stopping, I tried to smile at Annemarie while I said: "Annemarie, I think Micherle and I should go back to town and let you bicycle home, or your mom might be worried. It was so good to see you again, and please do not forget to tell your mother I have no bitterness in my heart toward her. It is the least we all can do for Rudy, to make peace and forget the past."

Annemarie and I shook hands, and we parted. Micherle walked silently with me back to the village.

Rudy was dead, most likely. Again that cruel bit of hope that can keep people in agony for years preyed on my mind. What did it really matter? He wasn't mine anymore even if he still lived. A wave of despair and hopelessness swept over me. Was it worthwhile to keep going even here in the West? It was almost more than my pride could bear to realize my main purpose in going on had been my hidden hope to find Rudy.

A familiar voice called me. I turned around. In the distance I saw a girlish figure on a bicycle pushing the pedals as hard as she could while waving her hand and calling. It was Annemarie coming after us at top speed. Breathless, she pulled up to where we stood. "Maria Anne," she pleaded, "my mother would like to see you. As soon as I told her, she sent me right back after you. Please come and visit with my parents."

Now I felt resentful. It was one thing to send a kind message — but it was another to go and see her, shake her hand, talk to her. What if I said the wrong thing? How far could I go in forgiving her before my hurt pride would take over? What if I tried to get even with her for her heartlessness in breaking us up?

My face must have shown my struggle, for Annemarie said softly, while her eyes pleaded, "Please, Marianne, come with me. Mother has changed, and if she wronged you, she has paid for it in more ways than one. You don't know how much it would mean to her to see you. Please, for Rudy's sake, come!"

I felt ashamed of myself. Surely I would go and see those two poor old people if they wanted me to. Why should I add to their sorrow by refusing? We turned again and walked with Rudy's sister until we reached a small village surrounded by hills and woods. Steeling myself, I climbed some stairs to their place.

Seconds later I stood before two people whom I hardly recognized. Though hardly able to hide my shock at their appearance, I ran toward the mother and put my arms around her. She could not speak for a while, as she and the father began to cry. She seemed to know what I was thinking and tried to smile. "Yes, my girl, I know we have changed. Life has dealt hard with all of us. Come and sit down!"

She had food ready for us, bless her heart, and the old Silesian hospitality! She had gone to the landlady and asked for two eggs. That took a lot of courage. Some bread was ready also.

I could hardly eat, for I knew that they needed the food for themselves. The father was blue-lipped and short of breath and cried every time he began to talk. My last feeling of resentment melted in pity. Rudy's name was scarcely mentioned. Neither side felt free to talk about him.

As we got up to leave, the mother squeezed my hand. "Maria Anne," she said sadly, "I didn't mean to hurt you and I did not know that my boy loved you so deeply. He tried to find you again, but you never answered!"

"Let's forget the past," I said quietly, "and be friends again. Even if Rudy were still alive, he and I would never be able to get together again for marriage, but I would like to be friends with you for the rest of my life."

"Please, my girl, write as soon as mail will go again and you have a regular address, for you might be all Rudy left us, if he is dead." The father's blue lips quivered.

I nodded. "I will write to you," I promised, and kissed all three good-bye. Micherle and I climbed down the stairs and stepped out into the evening. Micherle, shy around strangers, hadn't said much, but as soon as we were alone, she started to chatter. The food had excited her the most. To think that we each had eaten an egg, fried! We had forgotten how good eggs tasted. What nice people!

That night we found a barn in the fields and slipped in for the night. The next morning I knew that the time had come to make a decision. "Micherle," I said, "this lingering around is no good for us. I think we should leave this area and tramp to the south. All my life I've longed to see the Alps. Let's go and see southern Bavaria."

"Let's go!" said Micherle excitedly. After several days of

walking, and after bumming part of the way on some freight trains, we neared Munich.

I was getting more and more disgusted with myself. All my life I had dreamed of a visit to the beautiful land in southern Germany. Now, while finally approaching it, I didn't feel anything at all. Something had gone very wrong with me lately, and I couldn't figure it out. It was as if all feeling had left me.

Did Micherle notice my changed behavior? I hardly noticed when she told me that she had met a young refugee and he had asked her to go along with him to Heidelberg. It didn't matter; nothing mattered anymore. I nodded, and she left! Well, now I was alone! No more responsibility, no more need to talk to anybody.

There seemed to be no hope or help for me, and I was beyond the point of recognizing my need for help and trying to find it somewhere. Most likely nobody would have cared anyway. No doctors or nurses were available for all those thousands of refugees in every city. People either survived or went *kaputt*. When I had the opportunity years later, I told a doctor about those days and he said I had been at the verge of a nervous collapse.

A few days after my arrival in Munich I found myself early in the morning on a brooding street. My beclouded mind was wrestling; darkness seemed to press in from every side, and my head tried in vain to think. Past and present seemed to blend.

Was there still war? No, war had been over for five months. A strange silence covered the land. No more hammering of machine guns, no more explosions, no ominous droning of airplanes during the nights, no more screams and wild cries as bombs found their targets. It was so unbelievably still, so oppressively calm.

But the big city carried the unconcealed wounds and marks of recent destruction. Ruins and fire-blackened trees edged the avenues, throwing long, strange shadows in the new morning light.

I wandered aimlessly through the streets. The stricken city tried to awaken. Bricks and rubbish had been pushed to the sides, making a path for the crowds. People rushed and pushed eagerly to get to shops and counters where they would stand in line for hours to buy a few morsels of food, if luck stayed by. Working people made their way to their places of labor, streetcars overfilled with passengers clanged and banged impatiently. Bicyclists squeezed through throngs of pedestrians, frustrated and encumbered.

I stood and watched. There was no need for me to force my way; I had nowhere to go. With thousands of others I called "home" a little straw-covered square on the gym floor of an old half-destroyed school. And I was fortunate to have found that.

Having received my morning food, a bowl of thin soup and two pieces of dry bread, I was free to go and do as I pleased. Nobody cared if I didn't check in by nightfall, and many more new "numbers" waited for a vacant place on the straw as still more refugees flooded in from the East.

I watched the morning rush, studying passing faces — strange, emotionless faces, seemingly hard and unfeeling, without a smile. The memory of death and the present hunger were stamped on their sad eyes and bony cheeks. But it mattered little to me. I didn't expect a smile, not even a spoken word.

Looking up, surprised, I felt the sudden warmth of the sun through my thin, shabby jacket. Why was the sun shining? It had rained for so many weeks. Almost at every step of my westward flight, rain had drenched me mercilessly. Now the bright, cheery sun and those charred ruins around me didn't seem to fit together. I stood staring and wondering, trying to bring order into my muddled brain. My mind turned in senseless rotation the words *sun, rain, ruins, death, hunger.*

Oh, yes, I was hungry again! The two pieces of old bread did not last long enough, let alone the watery soup. Why, now, why did the sun shine?

A deep urge crept up my throat, an urge to cry, to let go, to feel again. But I could not do it; my smile and my tears seemed buried under an avalanche of horror. Oh, how much I wanted to feel those warm drops rolling down my cheeks. I tried and tried again, but I just couldn't cry. With a hopeless shrug of my shoulders I walked on.

Suddenly my eyes were caught by several printed announcements. Big letters notified the people that there would be a sacred concert that night. But where? At the far outskirts of the city stood a frail cathedral, cracked but still standing; the bombs must have missed it. Even the organ was still intact. A group of courageous string musicians were inviting everyone to an evening with Handel.

Music! Music? How long had it been since I had heard the sound of good music? It seemed so long ago, almost an eternity.

Music belonged to a past world, a world I had no place or part in anymore.

Would the people let me in? The sign said everybody was welcome. And what about money? I had none to spare. I had given everything of value to the guide who had led me across to the border. I had saved nothing but my life and the knapsack on my back.

I read the invitation again: "Free Entrance — No Admission Fee!"

This was unbelievable. Why would anything be free? Why would anyone make music for *me* voluntarily? I pondered the mystery. Yes, there would be a concert, real music, which I loved so much.

Suddenly I was part of the crowd. I pressed forward, elbowed my way into a streetcar, and asked with new self-confidence for the way to the cathedral. Surprisingly enough, people were willing to direct me without so much as a frown. I swallowed hard in astonishment.

For several hours I lingered around the cathedral until the people came and filed reverently, expectantly into the high, arched sanctuary. The air inside was heavy with incense.

Not daring to sit in a pew, I stood lonely and still with the latecomers. The building eventually was filled. My eyes searched wonderingly about the church. Everything seemed unfamiliar and different. I looked up and followed the curving lines of the Romanesque dome.

The entire inner ceiling was covered with an old painting. I recognized it as a reproduction of the famous Sistine Chapel ceiling, "The Creation of Adam" by Michelangelo. God is reaching out to Adam. As his finger touches the finger of Adam, the spark of life enters the newly created form of the man, and he becomes a living soul.

Yes, I knew the picture, but I had forgotten the implication. As I gazed up, my mind struggled to get hold of something I had learned long ago at Mother's knee — something that had been part of my childhood. What was it that I tried to remember?

The music began. Strings and organ blended softly and harmoniously. The sound swelled, becoming louder and stronger, filling the old building, ascending to the dome, embracing the old cracked picture and finally bursting out through the broken, stained-glass windows with joyful ringing into the wide, star-filled night.

And then I remembered the story of the picture. Mother told it again, and I listened. Standing alone among the hundreds of quiet strangers I suddenly felt warmth within me. The ice in my innermost being broke. The music and Mother's words forced their way through the cracks of my broken soul. My eyes grew hot and moist, and my heart began to sing. Tears of joy rushed down my face, but not wanting to disturb the other listeners, I did not lift my hand to wipe my face. My heart cried out, "Mother, I can feel again; oh, Mother, where are you?"

When the music came to its glorious finale, I gazed up again. In the painting, God looked lovingly and longingly at Adam, and the man looked adoringly into God's eyes. But somehow they both seemed to look down at me, and I imagined I saw their eyes smiling.

Slowly I moved out, as the surging crowd caught me and carried me through the large doorway in the back. Then I found myself under the dark, velvety night sky and looked up again.

My mind was still searching and asking questions. There were so many things I could not understand, but it did not matter anymore. My heart had tasted again one moment of peace. Maybe life could have a purpose after all, and maybe there was lasting peace somewhere, a peace I had known before and lost. Maybe I could go out and find it again. At least I could try!

I nodded a grateful good-bye to the dome of the cathedral, where the lights were going out one by one over the picture of God and Adam. I turned around, straightened up, and with new courage walked into the night through the ruins and rubbish. My heart sang, and it was a new song. Or was it an old, long-forgotten song?

13 Starting Over

The world looked different when I woke up the next morning. The inner pressure had eased, and when I closed my eyes I could again see the picture and hear the beautiful music. As I wandered through the city, I found things I had not seen before. Autumn had come, and stepping over the majestic Alps, had begun to paint the land in bright and happy colors, even in the damaged city. The sun seemed to apologize for all the rain of the summer, for the Indian summer brought bright sunshine, deep blue skies, and fleecy white clouds. I had found a small park with benches, trees, and bushes left, and from there I watched the clouds, breathed in the pure air, and listened to the busy noises of a resurrecting city.

Other refugees had discovered those benches, too, and as we met over and over again, we began to nod shy greetings. Refugees are usually not the most sociable people, so I looked up surprised when one day a young man walked up beside me and introduced himself politely. Decent girls, I believed, did not make acquaintances with men in the streets. Street acquaintances were for cheap girls only. I raised my eyebrows in surprise and wondered what to do. Maybe it was the music still ringing in my heart, maybe the smiling blue sky or the white clouds that tumbled dreamily with the wind; but this time I smiled and answered with a few friendly words. He was a refugee also, from my homeland besides, and after a short time we had become friends. How nice!

Suddenly Gerhard, my new acquaintance, asked, "Miss Appelt, did you say you had educational training during the last years?"

"Yes," I nodded, "one could put it that way if necessary."

He got enthusiastic. "Do you know that you might be able to find a job? The state department of education and culture here in Munich is looking desperately for elementary-school teachers. Maybe you could apply."

I shook my head. "No, sir, I have no chance. They will not hire Nazi leaders, and I had a high rank in the Hitler Youth. They would catch up with me sooner or later; besides, I would not want to lie!"

"But you don't understand, *Fräulein*. They give amnesty to Hitler Youth members. As long as you were not a party member you will be OK."

Suddenly I was interested. No, I had not been a party member, only a member of the Hitler Youth movement. Somehow life had been so busy that our school had never found the time to stage the important ceremony of enrolling us in the party.

"But I have no papers with me to prove my education or anything. How would anybody hire me for any job?"

"Never mind, *Fräulein*. Try it anyway and see. You don't need to tell them everything anyhow! The new Bavarian government is determined to reopen at least the elementary schools at the end of October, and there is a great lack of teachers. Nazi members cannot be rehired, by order of the military government. You have nothing to lose, young lady; try it!"

He was right — I had nothing to lose. But how would I go about it?

He seemed to read my thoughts. "I will be glad to help you find the right office," he volunteered. "How about tomorrow morning?"

I smiled at his eagerness. Why was he so interested in helping me? It must be the same incomprehensible motive that had compelled the American soldiers to help us, the Red Cross lady from Switzerland to organize refugee stations, the string musicians to make music for us — free. I couldn't understand it, but I had begun to accept it as something real and true even though I had no name for it.

Hitler had taught me many things: pride, perseverance, logic, morals, efficiency. But I did not consciously know what love was, kind neighborly love that cares without being forced to do so. My experiences with Russian soldiers after the war had erased the remnants of my faith in humanity, and I could only wonder when someone showed me kindness.

"Yes," I heard myself saying, "I will meet you here tomorrow morning at nine o'clock. And thank you so much for your kindness."

The young man shook my hand, and we parted, smiling.

I found a way to iron my best dress, stood in a long line to wait my turn for a shower, and got my hair done in a beauty parlor after endless hours of waiting, for there was no hot water to get it washed otherwise.

Arriving at our meeting place the next morning, I found the tall young *Landsmann* (man of my homeland) already waiting. He looked surprised and eyed me from head to toe.

"Do I look all right for that interview?" I felt uneasy under his searching gaze.

"Oh, yes," he said, blushing a little. "I think you look very nice." Then it was my turn to feel flushed with embarrassment. We began to walk toward the center of the city.

He asked if he could meet me the next day to see how I fared. Then he gave me more advice on what to say, and left. I walked up some broad steps into a building.

I felt scared and lonely. In my hand I clutched a paper, the only document I possessed — my Catholic baptismal certificate. All I was able to prove was that I had been born, baptized, and named after my poor mother.

Presently I found myself seated across a desk from an elderly gentleman, who asked in a friendly Bavarian drawl, "What do you want, my girl?"

I had planned my speech and reviewed it in my mind as I tried to sleep on the straw-covered gym floor — but suddenly I couldn't say it! No, here again was someone kind, friendly, and human. Why should I try to deceive him?

I simply told the truth. I described my training, my bitter disappointment when I learned that the Nazis had lied, my lack of papers to prove anything. But I assured him I had a great desire to learn all over and be of service if given a chance.

I lifted my tear-filled eyes up and — was it possible? The man wasn't by any chance wiping his eyes! Why should he?

"Little girl," he said, "would you be willing to take a special examination before we make any further plans?"

"Oh, yes, I will be glad to!" I nodded eagerly, drying my eyes.

The man did some telephoning, and I was sent to different rooms for testing. In the afternoon I returned to the first office and the friendly old man received me with a smile.

"You did very well on your examinations," he said pleasantly. "Now for the other parts. We can give you an emergency certificate, and you will be included in a further training program while you teach, to prepare you for your final state examination. There is just one question left: What religion do you claim?"

I hesitated, not knowing what to say. Did I have any religion?

The man continued: "You see, southern Bavaria is Catholic all the way through and the people resent teachers of other convictions."

"But, sir, I am a Catholic," I interrupted, and fumbled for my birth certificate.

"Can you prove it?"

I handed him the certificate. He studied it carefully, compared my application blanks and the document, stood up, and offered me his hand. "You are hired!"

I received further orders, a train ticket, and a letter of recommendation. I would leave the next day.

I must be dreaming again! No longer an unwanted refugee, I was a normal, respectable person again. I had become a teacher, hired by the democratic Bavarian government to teach the primary grades in Grossding-harding in the southern part of Bavaria. How could so many good things happen at once?

I met Gerhard the next morning to thank him and to tell him good-bye. He seemed sober and had a lonely look in his gray eyes, a look we refugees had learned to recognize as a part of our lives. I beamed and bubbled as I told him of my good fortune. We shook hands and parted. He looked sad. Weeks later it dawned on me that my leaving might have destroyed a small flame of hope in his heart. He seemed to be such a pleasant person! Our paths never crossed again.

The Alps thrust their snow-covered peaks into a gilded sky at the far southern end of the high plateau, which my train slowly crossed. My new school could not be reached directly by train; I had to walk several miles from the station. My principal received me in a very friendly manner after he had read the letter of introduction I handed him. He invited me to stay at his house until I found permanant lodging.

One unforgettable incident took place while I was a guest there. The principal's wife had served a simple supper, and I was invited. After the meal she took a large, red, yellow-streaked apple from the cupboard and handed it to me. Overwhelmed by this gesture, I broke into tears. The lady looked perplexed.

"Ma'am," I stammered, "I think I have forgotten how an apple tastes. Would you permit me to save this apple for a few days so I could enjoy the smell?"

"You eat it," she said, "and I will give you another one when you leave!"

I could hardly get myself to eat that apple, that wine-red, luscious, aromatic piece of wonder. I had not seen, smelled, or eaten an apple since I left the hospital the year before, and I ate it with reverence. She forgot to give the second apple when I left her home — she had her cupboard full of apples — and my disappointment was so great that I had to fight back my tears.

Teaching was fun! It took a while to understand the Bavarian dialect of those little farmer children, but we enjoyed each other from the very first day. What a way of teaching it was, though! Even chalk had to be used with care, otherwise I would run out before the next ration came in. But we made satisfactory progress, and the parents seemed pleased.

One first-grade boy, above the others, seemed to love me with all his little heart. His parents had a small homestead near the school. He was the baby, born after the other children had grown up and left. Whenever I stepped out of the school building where I had my own cramped room upstairs, I would find him sitting on the front step waiting for me. I had made it a custom to go for a long walk every afternoon. After the rainy summer, the fall was unusually sunny and clear, and into November and December the days remained bright and pleasant. I never seemed to get enough of the beautiful view of the Alps, which I could see from my classroom window. My daily walks became my homage to that breathtaking scenery. My young friend, Sepperl, walked with me, his soft hand slipped quietly in mine. He would talk or be silent, as he chose. It was obvious that his innocent little heart worshiped his first-grade teacher, and my heart was warmed by his evident affection.

One day, as I checked the homework, Sepperl had not done his assignment. "Sepperl," I said firmly, "if you don't do your homework you cannot go with teacher for walks anymore!"

His big blue eyes stared at me with a hurt expression. Slowly big tears covered the deep blue star-like eyes and rolled down the soft, round cheeks. I quickly turned away.

"You've got to be firm, Maria," I told myself, "or Sepperl will think he can get away with things because he is your little companion."

But those big, tear-filled blue eyes haunted me. After school I hurried to go for my walk so I could soften the blow for Sepperl. But Sepperl was not sitting on the steps as he usually did. "Well, maybe he is making up his homework," I mumbled, and went alone. The next morning Sepperl was not at school. Perhaps, like some of the others, he had come down with the flu. Poor little fellow! I cut out some pictures for him during recess. I would go and take them to him in the evening.

When I came back from my walk, a messenger waited. Would I go right away to see Sepperl, please? He was critically ill.

I flew up the stairs to my room for the pictures, and then to Sepperl's house. As I entered the small, dark home, I heard the wailing of Sepperl's mother. My heart skipped a beat! Why was she wailing so loud? Didn't she know better? Sepperl needed quietness and rest! I raced upstairs to his chamber and froze in horror. Candles had been lighted, and the mother and father knelt by his bed. Sepperl was dead.

Heartbroken, I threw myself over the limp little figure and cried, "Sepperl, wake up!"

But his face felt cold, and his eyes were closed. His little white hands were folded neatly and didn't move.

The parents led me downstairs and told me the story. They had thought he had a cold and had put him to bed. When the mother came back after a while to see how he was doing, he seemed to be choking. They sent for the doctor in the next town immediately. When after a few hours he arrived, he diagnosed it as diphtheria and could give little hope. The child suffocated. "He called for you, teacher," the mother sobbed, "but you were gone!"

I do not know how I managed to teach the next few days. At the funeral I sat with the relatives by request of the parents and sobbed so heart-brokenly that the mother tried to comfort me. Yes, she was a good Catholic and she believed that the boy had gone to heaven. But I had no hope. True, I attended the Catholic mass because it was the thing to do in that community, but I didn't believe in life after death or any other religious doctrine. All I could see was the withdrawn, grave, waxen face in a small, white casket. And when I closed my eyes, I could see his two big, blue eyes as they had slowly filled with tears. Why? O fate, why?

I lingered at his grave, not knowing what to do with myself. Suddenly I felt a strong hand taking mine and a friendly voice said softly, *"Schulfräulein,* your grief will not bring him back. Don't cry anymore, please!"

Looking up, I saw two sincere blue eyes, a mass of curly blond hair, and white teeth in a big, boyish smile. I recognized him as one of the young farmers of the area to whom I had been introduced some weeks before at a wedding dance. We left the graveyard together and walked along the same path I had enjoyed so often with my little pupil. As the evening shadows lengthened, I began to tell him about that incident in class. Franzl listened patiently, then spoke. He spoke without polish, with plain words, but his simple explanations comforted me more than any deep philosophy. My guilt and sorrow began to lift, and when at last I climbed the stairs to my room, I felt able to face life again.

He and I became fast friends. The community began to whisper as we appeared everywhere together. I felt a little worried about the whole thing. One of his friends told me that Franzl's parents gave him a hard time. He was the heir to one of the richest farms in the county, and I was poor as a mouse in comparison.

At Christmas he brought me a piece of heirloom jewelry intended to be worn by the future wife of that family's heir. My head spun! His mother had sent the gift to me. The son had won the family over, but did I want that?

Two weeks after Christmas I received an emergency visit from my supervisor. He urgently needed a new teacher for a village school twenty kilometers to the south. It would be no easy task. Since the government had put a refugee camp into the former dance hall of that village, the number of students had grown too great for the school's single classroom, and I would have to teach in two shifts. No books, no teaching help, eight grades, the responsibilities of a principal on top of the long teaching hours, dealing with the community and a stubborn school board — the job was enough to scare anyone. That's why the supervisor hadn't found a teacher for that place.

"Are you aware of my age, sir?" I asked.

"Yes, Miss Appelt." He bowed politely. "But I think you can do it."

"I will try, if you will back me up," I promised.

I packed my few belongings, visited a little snow-covered grave once more, and left a friendly community behind me — and a very unhappy young man.

Would my heart ever find a home again? I did not feel that I had been cut out to be a Bavarian farmer's wife. That old German saying sounded convincing that Alpine flowers do not thrive well in other soil; and strange flowers, on the other hand, tend to wilt in the Alps. I knew I competed as a strange flower among the native girls, and they had let me know about it!

Why had I accepted so hard a job? Maybe it had been a welcome escape. Maybe it was my nature. Certainly I had a challenge on my hands. I busied myself in my many new tasks from the day of my arrival. The presiding *Bürgermeister* of the village acted understanding and friendly and helped me get started.

14 WHIRLWIND

After a few days in my new post an intriguing idea struck me. The neighboring village had not been able to reopen its school for lack of a teacher, and suddenly I thought of Annemarie, Rudy's sister, in northern Bavaria. We had exchanged letters after postal service had begun, and I knew she looked for a job. I told my supervisor about her. He reacted with enthusiasm in spite of the fact that she belonged to the Lutheran Church, and I invited her to come and visit me.

They hired her at once, and from the beginning we immensely enjoyed working together. We planned, tried new methods, helped each other in many problems, and roomed together in my school apartment. The pupils made good progress, and the parents began to accept us as their friends. They customarily invited the two *Schulfräuleins* to weddings, dances, and church feasts. Soon we had a reputation as good dancers and our lives filled to the brim with social events. Life had turned almost normal for us, even pleasant, except for shortages of material things, but that was not important to people brought back from death.

Into this calm scene descended a bomb — or was it a whirlwind? There had been a school holiday, and I had gone back to my former school community to visit friends. There my blond farmer friend insisted that I spend some time in his house. Knowing the custom of the land, I realized he was trying to compel me to make a decision. A boy didn't bring a girl home to his parents unless he had honest intentions of marriage. I felt uneasy, but yielded to his urging and visited with his parents.

While we made small talk, the telephone rang. Franzl answered and looked surprised. "It's for you, Maria Anne!"

"For me? Who would call me? Nobody knows I am at your house but Annemarie."

It was Annemarie. She had found a telephone in the mayor's office. She sounded choked and excited. "Maria Anne," she stuttered, "I just got a letter from my mother. The International Red Cross has found my brother! He is alive and on his way to see my parents. I know he will come down to see us. What shall I answer my mother?"

What should I say? Franzl stood beside me, waiting and wondering. My own heart and head spun like a wild carousel. And Annemarie, at the other end of the line cried and laughed at the same time. I knew what it meant to her; she had worshiped her brother.

Well, I had to answer. "Tell your brother that he is more than welcome to visit you, Annemarie! After all, dear, he is the brother of my best friend, and I will accept him as such. Annemarie, I am so happy that he is alive. I know what it means to you and your family. You know my personal attitude; as long as he respects it, everything will be all right."

I had to be alone and collect my thoughts. I excused myself as soon as possible and in deepest turmoil returned home immediately. The past was coming alive again, and fear gripped me. But Annemarie bubbled over with joy. She had already sent a letter telling Rudy to come and had made a thousand plans.

He came! It was April, and a late snow had covered the land. Late in the evening, just as we were ready to retire, I answered a knock on the door and saw two men in navy-blue suits. Rudy stood before me, slim and haggard, while his friend, Riko, seemed to poke him from behind. Both looked cold and hungry.

"Welcome, and come in," I said with forced cheerfulness, and shook hands with both.

Our hearth beamed warmth, and we soon had hot food ready for the weary travelers. Rudy didn't say much, but sat quietly trying to warm his cold, wet feet. Annemarie busied herself getting places ready for the boys to sleep, and I tried to keep conversation going. I couldn't help feeling sorry for Rudy. He had changed so much. All his youthful assurance was gone, and he seemed depressed and lonely. I knew how he felt. His whole world had broken, just as mine had; only he had not yet managed to pick up the leftover pieces.

The tension eased after a few days, and Rudy and I slowly found a way to talk. I watched myself carefully so that my heart would not slip again, because I was more determined than ever not to fall in love with him again. Rudy had just the opposite idea, as I found out later.

He applied at the University of Munich to study philosophy and was accepted. Munich was only a few hours away from my school and Rudy had every reason to return to my place every so often since his sister lived with me. He had never been a man of many words but he worked his way into my heart again by his quiet determination and his gentle disposition.

The breaking up with my jolly farmer friend left me overly sensitive and I felt guilty and resentful, but Rudy's patience and his arguments won out. I had no choice — Rudy needed me! He loved me, I was finally convinced of that, and I had loved him for too long to be unreasonable, but what he couldn't understand was that I wasn't the same girl he had proposed to just two years earlier. The thought of marriage frightened me. I didn't feel ready for it and I wondered if I ever would.

When Rudy had put his ring on my finger that unforgettable summer before the war ended, I had been a young, sheltered girl, full of romantic dreams and plans. Now I felt weary and disillusioned about love and life and I dreaded many things.

I dreaded the physical relationship of marriage. Would I be able to shake the memories of drunken soldiers grabbing for girls? Would I be able to forget Helga's white face pleading for help? But I hid my fears and smiled and we announced our engagement and the wedding date. Rudy was radiant, almost like his old, confident self again. He didn't seem to notice how quiet and thin I was getting — my ulcers acted up again, and it wasn't just my fear of marriage that started it either.

Our engagement had caused unexpected trouble in other ways, too. Of all things, we experienced difficulties because of our religion. It was a cruel joke, for neither of us had any belief of any kind, but I was a Catholic by baptism and by convenience since my job demanded it. I had never had any Catholic upbringing, but now I attended the Catholic Church every Sunday. Carefully I had watched every movement of other churchgoers, learning the forms of worship and thus fitting myself into the community customs. Other than that I didn't even bother to give religion any consideration. Neither did Rudy. He was a Protestant, nominal only, but foolish enough to tell that to my priest. That was the beginning of "cold war" between the two! I stood in the middle.

The priest of the area, a feared and highly respected figure, had never been my friend. I avoided him. When I announced my engagement, he felt it his duty to stop our marriage. As was the custom, I had to attend a preparatory catechism for marriage. Since Rudy was not Catholic, he did not attend these lectures and I went alone.

How I dreaded every lecture. The priest reminded me of my foster father — so full of zeal, but with no love! He threatened with hell fire and condemnation if I didn't give Rudy up. I looked up, tortured, and pleaded:

"Reverend Father, please try to understand! My fiancé needs me. I cannot let him go, for his sake. He lost everything — his home, his career, his future. He might go the wrong way if I turn my back on him. Can't you understand? He is a human being — there is a human responsibility!"

But the man in the black robe shook his head. No, he couldn't understand and he threatened not to perform the marriage. That would have been a catastrophe, because a ceremony before the judge alone would not have been accepted as legal by the community. I *had* to get married in the church.

Rudy was no help. He still had some rough Navy manners that irritated me to no end. He insulted the priest, teased me about my sensitivity, and caused tensions in the community.

A very influential farmer whose many children I taught and adored stepped in at last and helped us out. He talked to his friend the bishop and we received permission to be married. Rudy was triumphant. Now the priest had to marry us.

Our wedding became a community affair. Pupils and parents showered us with gifts and attention. All my small pupils strewed flowers and lined the aisles with lighted candles as we entered the nine-hundred-year-old church, filled to the walls with people and flowers, the smell of incense heavy in the air. With a face of stone the priest united us. Rudy felt too happy to be mean and was more than willing to bury the battle ax, but the priest was not.

After an elaborate dinner, my husband and I danced the wedding dance according to an old Bavarian custom, while the other people formed a large circle and watched. When we finished our waltz, the rest of the dancers joined us. Long after we had left the dance floor, we could still hear the music of the brass band and the stomping of many feet, clear into the early morning. Yes, it had been a gala occasion for everybody. Villagers talked about the *Schulfräulein's* wedding for a long time — longer than we did!

We had no honeymoon; Rudy had to return to the university after the weekend, and I continued teaching. He did not like to leave me every Monday morning, because my health began to fail again. I became frightfully thin and pale and began to fear the darkness. The priest felt it his religious duty to threaten me every so often that our marriage would not last, and life seemed to get more and more difficult. Rudy and I had a hard time adjusting to our new way of life. We both tried hard, but slipped deeper into misunderstandings and estrangement. We were not the same young people who had wandered so happily among the flowering meadows just two years before.

After our first year of marriage, which was a nightmare, I was convinced I had made a mistake in marrying Rudy. Maybe I had no potential as a good wife. Maybe we were just incompatible. I thought I had found a new beginning, but it seemed only the beginning of a bitter end. Rudy and I were ready to give up.

15 THE OLD BOOK

In our little living room, just below the ceiling in the corner, hung a small crucifix. A Catholic farmer's wife had brought it to me as a gift before I got married.

"You can't start a marriage without him in your home," she had said, very motherly and very pious. She had told me to pray the Lord's Prayer and some Hail Mary's before the cross five times every day. Obediently I had hung the crucifix where she had suggested. I tried to be obliging and avoid hurt feelings, but I had never been able to say the prayers; it would have been hypocrisy. It was bad enough that I had to act religious in church, but I would never pray to that Jesus in my home. The Nazis had taught me he was an imposter, the illegitimate child of a Jewish girl by a Roman soldier. I would have nothing to do with such a person.

It had been another rough weekend between Rudy and me, and he had left for a week of studies at the University in Munich, where he had switched to studying law. I knew that my husband was desperate; he wanted to save our marriage. But I was too worn out to care any more. I felt glad that he had gone for another week. Everything seemed so hopeless. We lived in two different worlds and couldn't fit together. Our ethical principles clashed constantly. My past made marriage unbearable for me.

I couldn't forget the brutality I had seen, and estrangement held me at the same time Rudy did. How far apart can two people be while sleeping in the same bed?

Not until our marriage did I realize how great our differences were. I had little knowledge of the life Rudy had led up to the day of our wedding. It had been unusual, to say the least! After a short time in a prisoner-of-war camp he had established himself on the black market as a cigarette trader. His knowledge of the English language helped. He bought cigarettes from the Allied soldiers for one German mark apiece and sold them to nicotine-hungry German customers for five to seven marks. His business had flourished, and he was known in certain circles as the "cigarette king." At times he had thousands of cigarettes stored in his apartment. Never in his life had Rudy done manual labor; it was beneath him.

I hated this illegal business and insisted that a hard day's work never degraded anybody. But what would happen to Rudy if I divorced him? I had seen a lawyer already and he wondered if there might be a chance to annul our marriage. That sounded good to me. But what about Rudy? Would it leave him scarred for life? His love for me seemed to deepen in proportion to our insoluble difficulties; he was not ready to let me go.

I looked up at the cross. "You surely haven't done much for this home, Christ," I said defiantly. On a sudden impulse I stepped on a chair and took the cross down and put it in the closet. I didn't care any more what my motherly farmer friend would say. But the empty spot on the wall seemed to bother me more than the cross, and my mind would go back to that naked, bruised figure in the closet.

Five Lord's Prayers, the woman had said. Did I know the Lord's Prayer by heart? Sure, I joined every Sunday in church when the people chanted and I murmured with the students when we had morning prayer.

"Our Father," I thought. Well, I could acknowledge a God if I had to. That was feasible since Hitler had taught us to believe in a supreme power, as long as it wasn't that Jesus Christ. But "Father"? Never mind! Who needed a father, anyway? Someone who looked down on me, scolding, punishing, demanding — I could never please him even if I tried. But that wasn't my greatest concern. It was that man on the cross. Sure, my mother believed in him, but was he really there when she needed him? "God, where is Mother? I have nightmares and I dream every so often — I see her homeless, wandering from place to place, hungry, alone, lost, like the many old refugee women I passed on the way to the West. Mother is dying of hunger in my dreams. You, God, are you looking after her? I don't ask anything for me, but care for her *if* you are up there, God; don't let her suffer!"

I had said it aloud and my voice startled me in the stillness of my lonely apartment. What was wrong with me? Was I by any chance praying? Well, if it did Mother any good, I would say *ten* Lord's Prayers a day! I would burn a hundred candles, too. And I would do the same for Rudy.

Mother and Rudy, the two people I worried most about — I would do anything to see them happy. But religion was a fairy tale to me — and life was not!

My classroom had been my refuge and a haven of peace. My pupils and I understood each other. We loved each other, harmonized with each other. The more conflicts I faced the more I fled to my teaching for relief. But lately I wasn't even finding peace in the classroom.

Whenever I looked up from my desk I looked at a cross. By rules of the church, every school in our area had a large cross on the wall. The pupils would turn to it when praying.

I couldn't remember much about the cross-story anymore, just that the Jews had shouted, "His blood may come upon us and our children." I remembered what the SS teacher had said — the Jews were cursed for killing him — but why? Why couldn't I remember more about those things? The haziness in my head increased again and I felt trapped — caged like an animal by friction, pressures, and agony. Wouldn't it have been better if I had died during the war like my friend Fluntl? At least he had died feeling victorious — died for a cause — now there was nothing left to live or die for. Miserable existence!

Rudy walked in Friday night with a big smile. He had a new bounce in his step. What was he up to now? I put up all my defenses. No new upsets for me, please. My stomach already felt as if it had a hundred knives in it.

"Look what I have!" Rudy looked sheepish and a bit embarrassed. He unwrapped an old, black book and handed it to me.

"A Bible?" I felt blank and puzzled. "What are you doing with a Bible, man? And where did you find it?" I bit my tongue and swallowed the rest of my words, for I almost asked, "Did you steal it?"

Rudy had no qualms about taking certain things if he needed or wanted them. It was in the spirit of a lost war to help yourself to anything you could, except that I couldn't, and Rudy and I had big arguments about it.

Rudy seemed to know what I thought, and he hastened to explain. "I found it in a used book store — very cheap!"

"Why did you get it?"

Rudy hesitated for a moment. "I fell into conversation with a young fellow on my way to the railroad last Monday morning. He is only a kid, really, but he knows religion. He reads his Bible so much he knows it all by heart. He belongs to one of those sects and sounds a bit mixed up, but he says the Catholics are wrong and he can prove it from the Bible so I decided to start reading it to tell that priest off!"

I nodded. That sounded like Rudy, all right. He would go to any length to get even with the priest — even to the absurd extreme of reading the Bible. And he did! Every time I turned around he sat with that old book, and seemed very engrossed. That was fine with me because we had a smoother weekend. But not all smooth, of course — we had one big fight about the priest.

I wanted Rudy to let matters go and attend church with me. After all, my teaching job provided for both of us and his university studies, and I needed good relations with the priest to keep my job. But Rudy couldn't see it. So I walked to church alone and Rudy stayed home reading his old Bible.

As I watched the priest performing his rituals, I wondered. That man did what he felt was right. He was true to his convictions, and I had always begrudgingly respected him for it. But Rudy had convictions too! So did I. Was there no way to bring people together if they had differences of opinions? Why was religion a divider?

Not until a few weeks later did Rudy dare to tell me the whole truth about his new interest. He hadn't only started to read the Bible; he had also visited a Protestant preacher in his eagerness to prove the priest wrong.

"I asked the man to give me some hard facts against the Catholic Church," Rudy said, and I nodded. That was my husband, all right.

"Did he?" I asked, and felt scared.

"No." Rudy sounded perplexed. "That fellow said he couldn't do that. His religion was something too precious to be used to fight anyone with."

"Good." I felt relieved, but not for long.

"Well, I think I found a way to get my needed information yet. I joined a Bible study group in the city!"

"You are joking. *You,* with such people?" I didn't know if I should laugh or cry.

"Schatzi (little treasure), it's interesting, really! Did you know that the Bible is deeply entwined with ancient history?"

Knowing Rudy's love for history, I now understood his enthusiasm.

"I don't remember much about the Bible anymore, though I grew up with it," I said, deep in thought. "But you know how I feel about any history right now."

How did I feel? Bitter! I hated history and disliked teaching it. History had been one of my favorite subjects in Nazi training but now I detested it. History writers were manipulators, liars who tried to show their own side of the story, not true facts. Hitler had used history to prove that his Third Reich would stand a thousand years, but it had crumbled in twelve years. Fooey on history!

"Schatzi," Rudy said very gently, "those Christian people I meet with every week have something. I don't know what it is, but it's something special. They might help me to become a better person, and I want to change, Maria Anne. I want to in order to save our marriage!"

I was touched. I never had thought that Rudy would go to such lengths to keep me, but it was hard to picture Rudy as a religious person.

"I mean," Rudy said as an afterthought, "I don't intend to join any church, but I'll just get enough Christianity to make me a better person. Then I'll quit. I don't want to become totally involved, of course. After all, that would be intellectual suicide."

"Rudy," I said, "maybe I should study some, too. After all, I could use some changing for the better and learn to hold my temper. Maybe you could teach me what you are learning every week?"

But Rudy had a better idea. He found an old, retired minister who was willing to visit with us every weekend who would introduce both of us to religion and doctrines.

Precious old Brother Schneider! Will he ever know until we meet in eternity what he did for us?

It wasn't so much what he said, though he knew his Bible well, admonished us with conviction, and was very fundamental and convincing — it was his life that impressed us the most.

It was winter when he began his visits, Bavarian winter. We lived at the foot of the Alps and one night could bury us in snow up to the eaves. His shoes were leaky, his coat old and threadbare, but snowstorm or sunshine, ice or slush, that old man came walking miles from the railroad station to my schoolhouse, having a cheery *"Guten abend"* and no complaints though his hands were often stiff and his lips blue from the cold.

He brought me my own Bible, a translation by Martin Luther.

"What is it that makes the old man come out in the worst weather?" Rudy asked repeatedly after the minister had left us to visit other people in the mountains. "What is in the deal for him? It couldn't be just his great concern for my rotten soul. Or *is* he really that worried about our spiritual welfare?"

He was, and we knew it, though he was a strict man who had strange manners. He assigned us a passage to read in the Bible every week, and we read it to show our appreciation for his willingness to come.

He came until Rudy asked him not to return. Brother Schneider didn't ask why; he just said a kind "Good-bye," said a prayer, and left with a smile.

I knew why Rudy wanted to quit studying religion; it was getting under his skin. Brother Schneider was a godly man, but he believed tolerance to be of the devil. He talked just like the priest in one respect: in order to accept God, he taught, a person had to choose sides. And both preachers felt they were on the *right* side! Because Brother Schneider wasn't Catholic, he felt sure they were on the wrong side. That was one thing Rudy appreciated and fully agreed with. But he was not so much against the priest that he wanted to join another faith. As a matter of fact, Rudy's antagonism against the priest had almost vanished as he had gotten so interested in Christ's teachings. But join a Protestant or any other church? He could never go that far!

How long, however, can ice withstand warmth? Can winter hold the earth in bondage when the spring sun kisses the soil alive to flowers and fruit?

Rudy and I had left ourselves open too long to the warmth of the gospel story, and we could not close our minds to it any more if we had to. We could not leave our Bibles alone long enough to forget their message, and I didn't want to. For that matter, neither did Rudy!

We both admitted by then that the Bible *is* God's Word, and the agreement became the common denominator for our different personalities. We both realized that it was God who had brought us safely through the war, spared our lives, and brought us together in marriage. It was only fair and the right thing to do to serve him in return.

While we struggled for a final decision, God sent us some extra help — I found out that Mother was alive! The International Red Cross located her in West Germany in a refugee camp. Through her letters I found out that her husband had died and that all of her children except the oldest son, August, who had stayed in Czechoslovakia with his Czech wife, were safe in the West. We all had homes and each wanted to keep her, but Mother went to live with her second oldest daughter because she was sick and needed Mother most.

I longed so much to see her but I had to wait for long, long months. Traveling was so difficult and costly those days; it was next to impossible to get a travel permit without bribing and we were poor. Her letters made the waiting bearable and what she wrote warmed our hearts. God was so real to her — and so good. He had made all of his promises come true in her life while she had gone through the ordeals of banishment from her little home. In his grace he had laid the father, ill with cancer, to rest before the Czech order of expulsion came. Mother's letters reflected so much hope, serenity, and joy in the Lord that we couldn't help but covet her peace of mind. We wanted what she had.

By early summer we chose the side that seemed right for us and were baptized into church membership. We also took the consequences: it was only a matter of time (but more time than I ever expected) before I was without a job. Protestant teachers don't teach in Catholic communities in southern Bavaria. I knew that; I understood and respected it, and I left — but I had no place to go!

Somehow I had the idea that God would do something special for us because we had decided to serve him. I thought he would baby me and keep all hardship away because I didn't feel capable of facing a storm.

But God knew what was needed — and the storm came. I was bent over with the pain in my ulcerated stomach, undernourished and nervous, depressed and in tears most of the time. When the doctor confirmed my suspicion that I was pregnant, my heart sank. I felt completely unprepared to become a mother!

In the spring we moved into an attic room of an old farmhouse. A brick chimney that stood in the middle of the room spread heat three times a day, whenever the farmer downstairs made a fire. This was a blessing while the weather was cool, but not when summer came.

Rudy stopped his studies at the University at Munich. Knowing he had to support a wife and soon a baby also, he went out looking for a job. I stayed in our little room, praying and waiting.

What lonely days! It would have been wiser for us to leave the community, but we couldn't because the housing authorities would not transfer us. Besides, it would have taken a lot of money to bribe a landlord in the city to rent us a place to stay.

Every evening Rudy came home weary and discouraged. He could not find a job with so many odds against him. He was a refugee with a Prussian accent, and refugees were not in demand, especially *Saupreussen* (Bavarian slang for Germans from the north). Besides, as a former Nazi officer, he was watched very closely by the American military government. No former Nazi must be allowed to make a comeback in the civil service. Rudy had no references, or, for that matter, experience in any trade. His identification card classified him as a university student, and employers shied away from training students for a trade. Students didn't usually stay long enough to make the training worthwhile, but returned to school as soon as possible.

The odds were against us and we knew it. Rudy could not find any job whatsoever — not even ditch-digging or street-sweeping.

After several weeks Rudy began to get desperate. I had tried to keep a smile on my face; but the new life within me was growing, and I anxiously counted the weeks until our baby's birth.

We lived as frugally as possible, but our few marks' savings melted away like snow in the spring sun. One morning we had to sit down and face facts. We counted our money. We had six marks ($1.50) left. Besides our own money, we had some paper notes in an old envelope. It wasn't much, but it seemed like a large sum because we had almost nothing else. It was our tithe. We had saved it up for many months. We had not turned it in to our church treasury, mainly because we seldom attended church in the city.

That morning I brought the envelope out, after we had counted our own last few marks, and laid it beside the money box. Somehow, managing to hold my tears back, I said: "Remember what Brother Schneider told us about the tithe? It is God's money, and we must never touch it, not even when in need. He said the truth and we know it. Now, Rudy, the moment our money is gone we shall be tempted to touch what belongs to God, so we must not keep it under our roof any longer. You must take the morning train to the city, find the church treasurer, and give her the money." Rudy nodded, and his sad eyes revealed what he thought. Before he left we knelt together in prayer, and this was the gist of it:

"Lord, we have come to the end of our road. We have given up everything we had for our new belief, and it seems that thou hast forsaken us. If we have done wrong and this is our punishment, please show us why we are punished, because we don't know why! God, maybe we have believed a lie, made up by men. Maybe there is no God and nobody hears us as we pray. But if thou art, O God, reveal thyself soon, for we cannot go on much longer. Everyone laughs at us already, and our own relatives think we have gone crazy. O Lord, if thou art, bring help soon and listen to our pleading, for we ask in the name of thy Son, Jesus, in whom we now believe. Amen."

We rose from our knees with heavy hearts, but I smiled and waved to Rudy as he walked away. Then, as soon as he was gone I threw myself on my bed and sobbed. Maybe Rudy's father was right. Maybe it was all my fault. Rudy had accepted our new religion first of all because he loved me and wanted to save our marriage. Sure, he believed in God, but somehow his whole religious experience was tied to his love for me. I felt a great responsibility, since Rudy expected me to lead out in spiritual matters. Alas! Somewhere I had made a mistake, for I had led Rudy and our marriage to a dead-end road, or so it seemed. My heart cried to God, and my tears mingled with my prayers. Doubts and darkness pressed in on me like a fog. Six more weeks before the baby was due, and nothing was ready — nothing was left for us. O God, why?

When Rudy returned, I tried to be brave and calm for his sake, and even managed a smile when he stepped in.

To my amazement, Rudy's face was one big smile. "What happened, dear?" I asked, hardly daring to believe my eyes.

"*Liebling* (darling), I found a job today." Rudy took me in his arms.

Fighting the bothersome tears back, I begged for details.

Rudy said he had battled with temptation and discouragement as he walked the long kilometers to the railroad station and traveled to the city. He had prayed earnestly and had gone straight to the church office to find the lady who managed the church finances. He was afraid to keep our tithe money in his pocket while searching for work again.

The lady, surprised and pleased when Rudy handed her the money, asked the usual questions about our well-being. Rudy told her about our coming baby and his need for a job.

"Wait a few moments." The kind woman picked up the telephone and made several calls. Then she turned to Rudy. "Brother Hirschmann, I think we have found a job for you. Go to this address right away and ask for Mr. Bauer."

She wrote an address on a piece of paper and handed it to Rudy. He was too surprised to say much, but managed to thank the dear woman warmly before he hurried away.

Mr. Bauer interviewed Rudy briefly and hired him.

"Think of it, dear," Rudy reflected. "For so many weeks I have looked everywhere to find work, but not until we had turned in our tithe was God able to help us. It took only half an hour after I had turned in our tithe to find that job. Now I know God lives and cares!"

We prayed a different prayer that night, a prayer of thanksgiving and praise. Not even the oppressive heat of our attic room bothered us, so happy were we. We sat at the open window and watched the glimmering stars while our hearts conversed with God.

"God," I pleaded humbly, "forgive my doubts; for now I know that thou art; and not only that, but God, thou art love."

I thought the stars smiled as they twinkled. They reminded me of the time when Rudy and I had first met, and we had sat on that log to watch our friends the stars. Then love had begun to bind our hearts together, and now love was again weaving. But this time it was greater love, for God was in it.

16 THE AWESOME JEW

Things improved slowly but steadily for us after that evening when Rudy came home to tell me about his new job. Sure, we had rough going for quite a while, but Rudy was so willing to do almost anything, and I was used to pinching pennies. Rudy's was a humble, low-paid job, and for the first time in his life the only son of the rich Hirschmann house did manual labor. He had to wrap packages from morning to evening and then deliver the packages to the railway terminal. The factory in which he worked manufactured sport and ski clothing. The company owner had once been a European ski champion, whose name, plus the quality of his merchandise, helped the company grow. The number of packages increased, and Rudy often had to work overtime.

In due time our baby arrived. We named her Christel. The cutest girl who ever arrived on this globe — naturally — she was so tiny that people seemed to see only her long dark hair, big brown eyes, and long, dark eyelashes. We had named her after Rudy's mother, and the grandparents were so delighted about her that they could talk of little else. We soon realized we could not leave the baby in that hot, attic room or we might lose her, so when the grandparents offered to take the child and care for her, we accepted, though it was hard to give her up.

Rudy's boss had offered us a tiny storage room on the top floor of the factory as sleeping quarters, because the long train trip was difficult when Rudy had to work overtime. We accepted gratefully. Since the baby was in good hands, we could leave our chimney-attic room and the old farmhouse. We carried our few belongings to the city, furnishing our new room with two army cots and some boxes. We felt very fortunate.

After a few weeks of intense search, I found a job in a coat factory and was promoted to office work after a short time. With both of us working, we were soon able to buy ourselves bicycles and also pay the grandparents more for care of the baby. Every weekend we bicycled long miles to see our little daughter for a few short hours. Returning Sunday night, I would lie in bed unable to sleep, my heart aching with longing for my Christel. Again prayer helped relieve the loneliness and helped me to learn patience.

One thing that brightened my days were Mother's frequent letters. They were comfort and security — and they unlocked my memory fully, though many names and events had come back to me before I found her again.

At a time when we expected it least, Rudy was promoted from packer to be the new export manager. The pay was two and a half times what he had earned before, and a church member had just offered us a basement apartment in his house.

While Rudy began to build up his new export department from nothing, I began to set up our first real household the same way. Then came the happy day when we could bring our child home. She was two years old, and had never seen the city. After a few weeks of readjustment she was happy again and filled our lives with a new joy. She liked to go to church and impressed the women of the church with her model behavior. Christel was like her daddy — quiet, reserved, and gentle — and she became a favorite child to many. How proud we were to show her off!

Yes, things were brightening up for us. Later, Rudy found a little house for rent on the outskirts, close to the new plant the company was building. Christel's little brother had just arrived. With prayers of thankfulness we moved out of the city into that cute little house with its garden and big evergreen tree. The new

baby had fresh air and sunshine, and Christel played for many
hours beside his basket.

What a special moment it was when Mother at last came to
visit me after our household was set up. Sepp, who didn't live
far from us, had gone to bring her. He and I bickered from the
minute she arrived about who had a greater right to keep her the
longest! Of course, Sepp won out because he was the son — but
Mother stayed with me long enough to tell me all that had happened since we had parted so many years before.

Father's illness had demanded several surgeries during the war,
leaving him disabled and harder to live with than ever before.
Mother nursed him patiently. When the Russians marched in,
Father was on his deathbed. The Russians never molested Mother
nor broke into the house to plunder. Father coughed continuously
and the Russians assumed that he had TB, though it was not so,
and they were afraid of his germs. He died of cancer.

The villagers helped Mother bury him at the old graveyard,
and Mother was allowed to stay in her house for several months.
Then came the time when even the Germans who had not belonged
to the Nazi Party had to leave the village — Mother too. The
people were penned for days in railroad stock cars and finally
arrived somewhere in East Germany. By then the East German
government had erected some crude refugee shelters for those
"privileged" refugees who were "politically clean," and Mother
found herself in a hall on some straw for a place to lie down, and
very much alone. The community spirit disintegrated and everyone
fared for himself as survival became more crucial. It was the
old story — no food for the refugees.

"I had managed up to that point," Mother said to me, "but
that evening on the straw I felt hungry for the first time. The
camp officials tried their best. We received a cup of very weak
cereal coffee — plain — and they had a big white radish for
each one of us. But, *Marichen,* I couldn't eat that coarse radish
on my empty stomach. I tried but I just couldn't! I gave the radish
to a teen-age boy — he gobbled it down in a hurry — and I tried
to go to sleep. I cried, *Marichen,* and I prayed! I said: 'Lord,
your Bible has a promise that assures your children of bread and
water. I read it so often that those two things are certain for
those who trust you. You did give me the water tonight, dear
Lord, but you didn't send bread. Only a radish, and my stomach
couldn't handle that hot stuff. Please, Lord, all I want is a crust

of plain bread, no fancy meal, just what you promised, *bread, real bread!'* "

My heart cringed while listening to my aged little mother. I could see her there on that hard floor, on some smelly straw, all alone and helpless.

"I cried myself to sleep that night," Mother continued, "and when I awoke the next morning I reached automatically into my purse. You know it, girl, we refugees always held tight to our stuff even during our sleep because there was so much stealing going on everywhere. I checked to see that nothing had been stolen while I slept. Guess what I felt?"

I held my breath and didn't dare to say it.

"Bread," Mother confirmed; "a big crust of bread! I looked very nonchalantly into my purse so as not to draw any attention to myself and then I began to eat, leaving the bread hidden. I broke off a little piece to still my hunger, but I didn't find out until weeks later who had given me the bread. Guess who did it?"

I shook my head. Who would give bread away at such a time?

"It was Octavian's wife. Do you remember her?"

Octavian's wife. Hadn't that been a neighbor of Mother's when I was a child? A rather unfriendly woman who poked fun at us for our religion? "What?" I said. "You must be joking, Mother."

Mother smiled. "She mellowed after Octavian died and we became good friends after the Russians marched in. We would sometimes stay together at night because we both lived alone and she would even urge me to pray for her. But she never could bring herself to the place to pray or accept God for her life. Well, that woman had still her golden wedding ring with her when we arrived that evening. And she went out in the night and found a farmer who exchanged a loaf of bread for her ring."

"And shared it with you? That's unbelievable, Mother. That's not possible!"

"God impressed her, she told me later, when she confessed her good deed to me. She said it was like someone gave her an order to break a piece off of that only bread she had and slip it into my purse during the night."

"What happened when you had used up the bread?"

"That is another miracle, my girl. We were only a few days in that Communist camp before we were loaded into the same rail-road cars and sent over the borderline into West Germany. There we were received with food and put into a pretty decent refugee camp. I never starved again, *Marichen.* From then on I always had some food that I could eat.

It was incredible. The Communists actually sent a whole train full of refugees over into the American zone of Germany when on the other hand they shot at anyone who tried to escape across no-man's-land to the West. They sent my mother's train to freedom, and we found each other! Was there anything too hard for God?

I never told Mother of the nightmares that I had about her on my flight. She would have scolded in her gentle way: *"Marichen,* how could you have doubted that God would take care of me? Are not all his promises 'yes' and 'amen'?"

I told her only a few things about my life. I didn't want to upset her. She always sounded so courageous when she told of her own hardships, but she couldn't bear the thought of her children's past suffering.

"Mother," I said, "remember the text in the Bible where it says that God loved us when we were his enemies?"

She nodded.

"God never left me, either, even when I hated Jesus. He went with me through labor camp and everything else!" Then I told her about the night when a voice told me not to go into the straw barn. Tears ran down her deeply wrinkled face as she listened.

"Marichen, I prayed for you during that time. I prayed for all of my children several times every day. I didn't know if any one of you were still alive or if I alone was left. I had not much hope that *you* had made it since you lived in Prague and we had heard of the murdering of Nazis, but I prayed for you anyhow!"

"I prayed for you" — it echoed in my heart. Mother prayed for me, and all at once I understood why I was still alive.

When Mother left again to visit with Sepp, I felt less antagonistic toward his possessiveness. Mother would come back again some day and stay with me for a long time. I had her promise and the assurance of her love — and her prayers embraced me and my family though we had to part for a while.

Rudy's department had grown to such an extent that in the busy season he had eight people working under him. Rudy and I had grown very active in the church and we held several church offices. We were on our way to becoming a respected family of the German middle class, and we could forget our humbling experiences and enjoy life. All was well with God and the world — except for my ulcers and the occasional little squabbles that any marriage has, and we had found an antidote for the latter.

"Let's pray together," one of us would say, reaching for the other's hand. Every evening, regardless if we felt mad, sad, or loving, we prayed and forgave. We knew that we were incompatible in many ways, but prayer kept us together and helped me to become more warm and responsive as a wife. I was determined to forget the shadows of my past and be the example of a Christian wife and mother, and I felt rather sure that I was well on my way.

Then out of the blue came a flash of lightning to my soul. An elderly church sister faced me one day after church. "Maria Anne," she said solemnly, "I wasn't aware that your father is still alive. I thought you grew up an orphan."

I felt defensive and uncomfortable. What was that all about? Sure, she was a dear friend of mine, but why would she start to pry into my past?

"Who told you about it?" I asked.

"Never mind that," she said soberly. "You have been on my mind the whole week because you told someone that you hated your father! I must talk to you about that!"

I frowned and waved my hands impatiently. "There is nothing to talk about. I have a right to resent my papa; he never cared for me and I hardly know him. I suppose he is still alive somewhere back in Czechoslovakia, but for me he is dead. I prefer to think of him that way." I waved good-bye and turned to leave.

"Maria Anne," the little old saint persisted, "the Bible says 'Honor your father and mother.' It doesn't say, 'Honor your good father.' "

I walked away without a word. There was a storm in my heart and I felt angry and insulted.

The nerve some people have, I thought. How could she dare to put her nose into my personal life and offer her saintly advice? How could she know how it felt to be forsaken by a parent?

My ulcers acted up so badly by the time my family and I arrived at home that I couldn't eat. I put my two children down for their afternoon naps and lay down myself. In the quiet of the bedroom I argued with God. I prayed, I accused, I cried. What was my problem?

And then it hit me like a thunderbolt. The Man on the cross! I had never faced up to him. From the time I decided it was only decent to serve God in return for all his kindness, until the present moment, I had simply exchanged allegiances and gods. As a child I had lived by my mother's God-concepts and tried to obey her; later I gave my loyalties to the *Führer,* worshiped him and obeyed his word. When I had become willing to acknowledge the sovereignty of the Great Ruler of the universe, I had served him mechanically, as all my life I had been taught to serve; I was now trying to earn my way to heaven. But I had never trusted the Jew from Nazareth as my personal Savior!

Yes, I talked about Jesus; prayed to the Father in his name, read about him in my Bible, and confessed him. But he was far away in heaven and I was on earth, and I thought it good to keep that distance.

"Why, O God, why? Why is it that I don't know you, Christ of the cross?"

In the quiet of my little bedroom, pain-racked by my stomach, I found some answers that afternoon.

I had heard about Jesus' life; I was talking about it. I thought it admirable, but I didn't want to live it — I couldn't!

There were two things I couldn't give up — my pride and my hate!

Not give up my pride? Hadn't I humbled myself willingly, down into the dust, ever since I joined a Christian church? Yes, and I was proud of it! How deceitful can the human heart be! I had accepted Christianity as if it were a change of garments — from the filthy rags of a social outcast to the cleaner church outfit of good works and better behavior — but I had not sought Christ's robe of righteousness for my soul. How often religion is only an exchange of sins — from the coarse sins of immorality and arrogance to a respectable set which permits spiritual pride and anger under the cloak of lip service to Christ!

Yes, I knew why I had never been willing to come to terms with the Man on the cross — I had known it all along, but had never been willing to admit it! I would always just approach the cross, give it a short glimpse, and then run away because I could not stay and listen — listen to those words I was afraid to hear: "Father, forgive them, for they know not what they do." I couldn't face him under that crown of thorns, bleeding, hanging, while his words echoed to me through the centuries: "Love your enemies, do good to those who hate and despise you —"

"Son of God, I cannot do it! I cannot stop hating. I can only push it out of my memory and try to ignore it. And every time I think of it again my hands form a fist. Man on the cross, I cannot even understand why *you* let yourself be nailed to the cross. I would have never, never let them do it to me if I had the power you did. Didn't you have any pride? Jesus, why didn't you just take a bolt of lightning and knock them all out? Wipe them out, those miserable creatures! Oh, how I hate meanness and cruelty, and how I hate your persecutors and mine: that Czech overseer, those Russian soldiers who hurt my Helga. Jesus Christ, I am afraid of you! You're asking me to love my enemies, and I can't even have kind thoughts toward my father. God, you're asking the impossible of me — and I fear you, God! I can serve you in fear and give you due honor, but I don't know how to love. Christ, I am even afraid to love you. You might ask me to become like you; but I can't! Pride and hate are part of me. I will crumble if I let go of them!"

I felt better for having been honest with myself and God. But there was no hope left in me. I knew myself and I would have to live with it — that was all.

17 Jesus, My Friend

A few days later my aunt came from East Germany for a visit. She was the unmarried older sister of my own mother. She and I didn't know each other, but I felt it my duty to look after her; she was all alone. So Rudy went and got her, and I regretted it from the first hour she arrived.

We couldn't get along together. Maybe we were too much alike. Maybe I was on edge because I had lost contact with God. She was very religious and lived by the Bible teachings — but mainly the "thou shalt not" admonitions. Her "don'ts" were our daily bread but they made neither of us the better because both of us were worried about my sick soul.

I came down with the "grippe" and it was a relief. I had to stay in bed where she couldn't preach to me. I was sick for a few days and my recovery was slow. I felt bored, restless, and impatient to get up and take over my household again. Who knew what that peculiar old aunt would do to my children when I wasn't around!

My eyes fell on a little black book on my nightstand. Auntie had put it there shortly after she arrived and admonished me to read it. Of course, I wouldn't. Not in a million years. I felt much too rebellious toward her to do her that favor.

But I was so bored and time ticked away so slowly — it would be hours before Rudy would be home to talk to. What was that book about, anyway? It had an unusual title: *Die Quelle der Kraft* (The Wellspring of Power). It was a translation from the English, entitled *Alone with God,* written by an American missionary, Matilda Erickson Andross. Oh — from America! That made me less resentful toward the book.

America! Though I knew almost nothing about it, the word had a good sound to my ears. Only three times in my life had I met Americans. First was that morning when I had run by accident into that American barracks after crossing no-man's-land, and I would never forget those unknown American soldiers' kindness. My heart always felt warm when I remembered how they had helped us. The second time I had faced an American was when I was the principal in my little country school and we had been ordered to attend a district meeting. An American educator had talked to us about democracy. He had the cutest accent speaking German, and I had listened carefully. After his speech he offered to answer questions. I had several, but I was much too nervous and afraid to speak up before a crowd of people.

One male teacher stood up and said: "Whenever you referred to our German past or the philosophy of Nazi education, you sounded very hesitant. You acted like the cat walking around the hot mash."

The teachers in the audience smiled. The American guest speaker seemed a bit uneasy. "The reason for that is that I tried not to hurt your feelings. It has been only such a short time since you all taught under Hitler; I fully understand if you still feel very much as you did during Nazi times — it will take time to reorient your thinking toward democratic principles!"

I found myself standing and my heart was throbbing in my throat, but I had to answer him. "Sir," I said, and took a deep breath, "if you try to indicate that we are still Nazis, you are wrong. We are not Nazis nor anything else. We trusted once and paid with our heart blood for it. We got hurt, sir, and we are still hurting, and we are not willing to trust again — neither democracy nor any other system. So it isn't that we are against what you said; it just sounds too good to be true, at least for us, for we are like burned children who are afraid of fire!"

Applause rippled and I looked around to see for whom the applause was meant. It finally dawned on me that my fellow teachers applauded my words, and I sat down, terribly embarrassed.

The American speaker found me after the meeting and shook my hand and thanked me for what I had said. His obvious willingness to respect my view left me puzzled — what made Americans so tolerant with people of other convictions? I did not know the spirit of tolerance; it wasn't a meaningful word in my vocabulary.

The third time I faced an American was when an agent from the Central Intelligence Agency came to our basement shortly after we had brought our Christel home. We had applied through a church agency for a sponsor so we could emigrate to the United States of America, and the agent came to tell us that there was no chance for us — records about our past stood in the way as Rudy had engaged in direct warfare against the United States.

That was a dark hour in our life, and I had prayed and hoped for a miracle, but I had consoled myself — maybe God didn't want us to leave Germany.

And now I held a religious book written by an American woman. I glanced at the first page, and her style caught me from the first sentence. She wrote as simply as that American lecturer spoke when he explained democracy to us, and it fascinated me!

There was nothing of the fancy vocabulary and rhetoric I was accustomed to from German literature, lectures, and sermons. She explained it so simply that even my children could have understood, but her simplicity did not offend me, though I prided myself about my use of a wide vocabulary at all times. The simplicity of her book disarmed me in leading me like a child to see Jesus.

I had never thought of him as a friend but as a God and King to pay homage to. He was a Judge whom I would face (and I dreaded it). But this writer said Christ had all heaven waiting for us to bring special blessing into our lives. He had only thoughts of peace for us and great plans to use us in a mighty way if we could learn *one* thing: how to communicate with him. It was a book on prayer, and I wondered what she meant. I knew how to pray. Twice a day I knelt down and talked to God, always very thoughtful not to forget to give thanks first before I asked God for help, protection, and other gifts; always very careful to be reverent, respectful, and to use the proper vocabulary.

This writer said that there was nothing wrong with a formal prayer, but Christ longed for more than that!

She likened communication with Jesus to a telephone conversation — we on one end, he listening on the other. But the usual prayers of Christians were monologues, she said. We would say our piece, finish with "Amen," and slam the receiver down. Shouldn't we stop long enough to listen? Would not Christ talk back to us if we waited for an answer? The thought of it nearly overwhelmed me — but she quoted several famous people of British and American church history who acknowledged that Christ had talked to them, and it all sounded so terribly simple! She quoted Scripture texts such as "My sheep hear my voice." Christ the great Shepherd said it, and I wondered if I were his sheep. One sentence, however, hammered into my mind above everything else, and I repeated it over and over until tears flowed and I couldn't see the pages: "Jesus and I are friends!"

How simple, how beautiful, how unbelievable!

Jesus and I are friends! How I wanted to be able to say the same, but that was impossible. She was good, had been a missionary and a servant of God. Of course Christ would be *her* friend. But he would never stoop to be *my* personal friend; I had been his enemy and I was still a rebel in my heart — proud, hateful. He would never answer if I listened; or would he?

I finished the book, and when Rudy came home I asked him to move my cot out to the balcony of our little house. It was a warm night and he consented. I liked to sleep under the stars; it made me always so still inside and so small, and God seemed nearer than during the day.

Lying on my bed, I began to talk to him. It took courage because I wondered if he would be offended if I didn't kneel down, but I did it anyway.

"Jesus," I said in my heart, "I want you as a friend, but I am not so sure that I am good enough to be talked to by you. The book says that it doesn't matter how I feel; you can change me, even my pride and hate, if I let you — I just give you my will and that's all. But I understand if you can't talk to me, Jesus, because I turned so much against you as a Nazi."

"I love you, my child, and I have called you by your name," an inner voice answered.

I sat bolt upright. "God," I said softly, "*did* you speak to me, or was it just my own heart? Please, God, don't let anything or anybody speak again if it is not you, dear Jesus; I am afraid I am making a fool of myself!"

"You are mine," he said; "don't be afraid. I died for you and I have called you to serve me. You shall do great things for me!"

"O Jesus," I said into the night, tears streaming down my cheeks, "I don't deserve so much love and I can't see how I ever could do anything great for you. You know I am a human wreck, ulcers, nerves, and all. But, Jesus, what's left of me is *yours*. Even my bad feelings and my horrible memories. I give you all there is to give. Just be my friend and talk to me sometimes; that's all I want for the rest of my life!"

Jesus and I became friends that night when I surrendered my all to him the best I knew how. Not that surrendering to Christ is over in a moment. When a human being gives himself to Christ, it is the beginning of eternity, and it becomes a more meaningful reality from day to day with no end to its depth.

I wasn't a new person when I got up the next morning: it was still painracked, tired me, and my feelings had not changed. I couldn't love Papa even if I tried. I couldn't forgive those Russians and wasn't sure I should. There was just one difference: I had found a Friend to talk to every time I needed to talk, and he would talk back if I listened, and I could stop worrying about all my weakness since it was now his problem, not mine.

"Jesus," I said before I went to church, "if that saint talks to me about my papa, what do I say?"

"Don't worry about it; everything will change, be patient," my Lord comforted.

"Lord, change my hate to love," I begged every day. But it took a long time. Some people may change in the twinkling of an eye; I was obviously too stubborn for such a miracle.

My attitudes changed very slowly from hate to pity, from pity to compassion. God is in no hurry.

My aunt still irked me, but I had someone to talk to about it, so I didn't sass her so much anymore, and we discovered one great love we had in common: Jesus Christ.

How can people fight when they talk about Jesus? How can people hate when they feel sorry for those who don't know the Lord?

It came so naturally; I had nothing to pretend and to force

when I sat down one day to write to Papa. My aunt knew his address.

"Dear Papa, you are much on my mind lately, and there are some rumors that your wife is dying of cancer and that you have a lady friend and two children by her.

"I want you to know that I am sorry that I treated you so unkindly. Please forgive me!

"We as a family have never been together on this earth. I wish so much that we could live together in eternity.

"Papa, I long so much for you to know my Jesus. He loves you and is waiting for you. Don't worry that you were his enemy all your life. I was, too, but Jesus took me as his own. He will do the same for you. I love you, Papa! Your daughter, Maria."

I never would have dreamed that my papa could write such a warm letter back as he did. The old bitter Herr Appelt had mellowed, and he corroborated the gossip that he had two small children. One was a little boy named Rudy after the Navy man I had loved so much during the war. The girl was Angelika because she looked like a little angel.

Letters flew back and forth, and I watched a miracle unfold from beginning to end.

God's timing is always perfect. With my first letter God sent a man into Papa's home — a retired minister of the gospel from the church my father fought so bitterly when he was newly married to my mother. Papa became friends with that man of God. So did his girlfriend. They both accepted Christ and wondered what to do next. According to the Bible they lived in adultery. Papa got a divorce and married the mother of the children. Then they longed to share their new faith with the dying Czech woman Papa divorced.

They nursed her and cared for her and the children brightened her last days, but she was too bitter to accept God. She died angry. Papa's letters were filled with deep anguish — oh, to undo life's great mistakes, but so often it is too late, too late! We comforted each other, for Christ forgives even if our own heart condemns us.

It was so good to see Papa safe in God's hand — him and his family. One great question I still had in my mind was what my Lord had said to me that night under the stars when I found him: "You shall do great things for me!"

What did God mean by that? I couldn't do anything special for him, ever. My education was of no use. I was sick; we were relatively poor. The greatest thing I longed to do was to lead someone to Christ. But I had never been able to find anyone who would want to accept my Jesus except for Papa and his new wife, and it was really that minister who had led them to the cross.

"Lord, will I ever find a soul for you?" I said over and over. But no one seemed interested though I tried to witness. Maybe I didn't know how.

Every fall our church had *Erntedank* (harvest-thanks). Charity toward the poor and needy was greatly encouraged. In order to do more, church members were provided with stacks of Thanksgiving magazines and asked to go out to sell them, since soliciting is forbidden in Germany. The money went for disaster relief.

Selling magazines was not our cup of tea, so Rudy and I always paid for the magazines ourselves and gave them away. We did so for several years.

Now harvest time had come around again and the magazines were in our arms to take home.

"Jesus," I said when we arrived at home after church, "do we *have* to sell these magazines this year, or can we handle it the usual way."

"You better go out and sell them," my Lord said.

"I was afraid you would say that, Lord," I sighed. "Where do you want us to sell them?"

"In your own street, here on Weisspfennig Weg," God said.

"Lord, this *isn't* your voice talking to me. That is the devil's, isn't it? You don't want us to go in our own street, Lord, please. None of them are Protestant, and they think us strange as it is. After all, Lord, we have to live with our neighbors. Please don't ask us to make life more difficult!"

"Go in your own street," the voice said, and it was a clear order.

"You better convince Rudy, then," I said. "He won't like it!"

Rudy didn't like the idea at all. He hated to do any selling, but he finally agreed to go with me. We each took one side of the street, and the magazines sold fast. Soon we were done and were very relieved and pleased about our success.

We turned our money in and felt at peace with God and the world again. But who should come to us after church but my saintly, elderly friend and hand us a pack of magazines.

"What's this?" I frowned.

"Listen, I paid for those magazines." She nodded her hoary

head proudly. "But I'll *give* you the magazines to sell and you can keep the money to buy food for your love gifts to East Germany and Czechoslovakia."

She was so sincere and so sure that she was doing me a favor. I had no choice but to smile and give her a warm "Thank you." Rudy groaned softly after we were out of her sight. I couldn't help smiling about the way God was driving home a lesson.

"Fine, Lord," I said and felt good. "So you want us to do double duty this year to make up for the last lean years of service. You win, Jesus. We'll go. But where?" It was no problem anymore. I didn't mind going anywhere, and our own block was done.

"Go in your own street."

I hadn't heard right. Or was someone mocking me?

"Jesus," I said urgently, "I am not playing make-believe; I really believed that you were talking to me. But that is not your order. You wouldn't forget that we went there last week!"

"Go in your own street," the Lord insisted.

"Lord, do you mean our Weisspfenning Weg?"

"Yes. Go in your own street!"

I sighed. "Lord, how do I explain *that* to my husband?"

There was no other explanation and I felt utterly bewildered. Rudy raised his eyebrows while I stuttered my story to him.

"Honey," he said kindly, "the people bought already. They'll think we're nuts."

I nodded. I knew all that, but I either believed it to be God's order or not. And I wanted to believe it.

Rudy decided to act funny about it all, since I was just about on the brink of tears.

"Okay, let's switch sides. I take your side; you take the one I sold to last week. At least the people will not know what's up!"

That relieved my embarrassment a little and we went out.

It was just as I expected. Nobody bought and I found myself at the end of my side waiting for Rudy. By then I was sure I was off my rocker and I would never expect an answer from the Lord again.

Rudy came after a long time and I was more irritated because of the delay.

He beamed! "Schatzi, did you get into that house last week?" He pointed to a fenced-in, two-story apartment house at the end of the street.

"No, the gate was locked and a big dog was in the yard, and I was out of magazines, too!"

"Well, that's why we had to repeat our selling with switched sides, Maria Anne. For in that house lives a couple who need Christ!"

"You believe that God told us to go again?"

"I do now. I actually went to make you feel better; you seemed so upset. But now I see God's hand. You see, I got into the apartment house when someone walked out as I tried to get in. And I am not afraid of harmless little dogs!" Rudy winked at me. "I sold some, but at last I found a door in the attic and knocked. A woman opened the door a few centimeters and started to talk to me. She bought a magazine and invited us to come back when her husband is home. She once was a church member, but her husband is against religion, and she warned me not to push it upon him, or he would get violent!"

"What makes you think that they're interested in Christ?"

"I didn't say that. I believe they *need* Christ!"

I couldn't object to that, and we went back for a visit later when the husband was home.

Hans and Frieda were a lovely, elderly, childless couple. Hans shot questions at us as fast as we could answer in return. The conversation had *one* theme — God and religion. Frieda sat and stared at her husband. He seemed eager, overeager to talk about God.

When we left after long hours of deep talk, he took us to the gate and shook our hands.

"Please do come back soon, friends," he said, and there were tears in his friendly eyes. "I have waited for you for six months." Noticing our surprised looks, he hastened to explain. "You see, I felt for a long time that it was time to make peace with God and I asked him —" he pointed to the sky — "to send someone to explain things to me. I am a simple laborer who doesn't know how to figure things out. God finally sent you. I had almost given up hope!"

We assured him that we would be back and then we walked to our home silently. We both had much to think about.

"I am sorry, Jesus, that I doubted your orders!" I could picture my Lord smiling and I smiled back.

Yes, Hans and Frieda were the first two persons we led to Christ. They joined the church, became our most devoted friends, and Hans became a church elder. Frieda died a few years later, but Hans kept that newfound joy. "I'll see her again," he said, and squeezed our hands. He was so grateful to us.

Yes, Christ's words to me had come true. I had been a tool in his hand to do "great things" and I was satisfied. Now I could relax, enjoy the abundant life, and rest in him. My cup was running over. Rudy had a good job, we had a nice little home, two healthy children, lots of friends, and Jesus and I were friends. There was nothing more I could wish — except for that hidden longing left in my heart: I wanted to go to America. But there was no way.

18 Dream Land – and Nightmares

The propellers droned on in the black night, and the ocean below us like the shrouded stars above could only be suspected.

That I was sitting in an airplane on my way to America was only a dream — something I had dreamed so often that finally it seemed real to me — or was it?

My six-year-old Christel and little Michael slept in their seats; so did Rudy. To the left of me sat an old woman, dozing — while her fingers held tightly to a rosary twisted around her wrist. Poor little woman! She was so afraid of flying, petrified by the thought of being above deep waters which could swallow her if the plane had to go down. I had to admit that it wasn't too comforting a thought, but I wasn't afraid. It couldn't happen! God hadn't opened a door for us to the New World after so many years just to let us drown before we entered. Neither would he let the old mother beside me die before she saw her daughter in New York again and had a few wonderful years of a new life in that great land. God is love, and he has thoughts of peace for his children and great plans for all of us — for everyone in this chartered plane, for that matter, since all of us were emigrants to the United States of America!

What a whirlwind the last few months had been. Just at the time when I had finally resigned myself to the fact that we were not supposed to take off to a new land but find our home in Germany, our papers had come through in spite of our past records. A sponsor had been·found by friends who had left the previous year for that land of promise, and here we were, free like birds and ready for a great new future.

What a blessing that things had turned so fast for us, or we would have never gotten away at all. I still couldn't understand why everyone had tried so hard to discourage us from going. Though it was good to have so many friends who hated to see us go, and I could understand why Rudy's parents resented it, we were not leaving for good. We were just going to America to get ourselves better trained for God's ministry, then we would return.

I had never seen my foster mother so upset — ever — as when we visited her a few days before our plane left. Just thinking of it made me heartsick again.

Our furniture and belongings had all been given away. There were enough poor refugees around us who needed everything we had accumulated since Rudy's promotion at work. We had kept only two suitcases full of worldly possessions: the big suitcase had the clothing for our family of four. The smaller case was heavy like lead and full of books — the only thing I had not been willing to part with was our books. Books to me had always been like friends. They could be shared, but never discarded.

With our two children and the two suitcases, we had made our rounds in southern Germany to say good-bye to our loved ones. The last stop was my mother. We went to church together for the first time since I had left the little cottage as a young girl to go to Prague. I didn't let go of her hand while we shared the Lord's supper, sang hymns, and knelt for our last prayer together. The parting was that painful and frustrating.

"God just gave you back to me after all those long years of uncertainty and praying, *Marichen*. Why do you want to leave me now again to go so far away?"

Mother's voice was only a whisper; her breath was so short and labored from her fluttering, weak heart, and her thin lips now had a shiny tinge of blue.

"Mother," I said, trying to hold back tears, "I don't want to leave you. You know how much I love to be around you. But I am sure that Jesus wants us to go to the other land. It is his will, Mother."

"If it is, then I must let you go, *Marichen*," Mother said, nodding gently. "But are you sure you are doing his will? You could be running ahead of God, my girl, because you *want* to go to America; it is easy to call our own desires God's will, and you have always been very headstrong and impatient!"

"Mother," I said, tortured, "we prayed so much about it. It *is* God's will — and even if we were mistaken it's too late now. We burned our bridges behind us!"

It was again a train that took me away from her. But this time there was peace in my mother's face, and in the clattering of the wheels I called: "Mother, wait for me, I am coming back to you!" She did not answer, but just waved and cried and I tried to smile.

Now I listened to the night song of the propellers as the plane flew west, and my soul was troubled.

What if Mother was right? What if our move was not God's will and we had run ahead of him? Would Christ go with me if I was going my own way? I looked back east where home had been, and my heart called for comfort.

"Are you still with me, Lord? Or have you left me, in case we misunderstood you? Where are you, Jesus?"

The eastern sky began to glow, and light stretched out her fingers to touch the night while I listened.

"Fear not, for I have redeemed you; I have called you by your name; you are mine! When you pass through the waters, I will be with you, and through the rivers, they shall not overflow you; when you walk through the fire you shall not be burned, neither shall the flame kindle upon you" (Isaiah 43:1, 2).

"What a strange text to give to me, Jesus, to begin our new life with." Why should there be fire and water and deep rivers? Weren't we just about ready to enter the land of great opportunities, the land of milk and honey, the promised land of my dreams?

"That's the Statue of Liberty," Rudy said as our plane swept low to land. I hadn't time to look because my children complained of nausea, and the old woman beside me prayed aloud in her fright. I held her hand very tight and smiled reassurance to Chris.

"We are almost in America!" I said. The date was May 5, 1955.

An hour later on that special day in May, I found myself sitting at the railroad terminal in New York City awaiting a train to Michigan where our sponsor lived. I was dumbfounded, shocked, and frightened.

Was *this* America? Oh, no, that was impossible! The place was horrible, dirty, full of dumped newspapers, beer cans, and other garbage. Didn't a rich country like this have enough pride to keep a place up? And the people! Why did they dump stuff? Weren't they proud of America? Didn't they care?

Didn't they care about each other? There were so many people rushing or just sitting around, but nobody ever nodded or smiled. And their attire! How shocking!

Didn't Americans know how to dress for travel? After all, this *was* a terminal and people came here for that purpose. Oh, some people looked proper for the occasion, but most of them looked sloppy — like the station. And there were so many old people, mostly men, sitting on benches. They didn't even have suitcases or bags. They just sat and stared, looking as poor as German refugees, even unshaved, ungroomed.

One woman walked by, dragging a child. She wore short pants and no stockings. What a shocking way to appear in public, I thought.

My children nestled close to me. They were overtired and afraid. Since we had to wait for several hours, Rudy had left us to explore New York, and I felt helpless.

What a strange language. I hadn't thought of that before we left. I didn't understand a single syllable. Where did I have my dumb head? Just because I had grown up bilingual and always managed to communicate enough to get by — even with the Russians — I hadn't realized how different English was. And now, for the first time that I could remember, I knew not one word to read or speak. Our departure had come so fast I didn't have time to prepare myself at all.

An elderly gentleman sat down on our bench. I moved the suitcases closer to me and held tight to the children.

"Are you new in this land?" a voice said in German, and I looked up. The man smiled. I was so relieved to hear my own tongue that I fought tears.

"How did you know, sir?" I asked, smiling gratefully.

"You three look different and very lonely," the man said.

"New York people don't wear winter coats in May when it is 70 degrees. Where are you from?"

Glad that someone understood me, I talked unafraid. I even expressed my surprise about the dirt and that it all seemed so different, so uncultured, so to speak!

"May I give you some advice?" the old man asked.

I nodded eagerly.

"You will find this land altogether different than you expected it, *junge Frau,* but learn to say nothing until your first shock is over. Americans thrive on criticizing their own land but they resent it when others do it. Remember, it's *different,* not worse, than Europe — as different as the moon from the earth. Learn to accept the difference and your children will have a better future than you do!

I thanked the man for his kind advice and turned to Michael who stood before me making significant gestures. Oh, dear, *now* what would I do?

"What's the matter, lady, is something wrong?" The old man was kind.

"Oh," I said and burst into tears. "I know so little about English that I can't even find a restroom for the little fellow — and my husband is not around to help me out. He knows English."

"Well, you'll learn fast; don't worry. Go to those doors over there and look for W-O-M-E-N." He spelled the letters out in the German way. "That's the place for you and your little boy. I will stay here and watch your cute little daughter and your luggage."

I was apprehensive, but needn't have been. He was friendly, did as he said, and talked to me for a long time before he wished us luck and walked away into the crowd.

It didn't dawn on me until later that God had sent that stranger just at the right moment. I took his advice to heart and it saved us much trouble.

There was so much that was different for us that I sometimes had to bite my lips not to speak up.

When we finally arrived at our sponsor's place, even Rudy was flabbergasted. They were an elderly couple and he was in the construction business. They had a large house at the outskirts of town and they had prepared one bedroom for us.

"Mary," the lady of the house said, and Rudy translated, "I

hope the closet is big enough for you four. I have so much stuff in the other bedrooms I couldn't give you any more space to unpack."

"It's more than enough," Rudy said politely and gave me the word. I looked at him.

"Rudy, why do two people have that much stuff?"

Ludwig, the sponsor, overheard me, and he still understood some German since his parents had come from Germany.

"Tell your wife that it is hopeless. My wife is a pack rat and the only solution to our problem is a good fire. Wait until you see our garage. We have to park the cars outside — the junk is accumulating that much!" The big man laughed; my blank look amused him.

I looked blanker yet when I saw him step into his car to drive down to his mailbox, about a hundred yards from the house.

"We are lazy, Mary," he said. "I know I should walk, but Americans don't have their legs for walking, just to sit down!"

I guessed what he said in his German-English mixture and nodded. I had given up trying to understand reasons; I was glad enough just to make sense out of the words.

The first three words that made a lasting impression on my receptive mind were "dollars," "sale," and "diet." I picked those words out in an early conversation, and I got their meaning very fast but not their connection for a while.

Emilie, the sponsor's wife, took us to the grocery store the day after our arrival. It was a large supermarket and I had never seen anything like it.

"Rudy," I said, "ask her what people do with so much food. Doesn't it spoil?"

Rudy translated. She smiled. "Oh, there are many more stores in the big city, bigger than this market. Americans eat a lot."

That made sense, because both of our sponsors' frames were very well padded. She was much shorter than I was but at least twice as far around, and maybe double my weight.

"Tell your wife that Americans have to go on diets very often to lose weight," she continued.

"Vat is diet?" I tried to speak English.

"The reduction of the daily calorie intake clear down to one thousand calories a day," the fat lady said with a sigh. "I know I have to go on a diet again. So does Lue. The doctor said so."

Rudy explained. I sighed, too. What a strange land. I remembered we had been on ration cards in the American military zone of West Germany on 1200 calories per day (and often much less) for far too long. I could feel for her. But why do it in America with so much food around?

I followed Emilie's shopping cart. Michael sat on the cart, and Christel held tight to my hand, and we watched the lady pick her groceries. She would look around and always dart to some areas which had special signs: "Sale."

"What is s-a-l-e?" I asked Rudy in German. He asked her and she said something even Rudy couldn't follow, except that she used the word "dollars" and "cheaper" a lot.

By the time she was through shopping, I had learned the meaning of two words. "Sale" meant sweet stuff and toilet paper, and "diet" was the opposite of sale. For she had bought ice cream, candies, chocolate, marshmallows, jelly and toilet paper on sale, but not much low calorie stuff. Nor had she bought fruit, though Michael had reached for it. My children were not used to sweets, but loved apples and bananas. In Germany we had never been able to afford to buy as many as we wanted. We would buy *one* banana as a treat for all four of us.

"No," Emilie said to Michael when he reached for a banana. "They're too expensive. Wait till they're on sale."

Michael looked disappointed, and Rudy explained to me.

"But Rudy," I said, flustered, "she bought a whole box of chocolate which isn't as good, much more expensive even on sale, and less healthful than bananas. Ask her."

Rudy didn't want to and we helped to carry several bags of groceries out. But I felt helpless when it came to putting the stuff away. Every cupboard was already full and the refrigerator was stuffed.

Ludwig saw my bewildered look. "Don't worry, Mary," he said in German, "my wife is very thrifty. She never throws left-overs away. She puts it into the refrigerator until it rots, and then she empties the refrigerator."

That made less sense than the "sale" and I felt so ignorant by then that I went into the privacy of our little bedroom and had a good cry.

All I wanted to do at any time was cry anyway! I was so homesick and hot and sticky and lost most of the time. All I could think was that I wanted to go home. So did my children, who refused to speak English. Maybe even Rudy wanted to go, though he tried to act enthusiastic.

Rudy worked as a carpenter's helper for Lue, and had a hard time. He had never done such work, never handled an electric saw, never hammered a nail, never worked in moist summer heat.

Rudy was a perfectionist; he had never done sloppy work in his life. But Lue was a business man. Time was money. What did it matter if a board was nailed crooked? It mattered to Rudy! One day he was so tense and nervous that the electric saw slipped out of his hands and he reached for it, afraid that the tool might fall and break and that would mean loss of money for us. The saw cut into the bone of his hand, and Rudy was rushed to a doctor.

For the first time we experienced what it meant to live without socialized medicine and sick day compensation — a must in all of Germany.

I went to work so we could pay our rent — ten dollars a week for the bedroom we lived in.

The only jobs I found were strawberry picking and house cleaning. I did both, and we were never behind in our bills.

Rudy's hand healed and he went back to work, but our sponsors felt they needed the privacy of their own home, so Emilie rented a small basement apartment for us.

The apartment consisted of a bedroom and a kitchen. Shower and bathroom facilities had to be shared by four families. Lue acted embarrassed when he came to visit us.

"Don't stay in there," he said. "It's no good."

I shook my head. "It's okay; don't worry, we'll make out." I had no smile left, and Lue walked to his car.

But it was not okay, and I knew it. But what could we do? I had never heard of a slum until I lived in it, and by then nothing could astonish me anymore. I lived in a nightmare again, and waited to wake up — wake up in my little house in Germany where it was cool and smelled clean and where Rudy would come home on his bicycle from the office. But I never woke up. The horrible dream went on and on and on. Every morning when I got up to fix Rudy's lunch box, I got angry at the thick red dust on the old table. The same dust covered the outside of the tiny, lone window, high above the stove, and made it all dark so I couldn't see the sun and the sky beyond the basement entrance. I washed and dusted and rubbed to fight all the dirt, but it was hopeless because of the nearby highway, and I knew it.

I knew also that the highway was one reason Rudy looked so dreadfully tired. The big trucks shook the whole basement as they roared past the house and Rudy couldn't sleep with that noise. He was such a light sleeper and there were so many trucks on the road every night — every miserable, hot, and smelly night.

One night I was awake, too, and I got up to get a glass of water. As I pulled the string to the dim light bulb that was in a shaky socket above the sink, I saw a movement, some beady eyes, and a fat rat's tail. I choked on the water and threw up into the sink. Rudy came out and asked what was the matter.

"Rudy, did I see what I think I did?" I asked, and my stomach convulsed again. "Are there rats in this basement?"

Rudy nodded and held me tight. Yes, he had known it since we had moved in, but he had never mentioned it since he knew my abhorrence of rats. I sobbed on his shoulder and begged, "Please, Rudy, take me home again. I can't stand it any longer. We have made a dreadful mistake. God has forsaken us and we are doomed if we stay here. We all will die. The kids have lost their smiles and are so pale. You are getting thinner and more exhausted every day and I — oh, Rudy, I am afraid I am pregnant again! What shall we do, Rudy? Where shall we go?"

Rudy took me back to bed and I cried myself to sleep in his arms. Rudy had black circles under his eyes when he left for work the next morning and he looked so haggard and aged. I felt guilty for having added to his burdens. He was so uncomplaining and brave, and so very quiet. He said less and less.

What was there to say? We both knew it all too well. We couldn't go back to Germany. We had no money and hadn't even finished paying back our fare to America to the World Church Service. We did send a few dollars every week from Rudy's small pay check — Lue didn't believe in overpaying people.

I couldn't go to work because there was no one to tend the children. But I cleaned some rich peoples' houses once a week. They allowed me to bring my children with me. But our combined earnings were just enough to make ends meet. We were not able to save anything.

Christel and Michael always stayed very close to me. They acted like two forlorn little birds, and Christel refused to go outside to play. She hated the grassless red dirt around the apartment house and the traffic close by, and would hide her face in my apron.

"Mutti, when will we go back home?" she would ask in her quiet way, and her big brown eyes would wait for an answer, but there was no answer. I would look up to that tiny, dark glass where there was supposed to be the sky, and I would call for my Lord, but there was no more answer, either, since I expected none. Somewhere I had lost contact with my faith, my home, and my smile. All I had left was a little pride. I tried to keep that rats' hole as clean as I could and I never wrote back to Germany that America was rats, dirt, and loneliness. I always managed vague, general letters. Maybe it wasn't even pride. Maybe I couldn't bear the thought of how they would worry about us. Maybe I was afraid to dishonor my God. We had been so sure that we had followed his guidance, and told everyone who had tried to tell us not to leave that it was God's will for us to go to America.

But it was a mistake, Lord, wasn't it? You didn't talk to me; it was only my eager heart that fooled me, and now all four of us had to pay the consequences for a faith that had been presumptuous. But *why* did we make that mistake, Lord? Why?

19 The American Way

Our sponsors were very prompt and eager to pick us up every weekend for church. Both held important church offices and faithfully attended every church function that came around, even midweek prayer meeting. Emilie let it be known that she expected the same of us though we didn't live in their home any more, but I balked!

I was bitter enough to assume that she was not really concerned about our souls, but that she dragged us to church to show off her good works. After all, hadn't she and Lue taken the risk of sponsoring us — a poor emigrant family — to come to America for a better life than we had before?

"I hate to go to church in this country," I said defensively to Rudy. "I hate it!"

Rudy looked surprised. "Honey, in Germany you were the one who loved to go as often as possible. What's happening to you?"

"How can you compare our church in Germany to this place," I cried. "It's so different! First of all, I can't understand the sermon or anything else. Second, they even ruin the hymns I know in German. They sing so fast it's irreverent. How can a person feel worshipful when people sing with such fast rhythm? And the way they dress! The women come to church in red, pink, and bright yellow dresses, if you please — to the house of God! They look as if they were going to the *Oktoberfest* (beer festival in Munich), not to a worship place. I always feel out of place in my black church dress I brought from Germany!"

Rudy thought for a while. "Mary, even if you don't feel at home in the church," he said, "for the sake of the children we had better go anyway. They love to go. In this country they do a lot for the children and young people in the churches, and all the special teaching aids and pictures they have make it real to them."

I grumbled some more, but couldn't argue with Rudy. I knew he was right.

But I couldn't help myself; everytime I sat in church I compared it with our little church in Munich and tears flowed again. However, the greatest shock was yet to come. At the beginning of one church service, the congregation rose for the opening hymn while I listened to the introductory chords of the organ to know if it was a familiar melody. Well, did I ever know *that* tune!

"Glorious things of thee are spoken —" the Americans around me sang lustily in a marching beat, and I was dumbfounded. Didn't anyone know *what* song they sang?

They were singing the national anthem of Nazi Germany, "Deutschland, Deutschland, über Alles" (Germany, Germany, Above Everything) but with American words. It scared me; it seemed so sacrilegious, for in the new Germany this song was forbidden! I looked at Rudy. He looked a bit nonplussed himself though he tried to sing from the hymnal. Suddenly he bent over and whispered in my ear. "You know *that* song. Sing it in German!"

He had a mischievous gleam in his eyes, and then we both laughed. It struck us so funny. Emilie frowned at us. How did we dare to laugh in church, said her puckered face. But I couldn't stop giggling though I tried hard. Rudy's eyes danced and both of us found it hard to wait to let Emilie know what she sang!

Emilie didn't think it was funny at all when we told her after church. "That Hitler," she fumed; "how did he dare steal an English church song and make a Nazi anthem out of it!"

Rudy tried to explain in his limited English that neither had stolen from the other, but both got the melody from Haydn. But

Emilie knew what she knew and felt deeply offended. The whole thing seemed so ridiculous that I kept on smiling, and smiled right into the face of a tall, handsome gentleman who stood at the open door.

"I am Dr. Weaver," he said, and shook Rudy's hand and then mine. I was very surprised, for Americans are not handshakers like the Germans, and I missed it. I shook his hand very warmly and smiled some more.

"We would like to visit you this afternoon," the man said in a friendly way. "If it's okay with you," he hastened to add, watching my face closely.

I understood enough English by then to pick out the word "visit."

"No, I don't want anyone to come to our place," I said to Rudy under my breath in German. "I would die of shame to ask him in."

Unfortunately that man understood some German and caught the meaning of my words.

"Tell your wife not to worry; we will come by and pick you up for a ride in the country. Good-bye!" Dr. Weaver smiled and walked to his station wagon where his wife and a car full of young children waited.

The man kept his word.

"Tell him that I apologize that there is no decent chair for him to sit down," I whispered to Rudy when the doctor walked in. Rudy apologized and the doctor laughed.

"Don't worry, furniture does not reflect people's worth!" he said. His eyes seemed to take in everything.

Then we jammed into the station wagon and went into the country. What a ride! The car was filled with wiggly kids who made all kinds of loud noises, but the doctor's wife sat there all relaxed.

"We plan on a dozen children," the doctor announced, and Rudy translated. I swallowed hard. Well, they were on their way, but why would anyone want to have that many children? However, there wasn't much that made sense to me in America anyway. Whatever the topic, I had learned very fast to observe without questioning underlying motives.

The doctor stopped the car by a lake, and we looked at the beautiful scenery. Nobody got out.

"Rudy, don't we go *spazieren* (for a walk)?" I asked softly.

The doctor had heard again. "Oh, *spazieren gehen,*" he chuckled. "You Germans love that."

So we all stepped out. With my two children who hadn't said a word the whole ride, I went among the luxuriant, green growth to pick some flowers and leaves to take back to our drab dwelling. What beautiful leaves that one vine had! I reached for it.

"Don't!" The doctor's wife shouted. "Don't touch it!"

I jerked my hand back.

"Mary, no, no. This is poison ivy," the doctor said. "It is poisonous."

Rudy explained. I shook my head in disgust. This country was altogether too much for my taste. I hated it more and more! They didn't even have a place to go *spazieren* without some poisonous plants spoiling the pleasure of it. Who knows, maybe they had snakes, too!

I asked Rudy, and the doctor answered, "Sure, we have snakes. Pine snakes, rattlesnakes, gopher snakes, and a few other kinds!" Art Weaver obviously enjoyed teasing me. I was glad to get back into the car and go home.

"We'll come back next weekend and take you out to my folks," Art promised. He had suggested that we call him and his wife by their first names and we tried to do it, though we were not used to it. That was another strange thing in America. Everybody seemed to call the other people by their first names. Even the children did it. How disrespectful! I would *never* let my children do that, I thought. Grownups had to be properly addressed in my house.

Every day in our basement apartment our children talked about going for a ride again with the *Herrn Doktor*. We all looked forward to it, and the thought brightened the whole week. But would he really keep his promise? I hated to think how disappointed the children would be if he didn't mean it. So would I, for I saw no one else the whole week except my two small children and Rudy. But Rudy was always so exhausted in the evening from the unaccustomed moist heat he had to work in that after dinner he fell right into bed.

God be thanked, Art and Natalie kept their promise and took us straight out to Holly, where Art's parents lived.

What friendly people the old folks were! No wonder all their children were so congenial. We met the rest of that family tribe but it was hard to remember all those names. The whole homestead seemed to burst with people, children, sunshine, and laughter. And the food! For supper they brought out big watermelons from their own garden, but well chilled beforehand, corn, soup, apple cobbler, homemade bread sandwiches, salad, and later popcorn, apples, and homemade ice cream. The most interesting part for me was that someone called it a "light" supper.

I enjoyed everything except for one detail — the way most everybody talked to me! I understood very little English as yet, and I spoke even less than I could understand, but I tried my best to communicate. Whenever the Americans would answer me — often with a torrent of words — I would look up, puzzled. Instead of repeating it in fewer and simpler words to help me understand, they would repeat with more verbosity and raise their voices. They obviously assumed that if English was shouted, even an idiot could get its meaning! Well, I apparently was less than that. I couldn't. It would frustrate me no end.

Art was the worst. He would just boom into my ears.

"What is *schreien?*" (scream) I asked Rudy. He thought for a moment. His English vocabulary was rather basic too.

"It means 'cry,'" he told me.

When Art tried to explain something more to me, I looked up, proud of my new vocabulary and said with emphasis: "Don't cry at me!"

Now it was Art's turn to look puzzled. I raised my voice and shouted in his ear, "Don't cry at me!" He got the message and broke into a hearty laugh. He never screamed at me again.

There was one tall young woman among that big family that I liked from the moment we met. She was one of Art's sisters, and married to a doctor. He had his young practice in Holly, and the couple lived in her parents' home, upstairs in a small apartment, until their own new house would be finished. The frame was already up, Rudy told me.

Her name was Aileen. I had never heard such a name before, but I thought the sound of it fitted her personality. She was so gay, carefree, full of fun and warmth, and very considerate of my language handicap. I felt so grateful I stayed close to her and helped with the clean-up and the dishes, so I could talk to her a bit more. Once in a while she seemed deep in thought, and occasionally pulled Ken, her husband, to the side, then her father, to discuss something of obvious importance with them.

It never dawned on me that we were the topic of those family conferences until the following weekend when we returned for another visit and Aileen received me with a beaming face and the question, "Would you like to move and live with us for a while? We can share the apartment together."

I looked at Rudy. She didn't really say what I understood? Maybe it was my wishful thinking. Why would she say something like that?

Rudy asked her to repeat. We were not sure that we had understood. "Pardon us, please."

"I want you to get out of that basement," Aileen said slowly, smiling, "and come to our place — to live here. There is work for you, Rudy. They are building a big auditorium at the school nearby, and Mary can help in the house and garden whenever she feels like it. Your children can play with our little Vicki and the neighbor kids — that is, if you don't mind crowding. The apartment is small."

I stared at her while Rudy translated. Why would strange people inconvenience themselves that much to help us? And what about our sponsors?

"Rudy, what if the sponsor will not let us?"

Rudy translated. Aileen frowned.

"Mary, this is a *free* country. You can move any place you wish. Nobody can stop you! Your sponsors signed responsibility to the government for your financial independence for your first year here in the states, but you are not their slaves. As long as you pay your bills and Rudy works, you are free to go and do as you please! This is a free country!"

"This is a *free* country," I repeated. "Rudy, ask her if we in this country are allowed to move without informing the authorities first of our departure, and if we can move in here without first getting permission from the local burgomaster." Rudy translated.

"You are precious!" Aileen laughed her carefree laugh. "Of course you can! You don't know America too well yet! All you need to do is pack your stuff and come. Come as soon as you can!"

We did! I was dreaming, of course, but this time it was a good dream. The horrible, dark nightmare was partially over and I was in the sunshine. But how long before I would wake up to more gloom and deep shadows? My homesickness was still as intense as ever, but now I could pray again, and smile. Aileen saw to that, and so did the old folks and Dorothy, the unmarried youngest daughter of the house who was Dr. Ken's office nurse.

"Now, Mary," Father Weaver said, "you may use any of the garden and orchard products we have. Just go and help yourself!" But I was afraid to just go and take their stuff, so they brought it to me.

Aileen handed me a bag of sweet corn, freshly picked. I had never prepared corn before in my life.

"Vat do I wiz it?"

"You husk it and put it into boiling water." She motioned and pointed to the stove.

"Vat time?"

"Oh, how long do you boil it?"

I nodded.

"Just a few minutes. This corn is very tender."

I smiled. I would serve corn and salad for *Mittagessen* (mid-day dinner) when Rudy would be home from the construction site for an hour. Just as he came up the stairs I dropped the golden ears into the simmering water. Rudy washed up and sat at the already-set table, hungry and eager. I prided myself on having the meals waiting for him on the dot.

I poked the corn with a fork to check for softness. It was stone hard in the middle, so I let it boil some more. But it just didn't seem to get done.

Rudy and the children were finished with the salad and showed impatience. I raced down the stairs to Aileen.

"Aileen, Aileen, corn don't cook right; is very hard!"

Aileen came to see. "What is hard, Mary?"

"Corn!"

"Oh, Mary, are you waiting for all of it to get soft? It never will. The kernels are done, see? Serve it. Butter it well and enjoy it. You folks can eat as much as you want; you are not on a diet!" She sighed and smiled.

The word "diet" again! There wasn't another word that gave me as much consternation.

For instance, there was that apple tree right below the apartment, bearing early summer apples. The grass below was covered with windfall apples, but nobody picked them up. So I would go ever so often and "save" all those apples from rotting by converting them into apple-strudel for the people of the house. On the weekend I would make lots of it, since Art would come with his big family and Wilma with her minister husband and two children, and they all seemed to love apple-strudel. They could eat twelve pans full in one weekend.

It made me feel real good in many ways except one thing bothered me. All the women would eat it and moan while they ate because I was ruining their diet.

Crazy diet, what was wrong with the Americans anyway — especially the women? I finally asked Aileen with the help of my German-English dictionary.

"Aileen," I said very soberly, "this country has much food, more than other lands, yes?"

Aileen nodded, amused. "Yes, why?"

"No other people have it so good, but no other people feel so guilty eating as Americans do!"

"What do you mean, Mary?"

"Oh, such dumb word like 'diet.' I hate it. It steals fun out of your eating. You always worry when you eat!"

Aileen laughed but then turned serious. "You are right, Mary. We Americans are strange. But you see, we Americans also tend to get fat!"

I looked her over. She was a tall, stately woman. She didn't look fat to me; neither did the other women in the family.

"Aileen," I said, "it's better to be fat and happy than skinny and miserable. Look at me!"

"Mary, you are wise, but you will never change us. We Americans are different."

I nodded. You better believe it; that was the truth. How well I knew it!

"Aileen," I asked another time, "why do American women wear red, green, and yellow dresses to church? It's not reverent!"

"Why not?" Aileen smiled back. "Look at nature. Doesn't God love bright colors?"

I looked around. Dorothy's flower garden burst with bright hues of every red, orange, yellow, and blue shade I could imagine, and the various greens were lush after the last rainstorm. She had a point!

"Aileen, why do people sing hymns so fast in church?" I asked another time. "It's not very devotional."

Poor Aileen, I was on her neck most of the time, asking, wondering, complaining. But she was patient, and by her love and tolerance she little by little changed my attitude toward the American way of life.

One day Art took Rudy and me to a choir concert of Negro spirituals given in a black church. I was first astonished, then enraptured.

Rudy bent over. "Mary, if the German brethren would hear that, they would consider it blasphemy."

"I know, Rudy, but it's fascinating. I can't help but like it."

"Mary," Art whispered from behind, "how do you like *that* rhythm?" His eyes twinkled. He knew me well by then.

"It takes my breath away," I said. "I wish I were a Negro. I would love to be able to sing like they do." I smiled.

Art didn't smile back. "No, you wouldn't want to be a Negro." He looked serious, almost grave.

I wondered why he said that, but didn't question him further. It was another of those American perplexities for me. Would America ever make all sense to me?

Not that these were my only perplexities. I had plenty of others much closer to home — like my pregnancy. I could not doubt it anymore that another baby was on the way, though I refused to see a doctor about it. What nonsense, to go for medical checkups! Pregnancy shouldn't be treated as a disease — though sometimes I wondered. My right leg swelled and big varicose veins appeared. My ulcers acted up badly, and my back throbbed in constant pain. Time pressured us and I knew it. Fall colors announced autumn, and we had to find a place to live. We couldn't forever take advantage of those overly kind people. But where would we go?

We found another basement, but this time I had no fear to live in it. No more rats, no smells, and we had our own private bathroom. The big, new coal furnace kept it cozy and warm, even after the chilly winds brought a hard winter and much snow.

I had much to be thankful for, and Jesus and I had much time to talk with each other that winter. I spent much time alone with little Michael during the day. Christel had started first grade, and Rudy took evening classes after work to improve his English. We could not afford a telephone, so it seemed very still after the months of happy commotion and laughter we had just left behind. But in the sunny home where we had been guests for several months, shadows lengthened too.

Old Father Weaver suffered with cancer. Aileen's silvery laugh didn't ring as it had when I met her first, and Art's eyes had a new sadness. I wondered how it would feel to be a medical doctor and yet be helpless to save a beloved father.

The one who showed the greatest courage and humor was the patient himself. Rudy visited him on weekends because he loved to talk to the old man. I had to stay behind because I got too upset, and Father Weaver didn't like tears around his bed of pain.

"You know what Father Weaver said to me when I left him?" Rudy said one day, returning from the Weaver home.

"What, Schatzi?"

"He said that he knows with surety that there is a crown laid up in heaven for him. But even if there wasn't such a thing as eternity or heaven and he would have only the life on this earth to live over again, he would choose to be a Christian. Christianity alone can fill out a human life to its greatest depth and potential."

Rudy was deeply moved. He was still so young in his Christian faith, a mere babe in Christ, and he had faced so many hardships since we had become Christians. I knew what he was thinking. Would we *ever* reach such noble maturity in our lives? Such willingness to suffer without complaint?

"Jesus, let me understand the meaning of suffering," I prayed. "It seems so unfair to me to watch that kind old father waste away in such horrible pain. He was so good to us. He refused to take rent or any other pay from us. He shared his food, helped us with the furnishing of our place, has only words of courage and hope for those around him. Jesus, why does he have to suffer so much?" As my heart talked to Jesus that night, I felt so confused and rebellious, and I needed assurance.

"Some day you will understand, my child, you can trust me," Jesus said.

"Yes, Lord, I know that sometimes Christians have to trust though they can't understand, but I forget it so often. Thank you, Jesus, for reminding me!" I fell asleep in renewed confidence.

Another person who inspired us deeply during those long, cold winter months was *Tante* (Auntie) Erhard, as my children called her. She had been born in Russia, but her mother tongue was German. Her life story sounded stranger than fiction. She and her husband had remained faithful to Christianity in Communist Russia. Her husband had been drafted by the German army to become an interpreter, since he spoke Russian and German. Close to the end of the war he had broken away from the German troops and found the address of his wife and son in a German refugee camp in Poland. On the way to that camp the Russians snatched him and brought him before a Communist tribunal for treason. He was sentenced to labor camp in Siberia — at least that's what reliable reports rumored to *Tante* Erhard.

"Mary," she said telling me her story of sorrow, "I gave birth to my second son during those days, and shortly after his birth we were loaded into open cattle railcars to be transported to Germany because the Russians were pushing the frontline toward the West. It was in the deepest winter and we had no food or heat on the train. We rolled and were pushed around for days, and so many people died. The winds were murderous. Children froze stiff. Babies became like boards. The frozen bodies were just shoved out through the opening of the moving cattle cars as we rolled on. My new baby had no chance, but I told God that I had dedicated both of my sons to him and he could take care of us.

"I laid my baby on my warm bare breasts under my clothes, and kept my other son under my big coat. Then I waited. It was just a matter of time before my milk would dry up and I would not be able to nurse any more, since we had no food nor water. For three days while the train rolled and the winds howled, I waited and prayed. My breasts never emptied, Mary, and my baby never got cold or hungry. We arrived in another camp in Germany where I could take care of my sons. We had the bare necessities. After the war ended we came to the United States, and here I work for my boys. Someday, Mary, someday they will serve God. He saved them for a purpose!"

I looked at her worn face and hands. She cleaned houses and did all sorts of odd jobs. They were as poor as we, but what a spirit she had!

"As for my husband," she said, "something in my heart tells me that he is still alive. Someday I will hear from him again."

Poor *Tante* Erhard, I thought. She had no word from him for the last eleven years; wasn't she just fooling herself with wishful thinking?

"As for you, Mary, stop wishing all the time to go back home to the old country. We older folks might never amount to much over here, but think of the children. They'll have a better life and a future. They can get an education and serve God someday. It's worth all the struggle and misery; just wait and see!"

Her courage lifted me, and I needed lifts badly. The complications of my pregnancy got worse from week to week.

"Lord, I dedicate that child to you in a special way like *Tante* Erhard did hers. Please take care of it!" Things looked bad and I knew it!

Six weeks before she was due, our little girl was born. Rudy hardly made it over the slick ice to the small village hospital with the bald tires on our old Packard. Aileen came flying and delivered the baby before her husband, the doctor, arrived.

The nurse in charge put the newborn baby on the scale.

"What luck," she said. "She weighs exactly five pounds. We would have had to send her away into an incubator if she had weighed an ounce less; it is state law!"

"Luck," I thought. "No, it wasn't luck; it was God." How would we have paid for such extra costs? It would take us months to pay up the bills as it was now.

"She surely doesn't act like a premature baby," Aileen said while working over her. "She has a voice like a general. What will you name her?"

"Hanna Aileen!"

For once Auntie Aileen was speechless!

They kept the baby there for ten days, but I was allowed to go to the Weaver house after three days. While I was there, Aileen took me over to her new house which was almost finished. Her basement was made into a big rumpus room with a red-brick fireplace in the middle.

"I might as well prepare you; we have a shower for you!" Aileen sounded excited.

I thought I knew English quite well by then, but shower was a bath with water from the wall.

"What shower?" I said, rather puzzled.

"Wait and see." Aileen's face beamed.

The rumpus room was filled with women. The fireplace crackled and there was a party spirit in the air. To the side was a punch bowl filled with pink punch, and a big, beautiful cake in the form of a white cradle, waiting to be cut.

Aileen organized some games and had some music. On a big table were lots of gift boxes wrapped so fancy and piled very high.

"Mary," Aileen finally said after cake and punch were served, "it's time to unwrap your baby's shower gifts!"

"My baby's gifts?" I felt dizzy. "All of those boxes are for my baby?"

I hesitated to unwrap any of them. The paper and ribbons looked so costly I hated to tear all of that wrapping up. But I did as I was told. By the time I finished, there were seventy-two items piled beside me. There was also a new baby stroller and a bassinet.

"Thank you! Thank you!" I cried. I was so astonished I couldn't say much.

Everybody wished me blessings and luck. Then the people left, most of them strangers to me.

"Aileen," I asked weakly, "why did all those ladies bring me gifts? They didn't know me!"

"They are my friends, Mary, and they came because I invited them to do something nice for you. Are you happy?"

"Yes, I am. But why do people give showers in America?"

"Because we like it. It's the American way!"

"I like the American way," I said, and I meant every word of it.

Finally our baby came home to our basement and she looked out of place being dressed up so fancy at all times. She had more outfits and dresses than all four of us owned together. But we were not envious; we were all so terribly proud of her. We took her to church and I sat in the mother's room and I felt surrounded by friends — people who had brought me gifts and who bent over my baby to talk to her. She smiled back and gurgled her baby talk — in English, of course — after all, she *was* an American by birth. She belonged here!

Actually, I felt a bit sorry for her. It wasn't fair — one little American had come to live with four peculiar, square Germans. What an impossible situation for that poor child! She was so tiny and helpless; where could she find reinforcement? Wasn't there anyone else around to strengthen the American line and hold the fort in that family?

20 Call of the West

God must love little American girls, for he sent Hanna Aileen special support in shorter time than I thought possible. Only fifteen months later our second American baby arrived: another little girl. My husband named her after me.

Things were not the same by then. We had emerged from the basement and now lived in a dilapidated, two-story house beside the railroad tracks. But we were not alone; we had been persuaded by a young widower, Jerry, and his two small sons, to come and live with them in their "barn," as he called the old house in scorn. So all at once I found myself mothering two families, and it was a handful, to say the least! I was not unhappy with the unusual set-up, but there were moments when I wondered if I could stand my new mission another day without going crazy.

Jerry's boys were bed-wetters and had been with baby-sitters ever since their mother died shortly after the younger son, Marvin, was born. That meant that besides training two neglected boys I washed sheets every day as well as the diapers for one and later two babies.

That wasn't so bad because Jerry owned a washing machine.

But how would I dry the stuff? On the clothesline, of course, out in the sun. Then another train would puff past the house and the wind would blow all the black soot on my wash — and my wash cycle would start all over.

One evening my big family sat around the dinner table when we heard an oncoming train. Without a word Rudy got up and opened the back door. Then he sat down and continued eating while the train roared by.

"Why did you open the door?" I asked, annoyed. "All the mosquitoes will come in and pester the baby!"

"I had to open it to let the train pass through the house," Rudy said without cracking a smile. "If we are not mindful, this house will fall apart someday. It is shaking in every seam whenever a train hits!"

We all laughed and joked about it, but deep underneath we wondered. How long before the house would fall apart? Where would we go from there?

"Wherever you go, *Mutti,*" Jerry said pleadingly, "be sure and take us along. We need you!"

"Well, Jerry," I smiled, "you better look around and find yourself another wife soon or your two sons will think of themselves as Germans and belonging to us. I mean, we are speaking English most of the time for your boys' sake, but I want to switch back to German with my family, or they will lose their second language. Hurry up and get married again so we can return to normal in my family!"

Whatever I thought of as normal at that point, we never returned to it. Americanization had set in, and was changing us four Germans to the point of no return.

Rudy joined a Christian sales organization which was interested in promoting family devotion and healthful living in the American homes. He sold Christian literature and had become rather successful in a very short time. His work brought him together with many American people of all trades and kinds. Through him I got a secondhand insight into every class of American life. At times I was shocked at what I heard, other times thrilled.

Something hard to accept was the poverty and loneliness in which some people lived. America was a rich land; why such contrasts? One day while selling his books from door to door, Rudy found an old lady lying on the floor of her home. She had answered his knock with a weak voice, and he had stepped in to find her helplessly fallen down, unable to get up on her own. She had been there for three days! Rudy called for an ambulance and gave her a devotional book before he left her. She thanked him with tears. "God sent you to my door; you saved my life!" she said over and over. How Rudy longed to see her soul saved, too!

Another time he had entered a very fancy home on a referral and offered his entire family library set. The man of the house gave him his undivided attention, but shook his head at the end of Rudy's sales talk. "We are not religious in this house, Mr. Hirschmann. It would be a waste of money to get your books."

Rudy started to leave, but the man detained him.

"You seem to be rather educated yourself," the man said. "Why do *you* believe the Christian philosophy? Isn't it rather a crutch for human infirmities?"

In his quiet way Rudy gave an account for his faith in Christ. The man was visibly moved and saw Rudy out personally. Before they shook hands to part at the gate, the man pointed toward his Cadillacs and his big house. "Mr. Hirschmann," he said, "I would give all this and more if I could have what you have. It must be wonderful to live with such simple trust and peace. My life is miserable!"

Rudy found out later that the man he had visited was an executive in Detroit's auto industry. Assumed to be a millionaire, the owner of a mansion, several big cars, and a yacht — and he was miserable!

I put many names of people on my prayer list during that time, people I never met personally but who were near to my heart through Rudy's work.

Time flew. We had lived more than a year in Jerry's house and the new baby was almost three months old. The house still held up and the trains were as sooty and annoying as ever.

Aileen was packing. She and Ken had received a call into the mission field of the Far East and accepted it.

"Aileen," I said on the phone (I called her daily and wondered how she could stand it, but I was that enchanted with having a phone), "you mean you'll leave your new house, a well-established practice, and your poor, lone mother to go to the heathen?"

"Yes, Mary. We prayed about it, and we feel that God wants us to go. If God would call you, wouldn't you go, too?"

I thought for a moment. "Yes, I would," I said, "but I wouldn't have to leave as much as you do. You seemed to have so much fun furnishing your house, and Ken did so much of the building himself that the house is almost a part of you!"

"You are so right, Mary," Aileen said. "I love this house, but I love God more. Dad always dreamed of seeing his children go as missionaries. How much I wish he were still alive to see us go. I hate to leave Mother, but she wants us to go. If she had her way, she'd go too!"

"Aileen," I said, "I know you're busy, but I have another big question in my mind. Someone told us that California is a good place to live because it has mild winters and the heating bills are very small. Now in three months it will get cold again here in Michigan and I am not so sure we can survive another winter in this leaky shack. What do we do if we want to go to California?"

"You just pack yourself up and go," Aileen chirped. "There is nothing to it. Just load your new little VW and go west. It's the American way!"

"Thank you, Sis," I said, and put the receiver down.

That sounded easy enough, and it was the American way. And I liked whatever she called the American way; I really liked it.

That evening I called a big family conference and announced what Aileen had said. The thoughts were not new We had tossed the possibilities around in our talks before.

"Why don't we all pray about it tonight?" Rudy said in his deliberate way, "and we decide from there."

Jerry and I nodded. I had prayed about it before, but Rudy and I prayed earnestly that night for special divine guidance. All three of us felt the same divine consent and assurance by the following morning: "You may go to California."

Shortly after we saw Aileen and Ken and their two little girls leave for the mission field, we left Michigan, too.

I had no sadness when we packed. The telephone stayed untouched and the emptiness was profound — I missed Aileen's cheery presence that much.

Rudy built a big box as a luggage carrier for our black VW, and all our belongings went into it. He made another small box to fit into the luggage hole. That was baby's bed and diaper box.

The back seat was filled with blankets, pillows, boxes of food and a small camp stove. On top of everything, close to the top of the car, would be the place for our other three children. Christel, the eight-year-old, very serious-minded and mature for her age, would be my helper to keep Michael, the five-year-old, and our little Hanna entertained; they could talk of nothing else but the trip, even eighteen-month-old Hanna couldn't wait to leave.

Jerry was the capitalist. He drove a "big" American car and had to buy a used trailer to haul all his things, mainly his hi-fi equipment and his many records, also his king-size bed, because he was so tall he couldn't sleep in normal size beds.

Aileen's sister Dorothy, a good friend to both families, came to see us off.

" 'Bye," she waved. "Good luck to you all. Mary, when I see you again you might have short hair and drive a sports car!"

"Never, Dotti, never!" I called back. "You should know me better than that!"

I shook my head in defense. No, I would never cut my long hair. Sure, I felt out of place once in a while, since I wore my hair in long pigtails except for church when I put it into a bun. But part with my long hair? It was long enough for me to sit on, and Rudy loved it. As for driving a sports car — I would never drive *any* car! I was afraid to drive. I would be content to stay the tense, backseat driver I was, always ready to jump, scream, and grab for the dashboard, driving my poor husband up and down the padded walls of the VW until he would ask ever so often, "Do *you* want to drive?"

How did Rudy have the courage to drive across a whole continent with me right beside him? And how did Jerry have the courage to give up his good job at General Motors and strike out into the unknown?

What would Mother say if she knew what we were risking again?

Rudy had one hundred dollars in his pocket, and we owed more than a thousand dollars for the car to a dear old lady in the church. Jerry didn't have much more cash than we did. Neither of us had any savings — and we were on our way to —? We hoped Los Angeles, but we were not sure. It really didn't matter. We didn't know a soul out West, anyway!

I had been very careful not to mention our moving plans in any letters I sent back home. I knew better. Mother could get so worried and upset about us. She was waiting for us to come back home, and wondered why it took us so long.

I knew exactly what she would have answered if I had told her of our plans to go West.

"Marichen, why would any civilized person want to go and face those Indians and live in the nowhere? Don't you feel more responsibility toward your children than that?"

I couldn't help smiling when I thought of Mother's mental picture of America. American Western movies were the great craze in West Germany after the war. Those movies had colored the German peoples' image of the USA profoundly — even for people like Mother who didn't go to the movies.

The American West was Indians and cowboys for Mother, and she wouldn't have slept in peace if she knew we were facing such great dangers. I felt a bit apprehensive myself. Not of Indian attacks, of course. It didn't take me too long after arriving in the United States to figure out that the real America had no resemblance to the Hollywood-West of the movies. I wondered why America represented itself to the world in such twisted images; it had done itself a very poor favor as far as I could see it. But that wasn't my worry at that moment — I wondered instead what we would do when our hundred dollars ran out. So many things could go wrong; what if the cars broke down?

It was possible. Our Volkswagen was so overloaded and top heavy that we could see people in passing cars smile and point at us.

I looked out toward heaven. "Jesus, all I can do is to trust you! We are rolling again and the bridges are broken behind us. I have to believe that we are led by you, or I would panic. You know where we are going; we don't. Get us to the place of your choice, please, Jesus."

We slept at the side of the road or in state parks, and I prepared meals and sterilized baby's formula on the small camp stove. Every evening I washed out the diapers by hand. The next day I would dry the diapers by hanging them out the window one at a time in the hot summer wind.

We couldn't go fast because Jerry pulled a trailer. I liked that, because it gave us a chance to see the changing scenery, and I was less tense, therefore easier on Rudy's nerves. Rudy watched the road and his little car very carefully, as carefully as our money; we turned every nickel twice before we spent it. But in spite of it our money diminished fast. Would we reach California before we ran out of gasoline money?

It took us ten days to get across the continent — ten boiling-hot August days in an overloaded black VW without any type of cooling, with four small children squeezed high on top of bedding in the stuffy back. It might be the American way, dear Aileen, but surely not the easy one!

When we rolled over the Tehachapi pass down into the lower sun-parched mountains before entering the suburbs of Los Angeles, we could smell the hot brakes of Jerry's car and trailer ahead of us. I prayed in desperation, "Jesus, don't let anything go wrong now; you know we couldn't pay for any repairs or anything else. We haven't come that far without mishap to break down now. Don't let us be stranded in this murderous heat, Lord!"

God is good! We rolled down, down, down, and on, right into Los Angeles. But my heart was too numb to be grateful; I was that shocked about what I saw.

"Rudy, you mean to say we have arrived? Is *that* Los Angeles and the famous California and all the rest of it?

Were we out of our heads to come to a place like this? The air felt like a burning furnace and stank so badly it was hard to breathe. Nobody had mentioned smog to us until we arrived in it — and it was thick stuff! The freeways were so jammed with cars that we moved bumper to bumper at snail speed. We had hit rush hour traffic. Mother, if you only knew where your *Marichen* has landed now —!

I was glad she didn't know or she would have been sick about it. I was, literally! My head seemed to burst, my eyes watered, and my stomach was out of order more than usual. I was never without stomach pain anymore.

Rudy had written down the address of a German preacher who pastored a small church of German-speaking people in the middle of Los Angeles. After a long search we found the street and the church.

Bless you, Pastor Scheffler, for not displaying any shock or surprise when we turned up that hot August night before your door! I have often wondered since then how much this restless, torn world owes to those thousands of nameless preachers in every Christian land and denomination who preach Christ by their kindness and willingness to help, louder than any of their sermons could.

The pastor's smile was as broad as his waistline, and just talking with him made me feel better. The wife who had stood by his side for many years was just as sweet. They took us to his church. A small house stood to the left of the big church building and the pastor called it "Das Dorcas House."

"Make yourselves at home," he said, patting the children's heads. "There is a small kitchen with a water faucet, and two beds available in the adjoining rooms. Look around in the cupboards for blankets, pots and pans and cockroaches. Stay as long as you can't find anything better!" Then he turned to me. "You look rather discouraged, sister. Get a good night's rest. Tomorrow will look better to you. It is not always as hot and smoggy around here as it is now. You'll get used to it. Several German families like you have come to us in past years and wondered if they could stand it all. Today they are happy Californians and wouldn't want to live anywhere else!"

I nodded. I questioned that I would ever be one of those happy Californians, but there was no need to be rude. I felt so grateful that God had provided a shelter for all of us and I was already in the midst of preparing supper, washing sweaty, tired children, and sterilizing baby bottles. The future would have to wait.

The sleeping situation appeared a bit more tricky. How do nine people fit into two small bedrooms with two single beds? By taking the beds apart, of course! One gets the top, the other the bottom. Rudy and I got the top mattress, Christel and Michael got the springs with a cardboard on top of it. The babies had their own boxes. Jerry and his boys had similar arrangements in the other room, except that Jerry's legs were longer than his mattress. He claimed he liked it — it kept his feet cool!

"I think I shall like California," Jerry said the next morning. "It's a dry climate and the nights are cooler here than in Michigan!"

I gave Jerry a suspicious look. Did he really mean that, or did he try to brainwash me into liking this desertland? He didn't need to try; I would never stay around long enough to give California a chance.

The next morning Rudy contacted the southern California headquarters of the same sales organization he had worked for in

Michigan, and came back to the Dorcas house full of new courage.

"Honey, they are happy that we came to work out here, and very eager to help us. They are giving me a big, untouched sales territory to the east of Los Angeles. You will not have to live in the big city. They say it's countrylike in Pomona. You'll like it!" His smile looked so relieved.

Rudy's smile decreased in the following three days while we went house hunting in Pomona. We needed a big house for small rent, like the one we had in Michigan, but there was none, even if we had been willing to share it again with the sooty old trains. Neither was to be found in that city. I was too tired after three days of fruitless searching to go hunting again, so Rudy went alone the following day.

"I think we are buying a house!" he announced when he walked in that evening.

I stared at him. Had the heat damaged his brain? Our hundred dollars were just about gone and he hadn't started work yet.

"How does one buy a house without money? Please tell me!"

"The company is lending me a down payment for a new tract house, dear, and I found just the right size and price. It has four bedrooms, two baths! I want you to see it first, however, before we sign papers."

Of course I liked it. Roomy and new, it looked ever so empty. It did not have a stove, washing machine, curtains, or furniture; just plain walls and a dark brown linoleum floor. And so hot! There were no trees to provide shade. The yard was dirt, dry, chalky fill dirt with no topsoil, grass, or landscaping — dirty dirt to be tracked into the house by five pair of lively children's feet. It was easy to picture myself cleaning forever!

We signed the papers and moved in.

How do nine people live in an empty house? It's simple! They use the floor — to sleep on, sit on, play on. Of course, Jerry had his room sparsely furnished, and could even boast of a bed. But that didn't help the rest of us much. But who complained? We had a house!

Rudy's courage was great. He started work immediately and managed to dig up an old gas stove and a round table with six, non-matching, wobbly chairs, and even the remains of a couch.

"Why don't you sit down to eat with us?" Jerry asked innocently when the rest were seated for our first dinner around the table in our new dining room.

I busied myself between kitchen and dining area and took care of my crying toddler. We had no highchair and she felt left out.

"*Mutti* has no place to sit," Jerry's seven-year-old son Martin said quickly before I could find a better answer to change a touchy subject.

How does a mother convince six people to remain seated and eat the food before it gets cold when everyone wants to give her his chair? At the end I convinced the family that I preferred eating by myself in peace later, since the babies needed to be fed first.

The babies and the rest of us looked rather presentable, and rightly so, when we got ready to go to the church for the first time. After all, we were home owners and in business, were we not? I had washed everything by hand. The California sun dried things beautifully in short hours and I ironed on a blanket on the table.

The church was big, strange, and had too many people. All of us felt lonely. We missed the friendly spirit of our small country church back East, but that was to be expected. After all, we came to worship God! However, when a little, elderly lady came up after church and started to talk to us I realized that it was easier to worship God when a friendly face came around to greet us and to make us feel welcome. I felt so pleased that someone showed an interest in us that I got carried away and gave her our address and a warm invitation to visit us. I looked to the sky: "Lord, I had forgotten that my house was empty! How could I invite anyone without embarrassment? I hope she will not come! Keep her away, Lord!"

Nobody could have kept such a friendly, busy soul as sister Mason from visiting newcomers and strangers who came to church. Furthermore, God had no intentions of answering my groan to him anyway. She walked in the next day with a big smile, and I invited her to sit down.

"Please sit at the left side of our couch," I said, hot with embarrassment. "The right end of it isn't usable." At least not to sit on, I thought. Only to fall through to the floor, and the kids loved to do just that. It was a never-ending source of merriment with the boys, but how would she understand that?

Mrs. Mason never sat down. Was my couch not good enough? She had a fixed gaze on her face as she walked around the otherwise empty living room. Then she walked past the dining area into the kitchen, gave it a glance, and finally walked down the hall and peeked into all four bedrooms.

"Just as I thought," she said, emerging again from the hall back to the living room where I still stood too surprised to move. "Just as I thought." She gave me a faraway look and walked to the door. "I'll be back," she said, and hurried to her car.

"What was that?" I said to the children after I had caught my breath again. "What does that mean?"

Maybe Californians were even less inhibited and more informal than Eastern Americans. But still, what she did was almost rude, and she didn't appear to be a thoughtless person. Had I hurt her feelings to invite her to our humble place? It was clean, if that meant anything to her.

Two hours later the puzzle was solved. A truck loaded high with furniture and other stuff parked in our driveway, and out jumped Mrs. Mason and a man she introduced as her husband. Jerry, still without a job, was fetched from the back yard where he had begun to prepare the ground for putting in a lawn, to help unload. That evening when Rudy came home for supper, he walked into a furnished house! It wasn't fancy by any standard, but it looked mighty fine to us! Each one had a bed. Hanna had a crib and a high chair. Baby had a playpen. I even had a washing machine and many other things to make life easier for me. We had also enough chairs to seat everyone at the same time.

The living room boasted an old carpet, some easy chairs, and lamp tables with two lamps. The old couch had a new look with a throw cover, and I was so excited I laughed and cried at the same time!

That evening I asked Jerry to unpack all his electronic equipment and fit it into the newly furnished living room. There was even a small case for his many records. He did it gladly. Everyone in the house felt good and happy. The babies slept and the bigger children played with some toys given to them by Mrs. Mason.

Jerry tinkered with his hi-fi and put the needle on an old record. "Listen, *Mutti*," he said with his typical boyish grin. "I think you'll like this."

I listened to the happy notes of playful music chords and felt strangely touched.

"What is it, Jerry?" I asked. "It sounds like sunbeams dancing on water."

"You're pretty close, *Mutti.*" Jerry looked pleased. "And you should know *that* water.

I grabbed the record cover. "The Moldau," by Smetana.

"Oh, Jerry!" I couldn't say another word. I just sat down and listened. The past stepped into the room and sat down beside me.

I was young again and enchanted with a river that flowed from the south, rising out of the Bohemian countryside until her waves, like a magic mirror, touched and magnified Prague, my beloved city's beauty. Her ceaselessly flowing waters shimmered emerald green, her banks formed the endless neck of a harp, her bridges arched across like the drawn strings of that instrument, her water pranced, ready to play — ready to sing.

Vysehrad Rock — enveloped in morning mist and myth, the site of human settlement near Prague since earliest time, rises from the deep waters while the harp's sound ripples and murmurs old songs.

I stood again under the massive baroque arches of stone overgrown by a green wilderness of hanging branches and felt the cool shade of the old linden trees, while the wind danced with the sunbeams across the river and the gulls screamed.

Summer nights dropped the stars to the bottom of the river while the city of a hundred towers reached rigid fingers into the moonlit sky. The waters grimaced at their straightness and twisted their reflected shape and garnished the pointed steeples with lace.

Unceasingly the water's flow joins other rivers toward the distant sea, but in her bosom Mother Moldau carries the golden image of her most beloved city to the ocean. And the ocean dreams of her — as I do.

"Oh, Jerry," I said when the record ended and I stepped out of a dream, "how come I have never heard that piece of music before? Or did I just forget about it?"

"I have never played it for you before. Maybe I was afraid it would make you homesick," Jerry said hesitatingly.

Did people know me that well? I thought I had been hiding my homesickness rather well, though it had hit me with new intensity since we had come to California.

"Please, Jerry, don't play that record again for a long time to come. It tears open too many memories. I must learn to forget."

"What is it you miss the most, *Mutti?*" Jerry asked. "What makes you so homesick?"

I pondered the question and shrugged my shoulders helplessly. "Jerry, you might not understand if I answer. First of all, I miss people, mainly my mother and close friends. But since I can write to them, that is bearable. My greatest longing, however, is for Prague, my beloved city. The reason it hurts so much is that I might never be able to go back to her again, *ever*. Even if I go back to Germany I might be barred from Prague for the rest of my life. As long as the Iron Curtain exists I shall never be able to visit that city." I fought tears.

"Why is it that important to see a place again, *Mutti?* It's just houses and trees. I am not homesick for the places of my youth."

"Oh, Jerry, you are such an all-American boy. How could you ever understand what tradition, folklore, and the magic charm of bygone history does to a true European? America is such a young country, and all that seems to matter in this country is the *now*. But, Jerry, we are all as a link in a long chain, formed and influenced by generations before us. We hand the heritage of the past down to the next generation in the endless stream of time; therefore we are all part of yesterday and tomorrow! There is no other place I ever felt so much at home as in Prague. Tradition can be security, legacy, and inspiration. It was all of that and more to me."

Poor Jerry looked so overwhelmed that I had to laugh.

"Stop worrying your graying head about my philosophies, Jerry. We are all what we are; nobody can jump over his shadow. But I am trying hard to change my shadow. I try too hard to forget."

"Mutti," Jerry asked gently, "could America ever become *home* for you? I mean so that you will not be homesick anymore and feel that you belong here?"

"I don't know," I said, and thought for a while. "I really don't know if I ever will feel home again anywhere! I sometimes wonder if I shall stay a wanderer forever, a wanderer between two worlds for the rest of my life. What is home, anyway?"

Jerry didn't answer and I didn't expect any answer.

21 LAND OF THE FREE

By the time we had been in California five years I looked back on more weary wandering than I had ever asked or wished for.

We stayed in Pomona just long enough to take some roots, add another baby boy to the family, and see Jerry get married. Then we moved to northern California where Rudy had a promotion, another transfer, and I had major stomach surgery that left me emaciated, tired, and longing for a place where we could settle down for good.

That desire seemed to be fulfilled when we moved to Fresno. We found a charming older house with many built-ins and enough modern conveniences to ease my home duties. I liked that because I prided myself to be no longer a housewife, but working as a teacher in a parochial elementary school. Rudy didn't like it, but a sixth-grade teacher left unexpectedly just before school began, and the administration asked me to fill in and teach for a year. The teacher shortage had reached crisis proportions.

I enjoyed teaching and regained my strength in spite of forty wiggly students. I could have been content if it had not been for one bothersome issue.

"Why have you not become American citizens yet?" The question came up more frequently as time flew by. Even our oldest children asked it every so often and we shrugged our shoulders.

"What shall we do about it?" I asked Rudy one evening. "We have been in this land seven years now."

"Honey, you are the one who was so determined to go back home someday." Rudy sounded cautious and deliberate. "You disliked almost everything about this country —"

"Oh, Rudy," I interrupted. "I've changed my mind and you know it. Don't rub it in! This country has been very good to us in spite of our rough start. As for our kids, America *is* home to them; even Chris and Mike speak English without an accent. We'll never manage that claim for us," I grimaced, "but we have a good life here and the children are happy!"

"Let's talk it over as a family," Rudy said and we called our five children to discuss it. They showed strong preference for a certain country! Then we formed our family prayer circle and prayed about it. The following day we applied for American citizenship.

It's really just a matter of cutting through red tape and receiving a certain paper, I thought. But I miscalculated! First of all we had to pass our citizenship test and I got scared and studied for it with fear and trembling. My knowledge of U. S. history was deplorable, I realized. When it came time to appear I felt shaky, like a little schoolgirl. The official sat behind his desk and smiled, looking straight at me.

"Who was president when you came to the United States?" he asked, while drumming his fingers gently against the wood.

I was confounded. I expected to be asked about Lincoln, Washington, the Civil War, and a hundred other hard things, but not such easy stuff.

"Truman," I said, self-confident and a bit arrogant. After all, I wasn't that stupid.

Then I heard Rudy laugh. "Mary," he said and his eyes danced, "how could you say that, when your favorite president is . . ."

"Eisenhower," I interrupted. "Of course. I like Ike." I covered my face with my hands and looked through my fingers at the official. "Oh, dear me, did I flunk my examination? Do I have to come back again?"

The official smiled and shook his head. "No, you're okay."

"Thank you, sir. Thank you," I said and wondered if he let me pass because he was a Republican.

He asked a few more questions, and Rudy always answered quickly. He wasn't going to give me another chance to jeopardize my future citizenship!

It came as a total surprise when we were called back into that office a few days later. The same official was there and he sounded very apologetic.

"Your papers have been checked and the higher authorities are making an additional request. Since both of you have rather unusual political backgrounds, and since you, Mr. Hirschmann, have been in active warfare against the U. S. A., we are supposed to take some extra measures in your case. Now, please understand, this is not my suggestion. I am convinced that you are both very honest and straight people with the right motives in mind. But, you see, the others don't know you like I do." He ran out of breath and avoided our eyes.

"Sir," I asked quietly, "is there any chance that we will not receive our U. S. citizen papers?"

"Oh, no," he said. "Absolutely not! You will have to go through additional interviews and your answers will be taped. That might be just a bit annoying and time-consuming for you, but there is no reason why you shouldn't become American citizens, at least not to *my* knowledge!"

"Do I have to study more for those new interviews?" I asked rather anxiously. "What if I mix up Lincoln and Washington the next time?"

"Don't worry, Mrs. Hirschmann, there will be only present-day issues discussed and taped. You're absolutely safe!"

That's what he thought. If only he *knew* how dumb I was when it came to politics — dumb by choice, because I avoided political matters like a burned child that won't go near fire again. Would they let me become an American citizen if they discovered my total ignorance? The whole deal got much more complicated than we had anticipated and I had shaky knees.

"You will be asked *why* you want to become American citizens; I know that for sure," the friendly man said as he walked us to the door and shook our hands. We thanked him and went home.

Why *do* we want to become U. S. citizens? The question went round and round in my head for the next days.

Was it for the good life? For the plentiful food and clothing?

For the chances our children had? Sure, all those were good reasons, but not good enough for me. There was something else but I couldn't quite put my finger on it, or formulate it into words.

Someone else formulated it for me and just at the right time, too. I received another letter from my papa in Czechoslovakia. We had been corresponding regularly all through the years and we had become rather close to each other. Papa and his family had matured in their Christian faith and his letters reflected his new joy, but also frustration in living where they did.

Sometimes Papa was too daring in what he wrote. It worried me. If his letters should be censored by the Communists, he could be in real trouble. So far his letters had come through untouched. Thank God this last one hadn't been opened.

"Marichen," he wrote, "don't ever forget that God has favored you and your family in a special way. You are permitted to live in paradise already on this earth and once in a while we catch a small glimpse of your good life through your letters. I don't envy you for your material prosperity, though I long sometimes to be able to give our two children better food and warmer clothing. But you live in paradise because you're free! You are free to serve God and train your children as you wish. I can't.

"The other day my Rudy came home from school and seemed upset. I sat at the window and he came over to me and said, 'Papa, teacher said there is no God. The Russian astronauts have looked around in space and can find no trace of him.' Oh, *Marichen,* do I need to tell you how I ache in my olden days to see my children be turned against God by godless teachers? Guess what my smart Rudy said to me? He looked out and up into the sky and said, 'Papa, won't my teacher be surprised when she will see Jesus come back again?' *Marichen,* what shall I do? How do I protect my children in the future? We have no children's books for them, no pictures. *Marichen,* sometimes I am afraid that I shall not make it into the kingdom of God after all. You see, I can't overcome my hate toward the Communists. I hate them for trying to steal my children's hearts. But my Bible says that I must love my enemies and pray for my government. I can't."

I put my head on that letter and sobbed. Papa, dear old Papa, what can I say? I understand, but I can't help you, can I? We would love to share what we have, the books, the records, everything our children have, but I can't send it. They won't let it go through the Iron Curtain. "O Lord," I said, "it's not fair that we have so much and they have nothing. It is not fair to my people!"

I wrote Papa a long letter back, very cautious in my wording of course, lest I jeopardize him if the letter should be censored.

And a few days later I spoke my answers on an official U. S. government tape to the question, "Why do you want to become an American citizen?"

The official who interviewed us asked just that one question. After we had answered it, he shook our hands warmly and let us go. He seemed satisfied. So were we!

A few weeks later we appeared in the Fresno courtroom to be sworn in. We were not alone. A large group was adopted that day — or were we the ones who adopted the country, I wondered. Deep emotions welled up in me as we repeated our pledge of allegiance to the United States of America and to all it stood for.

A great truth dawned on me while I looked into the serious faces of my new fellow Americans. The reason why America was chosen by so many as their new homeland was not mainly because it offered a good material life, or that it was a melting pot for so many nationalities, or that it had advanced education for our children. The reason why I and so many others before and with me had become Americans by choice was that America offered freedom.

Rudy and I had become Americans by choice. Nobody forced us. We were *free* to decide, *free* to be free. After seven years of wandering we chose a new homeland. We belonged again because we wanted to — and Papa stood outside and longed to have what we had — the great gift of freedom of choice.

Little did I realize what change that small citizenship document would bring into our daily lives. I expected the glow of that special courtroom moment to leave again after a few days, but it remained.

People came into our house and congratulated us, welcomed us, slapped shoulders, smiled, wished us luck and God's blessings. Why? Because we belonged. I belonged, too!

Now it became "we" whenever I talked to "them" — the American people. I even showed an interest in politics and tried to take sides. What a different and special thing to choose between an "elephant" and a "donkey"! They both looked well nourished and equally good to me — but I had a new responsibility to make a choice. Oh, dear, what a hard choice!

I felt myself changing into an American, and often it came so spontaneously that the impact scared me. For instance, when my students turned to the classroom flag one morning to say their pledge. I had never said it with them before. After all, it wasn't *my* flag. But overnight it had become mine too, and I could say with my students: "I pledge allegiance to the flag of the United States of America —"

I felt a lump in my throat though I tried to be unemotional. I had promised myself never to love a flag again. It was best to stay cool and repeat the pledge without thinking, like many Americans. I did not wish to become involved again — I loved a flag and a Reich once, and how bitterly I paid for it! Go away, lump in my throat!

One day we teachers loaded the students into buses and took them to a school concert by the local philharmonic orchestra in the city hall. The air hummed with laughter and excitement.

The concert began with a crash of cymbals and a certain tune, and hundreds of youngsters sprang to their feet and sang: "Oh, say can you see —" I stood too, but I did not sing. I didn't know those words yet and I wondered if I ever would. I felt like weeping.

"Jesus," I prayed, "I don't want to cry!"

"Why not, my child?"

"I am afraid to be all emotional about a homeland, Lord. I gave all I had once before, and I got punished for it. I can't get all involved again. Will you help me to stay cool, please?"

"Mary, I gave you this new homeland; I brought you and your family here by *my* will!"

"Yes, Lord, I believe that. But it's not right to weep with pride and joy over a national anthem, is it? I felt like that as a Nazi, and it was wrong!"

All at once a flash of insight hit my troubled heart while I listened to the children sing. One nation *"under God,"* I thought. Then I understood and it made me free to be myself again. It was all right to love what God blessed, and I did not have to be afraid or ashamed of it. I could love with all my heart.

"Thank you, Lord," I whispered, and let my tears roll. My students looked up and their eyes questioned affectionately and I smiled through the tears and nodded reassurance to them.

Everything was all right; yes, everything! No need to hold back anymore, no need to ride a fence. It was right to be proud to belong to this nation, and it was good, and my tears were tears of joy, tears of gratefulness. I would go home and memorize the words of the American national anthem.

"Thank you, my Lord."

22 Heartache and Healing

What would Mother say if she knew that we
had cut our legal ties with West Germany? Rudy and I decided
not to say anything in our letters but tell our mothers personally.
A message came that Mother was failing fast, and Rudy suggested that I fly to her bedside during Christmas vacation. We
would have to borrow money to pay for the ticket, but Mother
had my solemn promise that I would come back to her. I would
keep that promise even if it meant debts and Christmas away
from home. I had God's promise tucked away in my heart that
I would see Mother once more before she died.

I mailed my letter announcing my coming and my heart sang.
"*Mütterlein,* your *Marichen* is coming, only eight more weeks until *Weihnachten* (Christmas) and we will see each other. There
is a lot I have to tell you, Mother. I can't wait."

I didn't know what to do first — passport, reservations, Christmas preparations, a school play, a helpful list of suggestions for
Rudy while I would be gone, a few more speaking appointments
on weekends. It always amazed me how our fellow Americans
in various clubs and churches convinced us that we must tell our
life story for them over and over again. When other families

relaxed together on weekends, we traveled miles to give our testimonies.

With only six more weeks until Christmas, nothing mattered, nothing upset me, nothing seemed hard. I planned and hurried and prepared and gave speeches — and still found countless moments to daydream in anticipation.

I would surprise Mother. My brother-in-law, the minister, would pick me up and not tell Mother that I had arrived at the airport. I would tiptoe up the stairs and into her room. "Mother," I would say softly, "I kept my promise. I am here —!"

Coming back from a weekend speaking appointment I found a letter from Gustel, my foster sister. Good, she was writing for Mother and answering my last letter which announced my coming. I tore the letter open.

Rudy found me in our bedroom crying so hard that I couldn't talk. He took the letter and read it, then he told Chris to feed the children and get them into bed. *"Grossmutter* (Grandma) is dead," he said quietly and led the children away from my bed.

"Jesus," I cried, "you promised me that I would see her again! Why did you let her die? Why did you let me break my promise to her? She waited so long. O my God, why did you let her die so soon?"

I felt bitter, almost hostile. I hadn't gone when I wanted to go because the teacher shortage was so severe that I couldn't leave the classroom. Now it was too late.

"Why, Lord, why?"

"Someday you will understand, my child," Jesus said.

"But you promised me that we would see each other again, Lord," I argued.

"You *will* see her again," God said patiently.

I cried until there were no tears left in me and my heart was numb.

"Honey," Rudy said after a few days, "our children have never seen you so inconsolable and upset; your mourning will not bring Mother back but will only give the wrong example to our children. Christians have a blessed hope."

"I know, Rudy, and I believe in it. But I broke my promise! How can I live with that thought? How can I ever laugh again? I let my mother down."

Thanks to God, time heals wounds. Only scars remain.

Just a few months later another letter came from Czechoslovakia. Rudy took me in his arms. "Mary, I carried this letter around for several days because I am so afraid to give it to you. Please don't get so terribly upset again! Papa died!" The letter was from my stepmother.

"Dearest *Marichen*," it said, "Papa's heart is now still. It was so tired and weak for too long. He died without fear or death-struggle. Before he closed his eyes forever he looked up and whispered something. I bent close to his lips and he said, 'Give *Marichen* a message. Tell her I am ready. We shall meet again over there.'"

I smiled through tears. "O Rudy, God is so merciful! Papa has overcome his hate toward a godless government. Papa died at peace with God. I am so relieved. That's what his message actually means; can you read between the lines?"

"You are a strange girl," Rudy said. "How come you are so calm this time? You seem almost happy!"

"Why shouldn't I? Papa is safe in God's arms, isn't he?"

Time goes on and sorrow becomes memory. Change is consistent on this planet and we all change with time. But we have the choice either to turn bitter through our experiences or come closer to God.

While flowers began to grow on two graves across the ocean, new assurance started growing in my heart. God knows best, doesn't he? Someday I would understand! Would Christians ever question God's wisdom if we could see the reasons and the end from the beginning? Didn't all things work together for good for God's children?

Maybe the time had come for Rudy and me to sit back and relax and enjoy the good life of America while growing gray together.

"Let's take it easy for a while," I said one day to Rudy while working in my flower beds after school. "I feel rather old lately!"

Rudy smiled. "I don't know if that is God's plan for us," he said; "I just got a phone call from Florida. They want to transfer us to Miami!"

"Oh, Schatzi, please don't accept. I don't want to leave California. I love it here!"

Rudy shook his head and raised one eyebrow.

"I know what you think right now," I said defensively. "All right, so I said I would *never* stay in California nor like it! I am eating my own words, all of them. Someday I might even cut my hair and learn to drive a car. But I want to *stay,* honey, and just be another average American housewife right here, in this house. Let's settle down and let the world go by!"

"Please, dear Jesus, I want to stay here!" I begged. But while I said it I knew that I could get no answer.

"Your will be done, God," I finally found the courage to pray, "and forgive me, Lord, if I have become spoiled or too attached to my house and good life; make me willing to go where you want us to go!"

Is there such a thing as a sacrifice for God and his will? I thought I made a sacrifice when I began packing. I felt sorry for myself while trying to be obedient, noble, and cooperative!

I am convinced that Jesus must have smiled while watching me grumble, wallow in self-pity, and give dutiful lip service to his will. For he had a surprise for me! Something so inaccessible I didn't even dare dream of it any more.

One of our main reasons for coming to the United States had been our dream of going to a Christian college. Then after we saw how much it would cost we had buried those ambitions. We would have to concentrate on getting our five children educated instead. I packed to move to Florida, and three months later found myself moving to a college community in northern California instead. Rudy's transfer orders were changed and his boss permitted us to live in Angwin, a place I had yearned to be for a long time.

All at once I found myself getting ready to go to school — and very scared! My U. S. citizenship made me eligible for a government defense loan, and the registrar granted me two years of undergraduate credit since I had taken courses here and there in the past years and also had proof of my years of teaching after the war in Germany. My oldest daughter, Chris, teased me; she was a high school junior while I was a college junior.

"Mother," she chided, "don't you dare bring home a C in any subject. We expect your best at all times!"

Those words sounded very familiar! My children have ways of getting back at me sometimes! I hid my fears behind a self-confident smile. "Fine, kids, the race is on. Guess who is going to win?"

"Mother will," Rudy said, and winked at me. He beamed confidence and reassurance.

How does it look when a middle-aged woman with pigtails

walks into a packed classroom of a hundred or more students —
late — clutching her U. S. history book? This was a lower division class, attended mostly by freshmen, and I had the attention
of every eye. The professor stopped for a long moment.

"There is a seat in the front row," he said pleasantly, and continued his lecture.

I started to take notes furiously but got bogged down fast.
Other students had a background of U. S. history in grade school
and high school. I had a dizzy head!

What was Plymouth? a car? a rock? a symbol?

What gave me the idea I could compete with bright American
youngsters — and how had I thought I could go to college where
they taught everything in English?

What would my children say if I flunked?

If I thought history was rough, my next course was rougher.
Child development. It shouldn't be *that* hard. I could boast five-
fold experience in that area — just common sense!

But I heard common sense expressed in a different vocabulary!
I found out, when it was too late for second thoughts, that I didn't
have an adequate English vocabulary for that class. But I had
signed up for a loan and classes and there was no sense wasting
time and money. I would make the best of it.

Then I was handed my first multiple-choice test. I had never
laid eyes on such a monster before. German tests of my past
had always been in essay form. My previous night classes had
tested with quizzes, true and false tests, and by demanding reading reports which I could do.

After I had given that multiple-choice test one look of blank
horror, I got up and put the paper on my teacher's desk and
walked out without a word. I couldn't talk or I would burst into
tears.

Good-bye, college dreams, I thought grimly. The whole deal
would have been too good to be true anyway.

"Jesus," I prayed in utter dejection, "why did you bring me up
here when you know me so much better than I know myself?
You know that I can't take such horrible tests. I am too dumb
and the English language is impossible to learn. I don't have
enough background to catch on in the first place!"

"Go see Dr. Hauptmann," Jesus seemed to say.

I marched into Dr. Hauptmann's office with the desperate spirit

of a condemned person trying to be calm while eating his last
meal before execution.

Dr. Hauptmann, of Swiss-German descent, was not only a German professor but also a child psychiatrist. We had met the
week before and I liked his jolly personality.

"Dr. Hauptmann, I shall drop out of college," I stammered
the agitated announcement. "I can't do it!"

Dr. Hauptmann showed no surprise or shock. "Would you
like to tell me why?"

"I don't know enough English." I broke down and cried. "I
can't figure out multiple-choice questions and I am terribly afraid
that my memory will let me down again. I turn all blank when I
get scared."

Dr. Hauptmann took a pencil and paper and drew a spiral. At
the center he put the word "anxiety." At the end of the circle
line the word "failure." Then he explained.

"You are getting yourself in a vicious circle, Maria Anne. Your
Angst (anxiety) pushes you toward inability to take tests or understand the meaning of a lecture. Now in order to unwind this
spiral, which end would you have to pull off first?"

"Meine Angst," I said.

"Can you?" the doctor smiled.

"Nein," I said in desperation. "I tried but it gets worse from
day to day."

"Okay, then, let's try the other end."

"But I can't fail," I interrupted. "I would die with embarrassment."

Dr. Hauptmann nodded. "Look, you *are* ready to quit.
What's there to lose for you? I want you to obey my doctor's
orders and go back into the classrooms for the rest of the semester
and just listen for the fun of it. Take the tests and see how *much*
you can do right — for interest's sake only. If you fail I shall talk
to your teachers and you always can withdraw up to a certain
date. Will you do that for me since there is nothing to lose and it
would be of value to me as a doctor to see the results? Stop being
so proud and eager to make top grades. Go for the fun of learning!"

"Ja," I said and got up. If the man only knew how much I demanded of my children — now I would have to eat my own words,
as usual!

I walked back to my child development teacher, an elderly,

very kind lady, and apologized for walking out. I told her why. She was so understanding it made me feel good.

"You may use your German-English dictionary when taking my tests; I trust you," she said warmly, "and I shall give you this first test orally."

Surprisingly enough, I knew most of the answers when she asked me, and I decided to obey Dr. Hauptmann! Even if I only learned something to benefit my own family it was worthwhile finishing the semester.

I didn't say anything to my children, though. It would be soon enough to confess at the end of my first and last semester, and hard enough to swallow my daughter's triumphant look when we compared report cards.

There was a text in my German Luther Bible, in the Psalms, which I loved but sometimes dreaded: *"Wenn Du mich demütigst, machst Du mich gross"* (When you humble me, you are making me great; Psalm 18:36).

I surely was at a great stage of my life if that text meant what it said. Too bad that the humbling part was so much easier felt and observed by everybody than the greatness! But at the end of the semester the only C received was in U. S. history. Chris was very mature about it. "Don't worry about that C, Mother. I have one in P. E.!" She had my full sympathy. Both of us sighed relief!

Later while I was in the kitchen, I heard Michael ask Chris in the living room, "You mean Mother didn't scold you for that C, Chris? Boy, what's wrong with her all of a sudden? She would have torn your head off last year!"

"Yes," Chris said, very grown-up, "but last year she didn't go to college, either; I hope she stays with it for a long time. They might even straighten her out yet! But don't get funny ideas for yourself, Mike. You'd better not take too many chances with your grades. You never know with her."

A year and two cut-off pigtails later, I donned the black graduation gown and that strange hat with the tassel, to march in with the seniors for graduation exercises. The world was a happy blur of sunshine, smiling faces, and wonder.

I was actually getting my degree, my Bachelor of Science, and my teaching degree from an American college, if you please!

After the ceremony, as I stood in the long reception line shaking hands and hugging people, Rudy walked up and laid a bouquet of long-stemmed red roses in my arms. He smiled so proudly I felt tears well up again.

What beautiful roses! But they looked a bit black in spots and were kind of droopy. I motioned to Chris.

"Honey, what happened to the roses?" I whispered so that her father wouldn't hear.

Chris giggled. "When he brought them home he tried to hide them and get the petals freshened a bit, so he put the whole box in the freezer. Then he got so excited about getting all of us on time to the graduation he forgot the roses. They felt stiff when I got them. He wouldn't even have remembered to bring them. You know how Dad is."

I nodded and giggled and was deeply touched. I would never have graduated if he weren't such a kind, understanding husband and Chris such a dependable second mother in our family. This wasn't only my degree; it was a family accomplishment and belonged to all of us.

I said so during a celebration dinner that night and Rudy grinned. "That's okay, *Mammi;* you earned that paper, and we all will get our own. You don't have to share yours!"

I knew what he meant. I had promised Rudy that I would take over the breadwinning after my graduation so that he could have his turn to go to college. We would pull each other to the degree of our choice.

"Rudy," I said very hesitatingly, "would you let me get my master's degree before we switch? I want to go into counseling so badly, and if I carry overloads I could make it in a year and a summer!"

Rudy smiled. "I expected that, little teacher; all you have been talking lately is your wish to learn how to counsel better; I knew what you were up to for a long time — but we expect *only* good grades from you, Mother, no more C's. Your language handicap is no excuse!"

The children chimed in and were jubilant. At least they could stay another year and summer without the possibility of being moved away. They loved where we lived and had made many new friends.

I threw myself with new enthusiasm into my graduate studies and enjoyed most classes, but more than any class I enjoyed the association with my young fellow students. Our big rambling house on top of a hill became "Hirschmann Hill" to many young people and our place their home away from home.

They enjoyed German *Kuchen,* potato salad, and other filling foods, but that special time of evening worship around the fireplace they obviously liked the best.

We sang a lot and talked. We argued and discussed. We prayed while forming a big prayer circle and always finished by reading my favorite chapter: 1 Corinthians 13, to me the definition of love in its highest form.

I wondered sometimes how much influence we really exerted and if our hospitality did any good. Was it just for our own benefit, since our whole family loved to be around people? But one evening a sweet blond girl who had never impressed me as a very religious person said, "Stan and I are getting married," (they had met in our home) "and I asked the minister to base his wedding sermon on 1 Corinthians 13, the chapter I learned to love in your home!" I felt rewarded.

One boy left as a student missionary after the school year. When he came to say good-bye he looked into my eyes and said, "Someday when I start my own home I shall have worship time in my house just like you do. I will also open my house to young people. I realize we make much extra work for you — but I will never forget the hours around your fireplace!"

Such words brought joy and encouragement since I was aware that our house had become the object of gossip to some of our neighbors. Can anyone hang a light in the night without attracting bugs? We had the girls and boys come and go, alone or together. Anyone was welcome and they knew it — even those with the bad reputations, and people whispered.

To know that Christ accepted people without discrimination became our comfort and strength. I learned more than psychology that year. I learned to do what seemed right to me and to defend young people, try to understand without judging — even the little old saints who were so quick to wag their tongues.

One afternoon shortly before my finals I struggled again with one of my hardest subjects, physiological psychology. All that memory work felt like a murderous threat to my poor brain. A lone college student had come to our house and sat on our front lawn in the shade of a bush. He had been around before but I didn't know him too well because he never talked. I felt a bit pressured and wondered if I should go out to welcome him, but decided to wait until he was ready to come in. I needed every minute for my studies.

"Go and talk to that boy!" Someone whose voice I knew very well by then spoke to me while I read aloud from my book.

"Lord," I said, "I have so much to study yet; could I talk to him later?"

"Go now," my friend Jesus said. "Right now!"

The boy was just leaving when I stepped out. "Don't leave, Jimmy," I called after him. "I came to visit a bit with you!"

Hesitatingly the young man turned around. I stared, alarmed. His face looked haggard and his eyes so sad that my heart went out to him.

"Jim, for heaven's sake, what happened to you? Are you sick?"

"No," he said with a helpless shrug. "I am not sick. I am dead inside."

"Sit down, honey; let's talk for a while!"

We did. He talked and I listened. Like a waterfall his words tumbled out. His fiancée had sent the ring back and his world had come to an end; everything was broken forever.

"I haven't eaten for several days, Mom H." Most students called me that. "I can't get anything down. I want to die, and today I had scraped enough pills together that I thought I could do it. I decided to pray once more before I downed the pills, but while I talked to God it seemed like something impressed me to come to your house. I didn't want to come. That's why I didn't walk in. I figured if I had to come to you, you would come out and get me. I waited for you, then I decided to leave. But you didn't let me go away, did you?"

"Never mind, Jimmy," I said, shaken to my roots, "it's just that I have such a tough skull that even God has sometimes a hard time getting through to me. I *knew* I should come out and invite you in. I was only too worried about a good grade to put you *first;* please forgive me!"

I got the boy into my kitchen and heated some soup and burned some toast — I felt that disturbed — and while I saw to it that he ate a few spoonfuls, I talked to him.

I told him that sometimes our greatest disappointments later become the solid foundations of great happiness for us. I shared some bits out of my life to prove the point, and Jimmy took it all in. Then we prayed together, and I asked him to promise me to flush the pills down the toilet.

"I will," he said solemnly, and I knew I could trust him.

After I handed him another sack lunch for the evening, since he told me that he didn't feel able to go to the noisy cafeteria yet, he walked away. I watched the slim, tall form of that young artist disappear and all I could say was, "Forgive me, Lord; forgive me for being so slow sometimes, so selfish! Isn't a person more than a good grade?"

The Lord must have smiled again, for I also got an A the next day.

That day I gave my Lord another promise. "Use my life to help troubled young people, O Jesus; I promise you that I shall go whenever you send me, regardless whether it is hard or easy, if it is pressure or joy; let me be a friend to the new generation, Jesus. Those kids need friends they can talk to. We adults are so busy with life, we are missing our highest calling that you, O God, gave to us: to feed your lambs, precious Shepherd! There are too many lost lambs around, too many lambs who need to be loved. Teach me to love them, all of them, dear Lord!"

23 Home, Sweet Homeland

My husband looked alarmed. "You mean to say that you want to teach dope addicts and juvenile delinquents, my dear?"

"Yes, Rudy," I nodded. "I saw Dr. Beard today at the school district office to find out about the possibilities of teaching high school dropouts, and I volunteered for such a job!"

Michael, the oldest teen-ager in the home since Chris had left for college, lifted his blond head. "Mother, *you* want to teach in that old, dilapidated high school near the college, where all the bad kids go? I don't think that you know what you're asking for!"

Rudy looked anxious. "Honey, you might get stabbed or end up poisoned with dope. Why do you need to go and ask for trouble? There are enough quiet, pleasant jobs available for you!"

I nodded again. Yes, I knew that. I had just ended my first year at a tame and very respectable school as a master teacher and things went very well indeed.

My husband would soon start his second year in school since we had returned to southern California to the college of his choice, and I had taught at the demonstration school of his college. I enjoyed it, since I loved to work with young people and it gave me satisfaction to guide those eager student teachers toward creative teaching, but I didn't feel that I had yet found my own niche in life. Something was missing.

"Mother," Michael said very seriously, "you are too old and set in your straight ways to make it with *those* kids; you are used to teaching little brats, but they are not dangerous like high school gangs!"

I got defensive. "Look, young man, who are you to tell me that they are bad or mean or anything else? You seem to be more attracted to them than I am, judging by the length of your hair and the heated arguments your father and you have about the pros and cons of marijuana and other assorted topics."

Rudy intervened. "Mom, Mike is right. The reason why we object is because we love you. What if you get harmed?"

"I've escaped worse things in my life before; I am not afraid!" I held my head high and walked confidently away from the discussion.

I didn't feel as confident as I acted when my husband took me to my new place of work after summer vacation.

Several big boys hung around my future classroom and gave our little Volkswagen suspicious looks. They had a wild appearance, and Rudy looked deeply worried. "Are you sure you want to go through with this, Mary? I will take you back home with me; you'll find another job yet if need be!"

"Oh, Rudy, stop it. You act like I am risking life and limb. These are not savages; they're civilized American youngsters, if you please!"

Oh, my poor conservative husband who already suffered agonies because his own son had long locks and refused to wear shirt and tie to church. The look of my future students made him squirm. He kissed me gravely and drove away — and I walked into my classroom with a smile — but shaky knees.

"Good morning," I said with a forced smile. Nobody answered. Eyes stared under half-closed lids in stony faces.

I swallowed hard and sat down. The tardy bell shrilled and I tried to call roll. A few pupils reluctantly answered "here" while the last stragglers ambled into the room. They came in with cool looks of appraisal toward me.

I smiled so big I felt my ears move and boldly thrust my absence report in the air. "Is there someone who would take the absence report to the office — please?"

No answer; just more fixed stares.

I turned to a bearded boy next to my desk and looked straight into his eyes. "Honey, would *you* be so kind as to take the absence list to the office, please?"

The boy's mouth dropped and he looked away for a long moment, then his lips crinkled in a mocking smile. "Yes, Mother," he sneered, took my paper, and walked out.

Spiteful laughter followed him as he slammed the door so hard that the old windows clattered, and I felt my ears burn hot.

"God," I prayed desperately, "help me remember not to say 'honey' again. You know I am in that habit because I can't remember names very well, but these are not little children like in the elementary school. Please, God, help me. It looks like Michael was right; I am not the right one for high school students!"

When the boy returned from the office I looked at him. "I apologize for calling you 'honey,' but I don't know your names very well yet and I have teen-agers of my own and I am so used to calling them 'honey' that it just slipped out. Please excuse me!"

There was a ripple of surprised movements and smiles from desk to desk. The boy grunted and appeared to be at a loss for an answer. All at once the air felt less thick with hostility and tension.

"Where're you from?" a girl ventured. "Your English is different."

"Which way?" I said, "by accent or by wrong use of words?"

"You sound funny," she said. The whole class laughed but it sounded less belligerent than before.

I admitted that I probably sounded strange with my rolling-rrr Germanized accent, and the students began to talk. One Mexican student suggested that he had the same rrr sound in his Spanish accent. He sounded pleased.

The bell rang in the middle of our lively talk and the students left for a smoke break.

When my next class filed in I could sense a difference of attitude; my first group must have had a few kind words to say about me since I was now treated with a distant friendliness and tolerant superiority. They even gave patient explanations when I tried to get them to begin their assignments.

"Look, Teacha," one big, dark-skinned fellow told me, "get it straight from the beginning. We ain't here to work. We don't do nothin', OK? So we *have* to come to school or the fuzz gets us, yeah? But nobody can make us work. Nobody, OK?"

"Yes, honey," I said, taken aback, and I squirmed. "Oops, I said 'honey' again." I waited for the reaction. None came; just silence, and the boy had a funny expression on his face, almost as if he felt pleased.

Well, since the students didn't plan to do classwork, we might just as well talk some more together. We soon had a good discussion going about cars, motorcycles, and things I knew nothing about. I couldn't even drive a car yet and admitted it to the students.

I received much sympathy and lots of advice, and I showed my appreciation toward their abilities. I respect experts in any field and admire technical knowledge since I have none — those kids towered above me when it came to understanding car engines and I listened closely to their stories. The bell rang much too soon for most of us. We had fun with each other!

Rudy came at the end of the school day with a dismal look on his solemn face. He was obviously ready to pick up the pieces of the former me and give me his: "I told you so, didn't I?"

I beamed into his sober face. "I had fun today. I learned much about car engines and motorcycles and how to make friends with high school kids. And you can stop worrying. The first day is over; there are only 179 school days left and I intend to enjoy every one of those days!"

Rudy gave me his indulgent "wait and see" look and drove me home.

Behind my enthusiastic front, however, nagged one deep worry, but I didn't give the males of my family any indication that something troubled me.

What would I do for 179 days with students who "ain't gonna do no work"? Pretty soon I would run out of interesting topics for discussions. What then?

I could still hear Dr. Beard's words when he hired me for the job. "Mrs. Hirschmann, the students you'll teach have had nothing but experiences of failure. Comprehensive high school has tried and not succeeded; don't try any of the usual teaching methods with them. Depend on your creative mind, not on your training. Try the unusual. We give you freedom to do anything new — let the sky be your limit!"

The sky looked bleak at the moment. I also knew that it would take more than a few pleasant discussions for me to be accepted by my students and in spite of the smooth first day I could sense the arms-length distance between them and me. We lived in different worlds and they tolerated me as a nice oddball. They even overlooked my stupid habit of calling them honey, but that was all.

My students and I played a game for the first week. Both sides had feelers out and we waited — for what?

"God," I prayed every night, "show me a way to break through! I've got to find a way to their hearts. They don't trust me, regardless of how hard I try to be warm and understanding. Their suspicion is harder than steel!"

In the second week it happened. Tiny, a big, tall fellow, had been called to the office just before the bell rang. He was one of the boys who seldom said anything. He just sat and stared at me while we chattered as a group. But lately I had seen his eyes light up and sometimes he even smiled when I make a joke. He was warming up to me. I never considered him a bad boy. He never bragged like some others about their mischievous pranks. He even had decent manners. He said, "Pardon me," "Thank you," and "Please." Not many knew such niceties.

I worried about Tiny since two policemen had walked past my window minutes before; it left the students agitated and restless and when the bell rang they stormed out into the yard. Moments later the policemen led Tiny past my window. He walked between them, handcuffed and dejected. He didn't look up when they walked by my window. I sensed his humiliation and sat motionless until they were gone. Then I laid my head down on my desk, let the tears run, and said aloud in the emptiness of my classroom, "God, did they *have* to handcuff the boy? He isn't a criminal, is he?" Then I had a good cry. I felt so helpless, frustrated, and as shackled as Tiny in my attempts to help teach and reach those mixed-up kids.

The classroom door banged shut and I got up to dry my eyes when all at once I realized that I hadn't been alone as I thought when I let my sympathies get the best of me.

Who had seen me cry? I couldn't be sure, but whoever had stayed behind must have told the rest of the student body — and from that moment I felt the confidence of the entire group.

They treated me with rough tenderness and gave me their

trust, a gift that I cherished more than gold. We communicated so well that I soon had a good collection of ideas about what to do next. First of all, those youngsters needed food.

The principal stared at me. "Mrs. Hirschmann, how can we feed them? There is no cafeteria in this place. They come at 8 and leave at 12:30. They get lunch when they go home!"

I shook my head. Males can be dense when it comes to practical things, I thought to myself, but I knew better than to express *those* convictions.

"Mr. Stanton," I said as charmingly as I knew how, "lunch food comes too late for our students. They need breakfast in order to have their blood sugar high enough for studies before noon."

"Any more suggestions, lady?" The principal gave me his busy signal.

"Yes. I want to start cooking classes in my room."

Mr. Stanton can laugh about a good joke, and he did. "Are you going to cook in your desk drawer?" he said with a grin.

I didn't crack a hint of a smile. I had too much to say before the bell would ring again.

"No," I explained, "but in my own big electric frying pan, if I have your permission, and —"

The bell rang and we had to discuss my new plans some more after school. By then the poor man had recovered from the shock and had a list of questions. "What will you do about groceries?"

"I'll find a way to get government surplus food. The rest I will provide myself."

"How will you wash dishes?" he objected. "There is no hot water in this old school."

"We will use paper plates, plastic ware, and heat water in the frying pan," I said.

"What will you do if the health department comes around and inspects the place?"

"They'll never catch us. I'll pray that they never find out. Meanwhile, let's cook until they do!"

The principal threw his hands up in despair. "You might as well do it; I should have known better than to reason with you. Germans are too stubborn to be sensible!"

"Determined, sir, not stubborn," I corrected him, "and you are not very flattering, may I add!"

I left in a hurry before he could change his mind, and got busy with my new curriculum.

The cooking class proved so popular from the very first day that the office had to set up a waiting list.

Within a few months the principal found donors for an old gas stove and a used refrigerator. We hauled in two rough but huge picnic tables to replace the desks.

"Are you aware what it costs to hook the stuff up? This district is too poor for it," the principal grumbled while dragging the appliances in himself with the help of my students. "These school buildings are condemned anyway, and we shall move out after the kitchen is set up."

I waited until the boys were out of hearing range, then I turned to him. "Stop acting like a tough administrator. Nobody believes it, anyway. You have a soft heart underneath it all, don't you?"

"The only reason I do it is to get you out of my hair," he said grimly.

"What hair?" I asked innocently, with a glance at his bald head.

The day the stove was hooked up we celebrated by baking cake — German cake, of course — and we took a big piece to the office to atone for all the commotion we had caused.

"We should never have hired you. You cause nothing but trouble and extra money," the principal teased when he came to look over the classroom.

"I know. You American school administrators have a foolproof method of running a school perfectly and never overdrawing your budget," I answered with a straight face.

"How?" He sounded pleased.

"By getting rid of the students and teachers. If you ever manage to take those last two flaws out of your school system, you shall have a *perfect* administration! However, before you get rid of me, let me suggest two other plans I have. Let's offer sewing and arts and crafts!"

"Who will get you sewing machines and art material?" Mr. Stanton asked. He sounded weary.

"You, sir," I said, and left fast.

By second semester everybody had forgotten how hard it had been to start all those programs. Truancy was diminishing and the students enjoyed the taste of food and success. I felt elated, except for the fact that we still didn't have hot water and that the refrigerator had a knack for stopping whenever it got very hot, mainly over the weekend. But these were inconveniences that could be handled. Other problems proved more insoluble, such as the bleak lives of my students.

In the relaxed atmosphere of a homelike school kitchen, the youngsters had no trouble sharing tales of their daily happenings after school. I got many glimpses into the thinking and habits of their lives, and at times it seemed almost too hard to face the hopelessness of it all.

It always grabbed me hard when girls became pregnant. Many did — too many! By school policy we had no permission to give sex education, and the girls seemed totally ignorant about reproduction and contraception.

To tell them not to do it was useless. The only things to highlight their monotonous and miserable existence seemed to be sex and drugs. And sex could be more easily obtained than pills when money was short.

One girl had attached herself very closely to my apron strings for several months and I tried to explain to her the consequences she might have to face as she freely mixed sex and drug abuse. She shrugged her shoulders and smiled, and stayed away from class after that. That's the choice I have, I thought, and it hurt. Either nag and lose them or feel guilty for not saying it, and see the sad results.

Vera came back after a few weeks, maybe because the probation officer applied pressure, but she acted listless and sick.

"Vera," I said when I had a chance to talk to her alone, "what is wrong with you?"

She shrugged her shoulders. "My stomach is so often upset. I throw up every morning."

"Is there a chance that you are pregnant?"

"I hope not," she answered.

"What do you mean, you hope not?" I insisted. "It sounds as if you have morning sickness."

"But someone told me that you get morning sick *after* three months of pregnancy, and I can't be three months pregnant. I had —" She stopped, embarrassed.

"Vera," I said, "will you talk to your mother today and tell her to take you for a check-up? You are on medicaid, aren't you?"

She nodded. "But I can't talk to my mother," she said. "She and I are not talking with each other."

"What do you mean, not talking?" I asked impatiently. "Did you have a fight?"

"No, Mrs. Hirschmann. My mother and I haven't said a word to each other for the last three months. Not one single word."

"You mean you don't say good morning, good night, or I am going to such and such place when you leave?"

"No. We are not talking. We do that whenever she gets too much on my case," Vera said nonchalantly.

"Do you want *me* to call your mother, Vera? You have to see a doctor, honey, and soon."

She nodded, and I saw to it that the girl had her check-up. I didn't need to wait for the results to know that I had another pregnant girl in my group, but with her I felt more worried since both she and her boyfriend were under sixteen and heavy users of drugs.

Vera's parents forced her to marry the boy, and I cried a whole evening at home.

How much chance did we teachers have to help those kids unless we could change their total environment? Our few hours of influence in the class couldn't make enough of a dent!

When Vera delivered her baby it had three ribs missing, and Vera's marriage ended in annulment. She seemed less upset than I felt and she tried to comfort me. "Don't take it so hard; that's life," she said. She appeared happy; she and her mother were on speaking terms at that moment and the baby slept most of the time — maybe too much for a normal baby? I wondered but kept silent.

Not everything happened that negatively; we had our victories, too — such as graduation day when we watched more than twenty seniors graduate, a first in that school. Betty, our pretty business teacher, and I gave each other silent signals as the names were called.

"That's your student," she would signal. "That's *your* name," I would wink back. We alone knew how much effort, pain, and babying it took to get some of those proud graduates to the finishing line, but it was worth it!

For instance, there stood *my* boy Carlos. His parents spoke no English but his mother cried through the whole ceremony. Out of seven children he was the only one who received a high school diploma.

What a close call that was! I had nudged, nagged, praised,

and threatened until Carlos had only one science course left. Since the school program based itself on individual work contracts, not on lecture methods, each student proceeded at his own speed. We teachers gave instruction and help on individual tutorial basis, which suited me just fine. Carlos had started in my art class and discovered how success tasted. We were both surprised at his talent. I knew that many of our greatest troublemakers had a creative streak, and art provided therapy and healing to their crippled self-images. Carlos outdid himself. He suddenly showed interest in other subjects, too, and ended up on the seniors' list for possible graduation — if we could master science and his terrible temper. Sure, I could tutor him through a science book but would he stay out of fights long enough to finish?

He didn't. In a fit of rage about nothing in particular he threw a pair of scissors. They struck the wall and broke, dangerously close to another student's head. That ended school for Carlos, with one subject to go for that coveted diploma.

I stormed into the office. The principal already waited to receive me.

"I expected you," he said, "but don't waste your breath. Carlos is *not* coming back. This time you're *not* getting your way. He is a potential danger to the other students."

"You are right," I agreed.

The principal gave me a suspicious look. "What are you up to?" He shifted and looked over his horn-rimmed glasses at me.

"Will you let me tutor him in my own house in the evening?" I asked meekly.

"If you don't have enough to do as it is, let me know," he growled while I choked back an angry retort. I couldn't afford to displease him, for Carlos' sake, and we both knew it.

"Go ahead," he said, "I'll never hear the end of it otherwise. You German women are so hard to live with!"

"What nationality is your wife, sir?"

"German!" he called after me. "Can't you tell by the way I talk?"

Of course I could, but what did it really matter as long as I got my way most of the time! Carlos, here we go!

Yes, Carlos graduated, and so did my Lana a year later. That graduation we had more than thirty students ready to receive their diplomas and Lana was one of *my* girls. She brought me a gift and a thank you card.

"Honey, this is *your* day for gifts," I said, deeply touched, but she gave me one of her sweet smiles which made her so very pretty.

"Mrs. Hirschmann, you are more than a teacher to me. You are mother, friend, and you saved my marriage, too. All I can say is thank you and God bless you!"

Precious girl! Her mother had died an alcoholic. She had kept her father's home since she was twelve years old. Her father was very aged and a bit senile. Lana got married before she turned seventeen and I helped her with the wedding plans. She made the wedding dress in sewing class and her wedding went smoothly. Her marriage, however, hit rough spots right from the beginning. I listened and stood by.

"Another one who seems to come out on top," Betty whispered while I took pictures of Lana receiving her diploma.

Some of those we had worked the hardest for, however, let us down at the end, and it left us hurt and wondering.

Betty, my fellow teacher and very close friend, had befriended a little Cuban girl in a very personal way. She taught Juanita how to adapt to American customs. In her own home Betty tutored Juanita through several courses and the girl responded beautifully until she started to take "reds." Juanita ended in a mental hospital, and I avoided mentioning her name to Betty. I knew too well the hurt that comes when we wonder why we failed.

What do other people think when the police helicopter hovers over the city for long hours, even days? Maybe they don't even notice. I didn't until I taught in the most despised school in the district, but the sound began to have a meaning for me. The helicopter searched for runaways. If the runaway was one of our students I worried and prayed for him and hoped the helicopter would spot him and send a police car after him before he could do something foolish.

Take Dina, for instance, who has leukemia and must take medication every day. She would get so frustrated with life that she would begin to shoot heroin and then she would run. "Go, helicopter, go," I cried inwardly. "Find her before it is too late. Dina must go back on her medication, or she will die."

Oh, Dina, life is a cruel puzzle for you, but sometimes it puzzles others, too — like me, and I am a grown-up person at that.

Yes, there were times when I began to wonder and got that old panicky feeling inside me again over certain issues. I would brood gloomily for hours.

Oh, yes, it was a fact that America had freedom and the best form of government in the world. But if that was so, why was there so much poverty, injustice, and lately even riots and violence in this country?

I loved America and I would get all defensive and furious inside when I would hear people disparage this country. I disliked the way the newspapers washed America's dirty laundry before the eyes of the whole world. Didn't they know that most people in other countries would never meet the real America, but judge our country by what the newspapers said?

On the other hand, was there not truth in it? Maybe I felt defensive about it because I was afraid. Could democracy be a delusion, as Naziism was? Did I defend and love something again that would lead me a second time to destruction? "God," I prayed, "give me wisdom. Let me not err again!"

I had been asked to lead the Sunday morning service in a nearby prison. It came naturally for me, through my new teaching job, to get involved with prison evangelism since some of our own students ended up in those institutions.

After several metal doors had been opened and locked again behind me, I reached the chapel. The chaplain greeted me.

"Mrs. Hirschmann, I am aware that you do some strong preaching, not only about God but also about your love for America, and I appreciate it. But it's only fair to warn you — we have an unusual congregation this morning. For some reason or other we have all the militant elements of the prison with us this morning. They might break up the service if you come on too strong!"

That's all I needed, I thought. I felt mixed up myself, unsure about why I loved this country so fiercely. I was weary from brooding about all of it so much.

The little prison choir sang, "Which Way, America?" I tapped my foot and sang with them. I loved that song and the choir leader knew it. Those catchy tunes really had a message. The rhythm was fast enough to arouse even those who slept — in more than one sense!

I stood behind the microphone without a pulpit and every eye watched me while my mind raced. "Jesus, please fill me with your Holy Spirit," I prayed. "I am all blank. I don't know what I am going to say!"

Peace flooded into my soul and I began to talk. I looked into the waiting eyes of those prisoners, aged twenty to twenty-five. They were labeled hard-core criminals. I told them in simple words why I love Jesus. "God in his love gave me not only peace and a new meaning for my shattered life, he also gave me a new homeland." Then I continued to tell them how I met the first Americans after crossing "no-man's-land" and how those soldiers taught me the meaning of love, neighborly kindness, and tolerance.

"You might not have been born at that time, my young friends," I concluded, "but maybe one of you has a dad who was there that morning, and I believe that the same American spirit is still around; I believe that most of the Americans even today would rather help than hurt — even you — and I thank you for it!"

I sat down. The chapel exploded around me and I wondered why. Then it dawned on me that I was being given a standing ovation. So-called hard-core criminals, charged with murder, felony, and other gruesome things, stood up and clapped, whistled, shouted. Some cried. Guards came running. I was sure that they thought I had started a riot. The chaplain motioned for silence. The prisoners sat down and it turned still. I watched it all — and noticed several rows of prisoners at the back who had not moved at all. They didn't clap or stand with the rest. They just sat and stared at me.

Those must be the militants, I thought. Into the new silence rose one of those fellows. He was so tall and husky he reminded me of that first American soldier who seemed to fill the door frame when I first saw him that long-ago morning after I crossed no-man's-land.

"Mrs. Hirschmann, would you answer some questions for us?" he asked politely.

I nodded. I was scared. I *knew* what he would ask and I was not sure I had an answer.

"I'll answer anything you ask," I said, and I prayed in my heart for wisdom and true insight.

The prisoner looked at me with cold eyes. "Since you think

America is so great, what do you think about us young people of America and our attempts to improve this country? What do you think about the protest marches and the riots?"

A flash hit me; it was one of those rare moments in my life when new insight is born into consciousness and light; the labor for it is over and the puzzle pieces are falling together into a new, clear picture of greater beauty.

"My friend," I said directly, "young people are the same all over this globe. They long for a challenge and a task in which to measure their strength. I have come from a country where young people feel as you do, but the only way they can protest is to throw themselves before a Russian tank. And the tank doesn't stop! Or they can pour gasoline over themselves, if they have a ration card for it, and then ignite it — and they had better burn fast or the authorities stop the suicide and heal the fellows to give them a trial and sentence of death! Yes, I am aware that American people are afraid of your riots and protests, but I am not. I watch these happenings on the TV news and all I can feel is astonishment — yes, even gratefulness, that I am permitted to live in a country that is so free it *lets* you riot as much as you do. I only wish American young people would do it a bit nicer!

"My young friends, I have long searched for the meaning of democracy and freedom. I thought Americans knew it, but they don't. Americans are the ones who seem to know the least about the value and philosophy of the freedom they possess. Listen, you fellows: freedom makes good people better and bad people worse. Remember that! Some of the rough things happening in America today are the price this land pays for its freedom. As for me, I prefer to pay the price and stay in this land. Those who can't take it should find another land; they might be happy to come back to these United States after a short time in another country!"

I was out of breath and I sat down. The chapel was so quiet we all could have heard a needle drop — but nothing dropped. A deep silence tied us together. The chaplain spoke the closing prayer and we filed out.

I shook many hands that day. Some of the fellows in the last rows greeted me too. One young prisoner had tears in his eyes when he grabbed my hands.

"Man," he said, "this is the first time in my life that I felt proud to be an American!"

"Thank you for coming. You did much for me," another prisoner said.

Did much for you? Friend, if only you knew what this service did for *me*. God sent me there for my own sake first of all. Everything made new sense to me and I felt like singing. I had peace again — peace with God and my country.

Sometimes falling stars drop out of our dream sky and become reality. Summer had come again and I was on my way to visit Germany. I had waited fourteen years for that moment and when it happened I thought myself dreaming.

My trip took me first to an Eastern university for a special workshop and then I would go on to New York and fly across the ocean to Europe for three short weeks.

While still on that university campus I gave a talk one evening in one of the big dormitories and afterward hurried to the door to get away before some listeners could corner me. Many unfinished assignments waited that night and I looked neither right nor left.

A little old lady stepped into my path and looked up.

"*Tante* Erhard!" I screeched with joy and hugged her closely. Who cared about assignments!

I did not know that she lived on that campus. Time and distance had interrupted our friendship; now we made the most of our reunion.

She owned a cute little home with ruffled curtains, an old-fashioned rocking chair, and a tiny kitchen that smelled like mint.

We exchanged pictures. Yes, Chris was in college, Michael finishing high school. The two girls were young teen-agers and Jo Jo a big boy and a football fan by now. Rudy was plowing toward his Ph.D. in German philology at the University of California.

"Where did time go so fast?" *Tante* Erhard shook her gray head.

Her sons had finished school and been married. One son was a minister, the other a college professor with a Ph.D. in chemistry. I admired their lovely family pictures.

"Oh, *Tante* Erhard, God gave you the desires of your heart! I'm so happy for you!"

"God spared my sons for his service. I knew it all along," she nodded with motherly pride in her eyes.

"And what about — " I hesitated to say it.

"You mean my husband? Maria Anne, I have word from him! He is alive!"

I was so excited I couldn't talk, but motioned for her to tell me more.

"One day I came home from work and I saw that strange letter in my mailbox. Before I opened it I knew already that it was a message from him. They kept him for twenty-five years in a *Schweigelager* (silent camp) in Siberia, Maria Anne! When they freed him he stayed in Siberia and started to look for us. Some one of our relatives in Russia knew that I had emigrated to the United States, so he wrote to the International Red Cross in Bern. They found our address for him and contacted us immediately; that foreign letter was from the Swiss Red Cross headquarters."

"Will he be permitted to come to America?"

"No, there is not much hope. I don't need to tell you why, do I? But somehow it doesn't matter. It is very hard to put it in words; we can write to each other and I can send him pictures and packages. The grandchildren are now the age our sons were when the war tore us apart, and now we are old and God has taught us patience. Soon, oh, so soon, we'll be united forever in his presence; what do a few more years on this old planet matter?"

"*Tante* Erhard," I said softly, "what would all of us do if we didn't have our blessed hope and the promises of God?"

"I would lose my mind, my dear. But there is a peace that passes all understanding, and God has given me that heavenly peace. I am content to trust him."

I remembered *Tante* Erhard's words when I stood at my mother's grave two weeks later.

All my bitterness came back to me but my foster sister comforted me. "For your sake it was better that you didn't come to Mother's deathbed. She was only a shadow of her self when she died. Her desperate struggle for every breath was agony for all of us who had to watch her. But her heart was in peace through all her suffering. She understood that you couldn't come so fast. You are privileged; you may remember her as she looked in her healthier days. Thank God for it — it's a happier memory!"

I thanked him. Yes, my Jesus knew best!

In three weeks I whirled through all of West Germany and Austria but didn't dare to go across the border to see my beloved city. I wondered if I should, but my stepmother Bertha and my brother Rudy and sister Angelika protested strongly. We had never seen each other and my little brother Rudy had a surpise for me. He stood a head taller than I and looked down at me. "Hi, big sister!"

I looked up. "Hi, little brother!"

They had come out of Czechoslovakia a few years after Papa's death, just before the Russians occupied the land of my childhood for the second time. Now they lived in West Germany.

We cherished every moment together and talked about Papa. Soon it was time for me to leave.

"Stay longer," my people pleaded.

"I can't. I must go home!"

"Didn't you come *home* to visit?" Angelika asked me.

"No, I am *going back* home and I can't wait," I said.

The big, silver bird hummed across deep waters through the night. "Make haste, jet bird; speed west. I long to go home, home to America!"

Rudy held me tight when I arrived at the airport. "I shall never let you leave us again!" he said.

"It was good that I went," I whispered into his ear.

"Why?"

I smiled through my tears. "Because I know now how it feels to come home!"

1967 -- Mom graduates with a master's degree in
Administration and Counseling and gives thanks to God.

1976 -- Hansi becomes known for her patriotic love for America.

1974 -- Hansi's children go to college
and she begins full time speaking and writing.

1975 -- Corrie ten Boom is Hansi's mentor.

1978 -- Hansi visits Egypt's famous places.

1978 -- Hansi visiting the Pyramids.

November 13, 1996

Today I am 70 years old. My heart is filled with awe and thanksgiving to Jesus Christ, my Saviour and Lord. I think of God's promise in Isaiah 46:4. I heard my foster mother quote it so often in her old age:

Even to your old age and gray hairs I am He. I am He
who will sustain you. I have made you and I will carry
you; I will bear you and I will rescue you.

Now I understand why she loved the text so much. It is by now one of my favorites, too. I have lived long enough to know that every word is true and so is *every* promise God gave to His children in His Word. It shall be my testimony now and through all eternity that Jesus *never* fails.

Time flies so fast, it seems like only yesterday I wrote the Hansi book and watched in wonder what God can do when we obey Him.

Writing it, I struggled with the English language, recurring nightmares and the never ending daily demands of a working wife and mother, but I prayed and wrote, rewrote and wrote again!

Before I mailed the finished manuscript to the publisher, I knelt and asked the Lord to give it Heaven's special blessing.

Little did I know what God had in store for me! The book became a Christian best seller almost over night, I became "Hansi" and the requests for public speaking mushroomed in proportion to the phenomenal sales.

When a little orphan girl from the hay loft turns into a successful author and public speaker within a few months, it sounds like a fairy tale --- and everybody lives happily ever after!

But the Christian life is not a rosy fairy tale, at least mine has never been. The brightest light throws the deepest shadows! Instant success and public recognition can create tension, conflict and broken relationships. It did so for my family and me.

I often wonder how much heartbreak might hide behind the big smile of a public speaker I listen to. I remember so well how I smiled through my first Christian Booksellers' Convention while crying through the nights.

But at the same convention God had something very special for me. I met Corrie ten Boom, the famous author of *The Hiding Place**.

Again, little did I know how important that precious old Dutch woman would become in my life.

Just a few months after "Tante Corrie" and I had become friends, the Lord directed me to resign my secure teaching position and step out into a faith ministry. By then I was a single mother and watched my children individually work their way painfully through confusion, rebellion, high school and college toward a life of their own.

Today all five of them are decent, hard working, successful adults; they married good mates and my grandchildren are, of course, the most adorable youngsters yet!

As for me, I learned to walk with the Lord in a new way! The ministry grew in spite of my inexperience with corporate and other matters. Corrie ten Boom stood by me with advice and encouragement. Her organization had been incorporated several years earlier.

She knew about the ups and downs of a Christian ministry. It was the grace and mercy of my Lord that kept me going, one day at a time. I learned soon not to lean on my own logic and understanding but simply to obey as I perceived His will for my life. The hardest thing for me was to accept the way I was treated as a public speaker by my audiences. It fell into two extremes. I received so many sincere and loving compliments from kind strangers, both by word of mouth and by mail. I wondered how to handle it and Corrie ten Boom gave me the key.

---

* She and her family suffered in a Nazi camp for hiding Jews

"Accept every compliment graciously like a flower, gather it together into a bouquet, at the end hand it over to Jesus!"

I have done that gladly ever since she shared it with me, but the other side of public reaction is harder to handle!

A servant of God might receive an arm full of flowers from a kind receptive audience but it takes only *one* critical, judgmental person who feels called to throw a stone and a hundred flowers cannot protect from pain and dark bruises. One nasty letter can cut so deeply that it destroys laughter for days.

Why are Christians so eager to shoot their own wounded? How is it that we in the Body of Christ are so quick to always assume the worst motives in someone else?

The answer to that puzzle I got from the Lord Himself one night when I cried myself to sleep. "Why, Lord" I asked, "I haven't done anything to that person!"

"Did the religious people treat Me any better", the Lord said tenderly, "did I do anything wrong?"

"No, Lord", I said, "You were blameless and loved everyone with a perfect love -- and they nailed you to a cross!"

Through the years I have learned to be still and let the Lord defend me in His perfect timing. God permits pain because so often our spiritual growth comes out of sorrow and heartache.

Nevertheless, the hardest thing yet is to watch when unkind people attack those I love very deeply.

Of course, for parents to watch their children go through heartaches is more agony than to be hurt themselves, but I find myself agonizing when innocent people in my circle must suffer just because they work with me.

God gave me a very special friend, a precious gift, when I was introduced to Betty Pershing more than 20 years ago.

Israel brought us together. Someone suggested that I should lead a tour group to Europe and include Israel. I had never given it a thought and I figured that I as a former Nazi would perhaps not be allowed to enter the Jewish State. I fully understood if it was so!

My heart had gone out to the Jews ever since I had to accept the fact that there had been a Holocaust. It took Corrie ten Boom to convince me. Before I met her I rejected the idea. I had never heard of such a thing during Nazi time and when the Russians reported the "freeing" of concentration camps, I thought it was Communist propaganda. It simply was inconceivable to my way of thinking that any German could have done such atrocities. Russians did it and I watched them - but never a civilized German!

When Corrie ten Boom spoke about her sufferings during the Holocaust, I had to face the horrible truth that I had followed and believed murderers and perverts, who even destroyed innocent children.

Tante Corrie's forgiving love helped me to come to terms with it. The Lord knew that I had not known about it during Hitler's time. If anyone would have told me I would not have believed it, I still did not believe it 28 years after W.W. II. When it finally sank in, I gave the Lord a solemn promise. Nothing I could do would erase a horrible past but I would stand by any Jew and Israel and give any help possible! I also understood if a Jew would reject my help and treat me with contempt! Maybe they wouldn't even permit me to visit their country?

It was the first question I asked Betty Pershing when we got introduced. I knew that she had toured Israel many times and was a staunch supporter of Israel and the Jews.

She reassured me. Israel was open to anyone who came in peace.

In 1976 Betty and I led our first of many tours to Europe and Israel and I learned to see the land through God's eyes, illuminated by Betty's teaching about the Hebrew culture. The Bible became a living Book and I left part of my heart in Jerusalem. (Betty's was already lodged there from previous visits.) God gave me a deep love for Israel and the Jews and Hansi Ministries makes no apologies for our total support of Israel and the many Jewish friends we now have. I still feel humbly grateful that any Jew is willing to be my friend and I pray much for the peace of Jerusalem.

Betty was a senior editor of a large Christian Publishing House when I met her and I knew that our small faith ministry didn't have much to offer if we tried to hire her. My hope was that she might work with me after she retired, since her company had a great retirement plan. But that was years in the future!

Just one year after our first Israel tour the Lord told me to call Betty and ask if she was willing to work with me.

I obeyed but had no doubt about the outcome. Betty would not walk away from a secure retirement, her church, her friends, and a regular pay check to join a very young and shaky ministry, or would she?

I presented the offer honestly, realistically, and as I saw it: "We have nothing to offer but the promises of God," I told her. "We have no retirement plan because we don't intend to retire. We go to our Eternal home with our boots on!"

Betty prayed about it and called back: "The promises of God are enough security for me. I'd love to come and work with you!"

She not only came to work but she shared the ups and downs of our vacillating finances. She drove a little motor home thousands of miles from state to state for our many double engagements on numerous speaking tours across the USA and Canada -- without a single accident.

Together we tried to provide a place for my children to come home to from their boarding schools or college dormitories. We laughed together and we shed tears, but mostly, we became prayer partners and the Lord knit our souls together as He did with David and Jonathan in Bible times.

I learned so much from Betty, she is such an exceptional Bible teacher. She claims the same about me, as I give the practical application of her Biblical insights. Through the years the Lord taught us to teach more and more as a team and gave us a spiritual oneness which became a source of great joy for us and others. However, as I said before, shadows are part of light, sadness is the other side of gladness.

Only God sees the heart of a person. Who can know the motives of people who have a vivid imagination and always seem to think in the negative? Do they really believe that they do God a favor by questioning everyone but themselves?

I remember the time when Betty and I presented a three-day seminar in a Midwest city. It had been organized by the Ministerial Association and ministers of various denominations listened in the audience. In the front row sat three gentlemen taking copious notes. They were the preacher and two elders of a local church from the denomination I had grown up in. I was surprised because they normally do not interact with the Evangelical churches.

At the end of the very successful seminar that particular preacher asked if he could talk to me alone. I agreed and he came right to the point.

In the churches of his denomination circled the story that I had given up my family to live with a woman. Did Betty and I have an unbiblical relationship?

I looked straight at him and said, "May I ask you first something else? What did you think of Betty's Bible teaching for the last three days?"

He smiled, "She is great. I made many notes. She surely knows her Bible!"

"Do you think the Holy Spirit was at work in the audience?" I asked.

"No doubt about it", he said, "I heard so many favorable comments. After all, the people came back the second and third day. That is not common in our community!"

"Could the Holy Spirit have worked as you observed, if Betty lived in sin?" I said quietly.

"If you wish to question me, I understand. After all, I was kicked out by your church leaders and nobody bothered to talk to me before they did it. But Betty has been in the Lord's service all her life, her reputation is blameless. Must she now live under accusations because she was willing to work with me?"

The gentleman gave me a long look. "I owe you an apology", he said, "of course -- God could not work through you if you lived in sin. I am sorry!"

He shook my hand and left. And I had another good cry during the night. "Lord, will this ever end?" I tried hard not to wake up Betty with my sobbing. "What can we do about it?"

"Just trust Me," Jesus comforted my heart, "I am your defender. When people think and say hurtful things about others, they show what's in their own heart, not what is in yours. They become tools of Satan, remember, he is the accuser of the brethren."

I do not know if Betty and I are still under such rumors. I can recall many other evils we have been questioned about through the many years. The warfare never ceases. Betty and I have learned the hard way that light irritates darkness and anyone who desires to serve the Lord fully is in for persecution, even by some "church saints."

We have watched churches split and godly ministers have breakdowns because someone feels called to let suspicion run wild.

I am sharing this not for Betty's or my sake but for the *many* wounded warriors in countless churches around the world. I have never seen God's servants under more stress and attack in all my years as right now! Sometimes it takes only *one* zealous defender of his or her *own* conviction to destroy the faithful work of many Christian workers. The most painful thing is that it is so often done in the name of a loving Christ.

The darkest hour of every night is *always* followed by a new morning and Christ's gift of Joy. The key to healing is forgiveness. We must forgive for our own sake; our wounds cannot heal otherwise. The Lord is so faithful to keep His promises but for some things to happen, we have to do our part first. We must choose to forgive, no matter how deeply we hurt or however we feel. Spiritual wounds can only be healed by the Holy Spirit.

Very often it takes time. We must learn to wait upon the Lord. Psalm 37 will always be my favorite Scripture. Yes, we often wait, puzzle and wait for God to answer, but He *will* give us the desires of our heart in His perfect time!

I shall never forget the year of 1982. America was in recession and I watched many fine Christian ministries fold financially. It did not look like our small organization could weather the economic drought either. Betty and I drove across our nation trying to encourage God's people, while I felt more and more drained. When our speaking tour ended we drove back home weary in soul and body. I told the Lord that I wanted to quit. I cried while Betty drove hour after hour. I asked the Lord why I felt so exhausted, when I knew that He carried me in His arms. He showed me a new thing! Yes, Jesus *did* carry me but I grabbed hold of His garment so tightly, my knuckles shone white.

"Why don't you let go?" He told me, "I am holding on to you and I will never drop you. I am able to keep you from falling!"

I asked the Lord why I had such a hard time to "let go" and He showed me that my experience with people had made me afraid to trust. Even at best humans let each other down, so we must never put our trust in people but in God alone.

I wiped my tears and asked Jesus to help me let myself be carried by Him alone and rest in His love. I also promised I would continue in His service until He told me to stop.

It was only weeks after that encounter that my Lord gave me another great desire of my heart. Betty and I received an invitation from a senior Chaplain of the US military to come and visit every US base in Turkey. I had been praying for years to have the privilege to serve our American Defense Forces. I owed American soldiers such a great debt for their kindness to me when I fled to the American Military Zone in West Germany.

Our trip to Turkey changed our lives and the ministry forever. We knew we had found our special calling as we traveled from base to base. We could not help but fall in love with those very special people, who are willing to defend our nation and freedom at a moments notice.

Since then we have visited many, many bases around the world and across America. Our love and admiration has deepened and we are often saddened when we see how little America appreciates her military and their families. So much sacrifice and hard work and even the demands to live in undesirable places is accepted by them in order that we may live in peace and freedom.

By now we have become "Grandma Hansi and Betty" for many military chapel families overseas and at home. We still travel far and near to encourage and thank them for their faithful service under ever mounting pressure and stress.

Lately, we have been directed by the Lord to also give encouragements to believers in many churches in America and around the world. Christians everywhere are coming under hellish attack. Storm clouds darken the sky over America, not only literally but spiritually. We are talking about a "Post-Christian era" of our nation -- and rightly so!

Is it a time to be scared of the future? No, it is a time to rejoice, because our future is as bright as the promises of God. Our Lord said that when we see all these bad things around us, we should lift up our heads and rejoice for our redemption draws near. Who could doubt that Jesus will come soon to take us home?

I often watch a glorious sunset from our porch. Our Lord's wonderful Love has seen fit to let Betty and me live in Hawaii. It's a great place to come home to after tiring tours and long flights. The orphan girl who froze so much in a hay loft lives now in a house that is always warmed by the sun. Kona has the most famous sunsets. I never tire of watching the blazing evening sky. It is always a foretaste of Christ's glorious soon coming to my eager heart. Oh yes, come Lord Jesus!

Closing this chapter I do want to thank you for buying this book. You see, my precious Lord and divine Husband Jesus, the Christ even gave me my most hidden desire in my old age.

As a child in a dark hay loft I would dream of having an orphanage someday, when I would grow up. I pictured rooms full of beds with soft pillows and warm covers. Each room was named after a flower and decorated accordingly. The girls wore pretty dresses and everybody had three meals a day and could eat as much as desired, there was even seconds on hot chocolate!

Grandma Hansi had buried her dream as the years flew by, we never operated with enough funds to consider such a thing -- and where were the orphans who needed my dream house?

I found the orphans this summer! The Lord directed me to visit Poland and Belarus (formerly part of Communist Russia). I went reluctantly but knew I had to obey and go. I have horrible memories connected with the Russian occupation. Would my nightmares return?

I went with a small group of American Christians and found wonderful Christian believers in both countries. They showered us with their love and appreciation. The audiences smiled and cried with me when I spoke to them through an interpreter.

Their precious faces replaced old memories of merciless cruelty. A great healing began in me.

I found many orphans in both countries but what I saw in Belarus shall be with me every day of my life on this earth. I never saw more poverty! Belarus is now in worse economic shape than when it was under Communist Russia.

Belarus got 70% of the radioactive fallout from Chernobyl. The devastating meltdown, which aroused the horror of the whole world in 1986 might enter our history books, but the world has forgotten the people who still suffer from it. One fourth of the soil in Belarus is still so radioactive, it cannot be farmed. The greatest harm is done to the children. Today Belarus is not only the land of deformed children but nobody knows what will happen to future generations. Any couple desiring children takes the risk of having a handicapped child. So many abnormal children are born that the government has children's homes for kids given up by parents who either do not have the means or courage to keep them.

I visited such a place and I shall never be the same again. The stunted growth is frightening. I held a child in my arms whose hands were an inch long. She was one year old. A boy without legs, many miniature toddlers, some of them mentally alert but so starved for love and attention, they did not want to let us go!

The one bright spot amidst the stoic endurance and the dark hopeless mood of the people is a new freedom of religion. For the first time in more than 70 years Christians are permitted to meet publicly and even build institutions and churches. Poverty hinders them from taking advantage of their new liberties. In all of Belarus there is neither a Christian nursing home or any Christian Children's work.

Well, Grandma Hansi got once more her marching orders. By God's grace and the help of God's family around the globe we shall at least begin the work of helping the children of Belarus.

I believe that humanitarian help alone can be cruel. To feed starving people and then let them face their destitute future without hope is not true help but it only prolongs agony. The fear of future hunger becomes more devastating if people know how a full stomach feels. With the physical help must come a message of hope and promise and the assurance that God takes care of His kids. Handicapped children can be nourished and helped with decent foods and supplements but they also must experience love and unconditional acceptance.

Belarus has enough loving, eager and qualified Christians to preach and serve among their people, if we give them the financial help to build, feed and teach.

I am fully aware that our ministry can make only a small dent within the great needs on this earth, but if *all* of God's children would ask the Lord to show them what their own part is, we could win many battles.

Betty and I paid for the reprint of this book with our own savings. We have never taken royalties from any of our books and tapes. The money has always gone back into God's work. The profit of this book will go 100% to our future project in Belarus. Our friends encourage us to call it:

Grandma Hansi's Children of the King

Will you please pray with and for us? It is a tall order for two lil' old ladies in tennis shoes, but we serve a most powerful and mighty God who loves children!

First we must build the facility. Then we need to set up a program whereby each child can be sponsored by a loving donor. We will make sure that the giver will become a real person, a parent substitute and each orphan can feel that he or she belongs to someone.

Tours need to be set up to give people a chance to experience, share, touch and hug a world, not known to the average Westerner.

Oh Lord, there is so *much* to do!

If you want to get in touch with us, here is our address:

Hansi and Betty
P.O. Box 2133
Kailua Kona, Hawaii 96745-2133

You may also request to be put on our mailing list to keep informed about our progress.

Now to Him who by His power within us is able to do infinitely more than we ever dare to ask or imagine -- to Him be glory in the church and in Christ Jesus forever and ever, Amen! (Eph. 3:20 Phillips)

Securely held in Christ's Arms,

Grandma Hansi

1996 -- At the Good Fence at the border of Lebanon.
Left to right - Jewish guide, Hansi and Betty.

Hansi's trip to Poland in 1996.
Visiting the destroyed headquarters of Adolf Hitler.

1996 -- Chernobyl causes growth stunts.
Hansi holds a baby <u>one</u> year old, her hands one inch or two!

Belarus -- A very alert little boy,
without legs, watched Hansi's every move!

Hansi will never forget the children's faces in Belarus.

1996 -- Betty and Hansi leaving a
surprise party for Hansi's 70th birthday.

The group which walked in to surprise Hansi for her 70th birthday party.
Back row: Maria, John D., Hanna, John, Michael, Betty H.
Front row: David (Maria's son), Christiane, Casey (Mike's daughter), Hansi, Betty